An OPUS book

PHILOSOPHY AND THE BRAIN

Philosophy and
the Brain

J. Z. YOUNG

Oxford   New York

OXFORD UNIVERSITY PRESS

1988

Oxford University Press, Walton Street, Oxford OX2 6DP

Oxford New York Toronto
Delhi Bombay Calcutta Madras Karachi
Petaling Jaya Singapore Hong Kong Tokyo
Nairobi Dar es Salaam Cape Town
Melbourne Auckland

and associated companies in
Beirut Berlin Ibadan Nicosia

Oxford is a trade mark of Oxford University Press

First published 1987 by Oxford University Press
First issued (with corrections) as an Oxford University Press paperback 1988

British Library Cataloguing in Publication Data
Young, J.Z. (John Zachary).
Philosophy and the brain.
1. Man. Mind related to brain
2. Man. Brain related to mind
I. Title   128'.2
ISBN 0–19–282167–9

Library of Congress Cataloging in Publication Data
Data available

Set by Colset Private Ltd., Singapore
Printed in Great Britain by
The Guernsey Press Co. Ltd.
Guernsey, Channel Islands

Preface

Although I have been interested in philosophy for a long time I never thought that I should be so rash as to write a book with such a title as this. There is a proper tendency by philosophers to despise those scientists who venture into their difficult subject, and I am indeed conscious of superficiality and misunderstanding. But I have taken the risk because I think that new biological knowledge can give important insights to old philosophical problems. Consideration of the nature of information as the essential basis of the continuity of life illuminates the whole concept of knowledge. Facts about the activities of the brain provide understanding of the individual as a responsible agent and so illuminate the problems of body and mind, intentionality and determinism. Investigations of the systems for encoding and representation in the brain show how perception is a search for information relevant for living. I believe that many difficult concepts, such as purpose, choice and value can be better understood by examining their counterparts in the brain and their manifestations in other animals as well as man.

I have tried to provide the information needed to understand the significance of biological discovery in a form that is accessible to philosophers. Conversely, I hope that biologists may see the relevance of philosophical discussion to their practical enquiries. My discussions do not go very deep either philosophically or scientifically, but they probably go rather beyond the limits reached by the practitioners on either side and so may help both parties.

Whatever professionals may think, there is no doubt that laymen and students enjoy reading about the more general views of scientists. Many people have told me of the stimulus that they gained from my first stumbling efforts in the Reith Lectures in 1950 on 'Doubt and Certainty in Science'. The present book is an attempt to attack the philosophical problems more directly — head-on. This obviously makes it even more open to criticism, which I am sure it will receive and deserve. Nevertheless I hope it will call attention to some important implications of modern biological knowledge that are often overlooked. It may also perhaps indicate to neuroscientists some problems that they might attack but are apt to ignore, as they probe with their microelectrodes. Most of all I should like the book to be of help to students and lay people who are concerned about fundamental problems of life and human nature. Knowledge of the brain can help to improve one's appreciation of life and to alleviate some of its troubles.

The book has arisen out of three Shearman Lectures given at the invitation of the Departments of Philosophy and History and Philosophy of Science at University College, London, in 1982. The lectures were called 'Philosophers use your Brains', but this seemed altogether too arrogant and provocative a title for a book. I am very grateful to Professor P. M. Rattansi for the invitation and for his chairmanship of the lectures. I also owe a great deal to the encouragement of Professor Ted Honderich who has read and criticized much of the text. His comments have shown me how widely my approach deviates from that of a professional philosopher. I am also very grateful to Professors Charles Philips and Lewis Wolpert and Dr J. O'Keefe, who kindly read parts of the manuscript and corrected me on many points. My son, Simon Young, read much of the early part of the book and provided me with penetrating criticism. Finally, I must thank Raye Young, who not only typed and retyped many pages but gave help, encouragement and shrewd comments throughout, especially on questions of style and taste.

J. Z. YOUNG

Brill
February 1986

Contents

PART I. CODING AND REPRESENTATION   1

1. The problem   1
2. Purpose, direction and history   3
3. What's in a brain?   8
4. Mentality is not separable from the brain   11
5. The brain as an agent. Brain programs   17
6. Living and knowing   23
7. Information   26
8. The maintenance of order. DNA   33
9. Embryology, adaptation and evolution   40
10. The languages of life and of the brain   47
11. Intentionality   51
12. Representation and computation in the brain   61
13. The origin of signals in the cortex   68
14. Changes in the brain before an intentional action   73
15. Some sites of linguistic activity in the brain   75

PART II. PERCEIVING   79

16. Perception as a search for information   79
17. The senses in the skin and their cortical centres   86
18. Taste and smell   98
19. Pain and internal sensations   102
20. The senses of posture and balance   105
21. Hearing   108
22. Vision   116
23. The visual cortex   121
24. The eye's search for information   128
25. Some theories of vision   137

PART III. LEARNING   148

26. Memory   148
27. Memory as a process of selection   156

28. The hippocampus and memory 161
29. Memory and development 168
30. Summary of some essential features of memory systems 170

PART IV. VALUING 173

31. Wants, needs and values 173
32. The hypothalamus 178
33. Some examples of regulation 184
34. Emotional responses 187
35. Ethics 190
36. Social man 201
37. Beauty and the brain 205
38. Freedom and determinism 207
39. What am I? 214

Notes 217
Index 225

PART I

Coding and Representation

1. The problem

Everyone agrees that all knowledge and thought are somehow related to the brain, but many thinkers pay little attention to this fact: the word 'brain' is not mentioned in the index to Gilbert Ryle's *Concept of Mind* (1949). When philosophers think about thinking, they mostly examine their own thoughts. When scientists think about brains they refer not to their own brains but to observations made by neuroscientists. All of us remain confused about the relationship between these subjective and objective ways of thinking about ourselves. The separation between the two approaches has a long history in religion and culture. Many people still claim that there are problems of philosophy and theology that can and should be discussed without reference to the brain: some would think that the separation is obvious and desirable. I believe that consideration of the information now available about living organisms and brains can help us to achieve a more satisfactory theory of knowledge and philosophy of mind, which might bring relief to many worried laymen, philosophers and scientists.

The apparent difficulty shows the weakness produced by our intellectual and social system that separates thinkers from observers, philosophers from scientists. The difference between them (roughly defined) is that when the philosopher examines his thoughts he uses mentalistic words, often of common speech. It is very difficult to agree about the use of these, because of the privacy and variety of their subject-matter. On the other hand, scientific discourse almost by definition depends upon words that describe observations that can be confirmed and agreed by all appropriately trained humans. Clearly it is desirable to use discourse about which we can agree, and this suggests that we should use scientific methods where possible. Armstrong puts it perhaps

1

too strongly: 'Only in science do we ever reach an intellectual consensus about controversial matters.'[1] We certainly must not assume that science has a magic formula for solving all problems. On the other hand it is now clear that there are serious deficiencies in the philosopher's classical methods for reporting his own and other people's mental activities. Beneath our conscious thoughts or perceptions there are layers of information-processing, which greatly influence what is thought or seen. Moreover there seem to be limits both of introspection and rational enquiry which may be partly innately determined and which neither philosopher nor scientist can transcend. We must be ready to recognize these and devise a philosophy that accepts them.

The question is whether the two approaches refer to the same subject-matter or whether the scientific method inevitably omits something. Indeed some people may say it omits the most important things, namely human feelings and spiritual values. I hope to show that it not only includes them but enlarges them. This will seem paradoxical if knowledge of 'material facts' is held to be totally different from thinking abstract thoughts. But are these really such different activities? Many philosophers, including Kant, have observed that thinking of all sorts depends upon use of certain fundamental conceptual powers or methods. We shall take up this idea and show that objective scientific investigation of the brain equally requires the use of many abstract concepts, such as information, representation, aim and value. If this is so it seems there can be no useful arbitrary distinction between the operations of scientists and philosophers. Perhaps after all they can use a common language.

Knowledge of the brain is still imperfect, but I hope to show that it is already adequate to allow a useful extension of the meaning of many of the words that are fundamental to discourse about ourselves and the world. Words such as 'knowledge', 'perception', 'aim' and 'value' can be made to acquire fresh and richer meanings. Above all we may be able to find some explanation of why we make the distinction between mind and body as we do, and so come a little closer to a satisfactory unified view of our nature, clarifying our use of this dichotomy, even although we cannot abandon it altogether.

I propose to outline some areas in which there is at least an overlap. Of course no one would suppose that we can achieve a system that answers all questions. We humans are indeed ignorant and confused creatures, and we are surrounded by mysteries. Some people no doubt prefer that philosophy and theology should remain apart from science, and it is not obvious that it will be easy to bring them together. All three have long histories and complicated terminologies. Their techniques and methods of arguing have been devised for different purposes. It is naïve to suppose that they can *easily* be combined, or even that they should be. Our thesis will be that they are not incompatible, indeed that new knowledge of the brain helps to understand old problems of philosophy and even theology.

2. Purpose, direction and history

i. *Two fundamental facts*

It is clear therefore that the discussion will revolve around the old question of the relations between the mental and the physical. This has been much explored by philosophers without resolution, but it may be that biological knowledge can help towards a satisfactory solution. Even excellent recent examples of the discussion fail to emphasize some fundamental facts about living processes that are important for a proper understanding of the problem. Indeed it is not too much to say that these facts may help towards a better theory of the nature of knowledge: a large claim indeed.

Two things in particular are missing from most lay and philosophical treatments of life and mind. First they do not show appreciation of the *intense and complex continuous internal activity that directs organisms to search for means of survival*. This incessant *pursuit of aims* is the essence of the maintenance of life. The search is not random but is directed towards the achievement of particular immediate targets that are pre-set for each creature. Secondly, this continuity of life is made possible only by calling from moment to moment upon the *stored information derived from past history*. As the philosopher Collingwood once put it, 'Life is history.'

ii. *All living involves selection and choice*

Much of the concern of philosophers about the relations of the mental and the physical arises from trying to reconcile the determinism of physical phenomena with the impression that human beings are free active agents, making choices and decisions as to how to act and live their lives. I shall have much to say about this and shall discuss in what sense actions are free (Ch. 38). There seems to be an impression that these capacities to choose, decide, and act are uniquely human. Biological discovery, however, increasingly shows that in this respect humans are manifesting characteristics that are common to all living things. Of course the choices and decisions of humans are conscious and forward-looking and we do not know how far this applies to other creatures. Anyone who has already 'decided' that these words, 'choice' and 'decision', can only be applied to humans should read no further. No one disputes that human beings are conscious; the problem is to discover the relation between their conscious choices and the similar purposeful actions that occur in all living nature. Throughout this book it will be maintained that much can be gained by stressing the *continuity* between the activities of humans and other living things. The differences involved in our consciousness and use of language are clear enough and should not be forgotten, but my thesis is that we can gain much by tracing the continuities between ourselves and the rest of nature.

iii. *The aims of living*

It may seem strange that I assert so categorically that living things are purposeful and pursue aims. There has been a prolonged attempt by biologists to eliminate teleology from their science, as it has been discarded from physics and chemistry. Some people are so frightened of the concept of teleology that they use the name 'teleonomy' instead: but this, as the Medawars rightly say, is a mere 'genteelism'.[2] It can be argued that the explanations that are used in physical science are incompatible with explanations in terms of 'purpose' and this forces us to face a paradox that cannot at present be wholly resolved. Living things undoubtedly act in ways that ensure their continuance: in this sense they show purpose and aims. These properties are the result of selection during the long history of evolution, which has provided each organism with a repertoire of programs of action ready to meet contingencies that are likely to occur in its environment. Indeed we shall later study the systems in the cells and in the brain that provide standards or targets for purposeful action. Yet clearly living things are physical systems: they are made only of a small selection of the ninety-two natural elements that make up the rest of the earth. No peculiar 'living elements' or 'living energy' are present. Moreover, in nearly all respects the combinations of these elements in living things behave like those in the inorganic world. Every year we gain greatly in power, in medicine and agriculture and other ways, by treating living things as physical systems. But yet they persistently show these actions directed to survival.

This problem has been examined in detail by Sommerhof, who shows that goal-seeking can be regarded as 'an objective system-property which is the very nature of biological organisation'.[3] This property can be expressed in terms of a concept that he terms 'directive correlation' between the various actions of an animal or man and the changes in its environment. He points out that the essence of the 'adaptiveness' of living organisms lies in the fact that they show 'a conditional readiness . . . to meet certain contingencies in certain appropriate ways'. A clockwork toy bird pecks a grain, but a real bird changes its action if the grain moves. This implies that the organization of the bird has the property that Sommerhof calls 'directive correlation' between its own actions and changes in the environment. This is the system property that ensures the achievement of its goals, either immediate such as pecking the grain or more remote such as survival of the bird or perpetuation of its genes. This correlation is made possible by the information that is available to organisms from their past history. The power to store information in this way is a unique property of living things and is not found elsewhere in nature. We shall have to examine this property thoroughly and study how it affects our views of the application of such concepts as 'causation' and 'physical law' to living organisms.

iv. *Living purpose and conscious purpose*

The next difficult question is whether we can usefully compare these teleological activities, present in plants as well as animals, with the conscious purposeful actions of human beings. A good

way to decide this is to examine carefully what is implied when
these words are used, as has been done by Taylor. His interpretation is subjective and very different from mine, but his
words can be applied to an objective brain. He stresses that the
fact that a system is acting purposefully does not justify our
saying that it is alive. 'There is more to explanation by purpose
than simply the teleogical form . . . [it has] special features of its
own.' The features in question are that when we speak of purposeful actions we imply that they are intentions of agents.

Thus systems to whom action can be attributed have a special status, in
that they are considered loci of responsibility, centres from which behaviour is directed. The notion of 'centre' seems very strongly rooted in our
ordinary view of such systems and it gives rise to a deep-seated and
pervasive metaphor, that of the 'inside'. Beings who can act are thought
of as having an inner core from which their overt actions flow.[4]

This quotation gives a very good idea of what is usually implied in
the concept of an 'agent', and it is striking that biology shows
quite clearly that *all* living things indeed have such a central core,
in the coded genetic mechanism of their DNA (Ch. 8.ii). It is
precisely this centre of each cell, working with the rest of its
protoplasm, that gives living things their powers to take purposeful action. It would obviously be absurd to say that plants or
lower animals act 'intentionally', and we shall return later to the
problems involved in the use of the words 'intention' and 'intentionality'. The point here is that all organisms act under direction
from a core of instructions, and it is useful to say that they are
'purposeful'.

Taylor's remarks also capture the way in which I believe we
should think about the brain as an agent, the centre of the life of
the individual, and if it is not too confusing we should think of
the DNA as the agent within or behind the brain. But we must
think of both these agents not merely as physical objects but as
dynamic structured systems, informed by their past history, continually varying the instructions they send in the attempt to
maintain the life of the organism. If we can achieve such a point
of view we should not find difficulty in reconciling what Taylor
calls the 'participant attitude' or the 'transparent desire' with the
fact that they arise in association with the brain.

Taylor claims, like Sommerhof, that we call an action purposeful if it is varied in order to achieve the aim in spite of the

circumstances. As we examine living activities and brain actions we shall find repeated evidence that this is exactly what happens. As I have said already, organisms are provided with repertoires, which I shall call programs, of possible actions, from which they select those that are appropriate, as far as possible, to the conditions (Ch. 5). As in the case of 'codes' we use the term 'program' for a physical system which, by virtue of its history, provides the 'information' or 'instructions' that ensure continued living. The operation of many neural programs is conscious but others are not, for instance those that regulate breathing or the actions of the stomach or heart.

Taylor would probably not be ready to admit that these programs are 'actions', because just after the passage cited above he adds a further criterion for purposeful action: 'What is essential to the notion of an "inside" however is the notion of consciousness in the sense of intentionality'; and so 'there is some sense in which the notion of desire involves that of consciousness or intentionality . . . the idea of what is desired.' This would seem to limit him to the definition that only humans are 'purposeful agents', but he quickly withdraws from this because, very sensibly, he would not wish to exclude 'at least higher animals', which are obviously purposeful. So if, as I accept, consciousness is not to be the criterion of purpose, we are left without any serious objection to the use of the concept of purpose as applied to all living things. I believe that this will be found a great relief to many people and will improve the descriptive power of biology. Of course, as I have said, this simple statement does not solve all problems that are connected with the difficult concepts of 'directedness' or 'intentionality'. It is clear that a plant's growth is 'directed', and I should be prepared to say that it was 'purposeful', but not that it was 'intentional' or 'conscious'. 'Intentionality' is a special property of the activity of some higher creatures that have brains capable of forming representations of future events, perhaps always associated with consciousness. I shall devote much further attention to them later (Ch. 12).

v. *Living agents*

Biologists know that animals and even plants are not puppets, manipulated by the environment. They are *agents*, provided with targets and a remarkably strong inner motor tendency that causes them continually to strive to achieve the aim of remaining alive, as has been emphasized by Thorpe.[5] Moreover we shall find that it is difficult, perhaps impossible, to give a clear meaning to the statement that the course of the search is 'completely determined' (Ch. 38). Many matters will become clearer once the full implications of this living activity are realized. Certainly many mysteries remain, not least how living things first came to have this activity and this purpose.

The brain in particular is not a passive object but a ceaselessly active system. The problem of defining bodily and mental relations therefore is to find out how the purposeful activity that we recognize in our own mental and personal life is related to the purposeful actions of our bodies and brains. There are obviously many difficulties of terminology and detailed knowledge (and ignorance) involved in such an enquiry: it is not easy to know how to proceed in meeting them. Some philosophers seem to wish to rush on at once to solve the hard problems. They may call attention to the difficulty that faces any attempt to find out and describe events in the brain that correspond to our more complex human activities, such as thinking about thinking. Such problems are indeed baffling and we cannot yet provide complete answers to them. However, if we begin by paying attention to facts that we *do* know, we may come gradually to see how these harder problems are soluble. In particular if we consider how the brain operates as we pursue our daily lives we may find a terminology that helps to provide a basis for solution of the more difficult questions asked by philosophers, which involve study of the nature of coding and representation in the brain. I propose therefore first to emphasize the closeness of the connection between mental activity and the brain.

3. What's in a brain?

In order to understand what is meant by the word 'brain' as it is used by neuroscientists, we must bear in mind the evidence that this organ contains in some recorded form the basis of one's whole conscious life. It contains the record of all our aims and ambitions and is essential for the experience of all pleasures and pains, all loves and hates. In the brain lie the texts that make possible all one's knowledge. If I ask you the date of the Battle of Hastings, you reply '1066'. Where was that information before I asked? It was not in your 'mind', which then contained (perhaps) 'This is a strange book I am reading.' The date was somehow recorded in the brain, ready to be recalled when needed.

Included in the brain are all the rules and instructions for the actions of speech and writing by which we communicate with others. This implies all the conventions of logic and mathematics by which we reason. Moreover, somehow recorded and represented there are the data that allow recognition and recall of all sorts of shapes, of faces, of scenes and of pictures. In the brain again, in some notation, are some versions or 'scores' of the music that we can recognize and can sing or play on an instrument. In short, the brain contains, as I say, all one's capacity for conscious life.

Some philosophers may find that these are extreme claims, incautiously expressed. I agree that great care is needed in explaining in what sense it has meaning to say that the brain 'contains' 'information', 'instructions', 'codes' or 'scores of music' and these concepts will be discussed at length. Indeed it is the business of physiologists to justify such usages, and to improve them by the development of new terminologies where necessary. We shall spend much time discussing how these words can be used. I believe that those who have studied the brain extensively such as neuroscientists, neurosurgeons and neuropsychologists, will agree that these statements are meaningful. These experts do not find it necessary to worry much about questions of brain and mind. They feel that with more attention to the brain many of the difficulties of terminology will disappear. Some even accuse philosophers of continuing to pursue unnecessary semantic complications, which they say can confuse the issues and delay solution of medical and social problems. Such thoughts may be simplistic but they are widespread and they show the need to explore what is involved in speaking of body and mind and the relations between them. In this book I shall seldom use the word 'mind', but prefer the adjective 'mental', for reasons I shall explain in the next chapter.

Meanwhile it may be useful to mention briefly a few of the types of evidence which show that all these powers depend upon the brain. These include the histories of those unfortunate people who suffer damage of the brain through accidents, tumours or strokes, with a resultant loss of some or even all of the ordinary capacities for emotion, memory and learning that most of us have. Moreover, physiologists and surgeons operating on the brain for the relief of epilepsy have shown how access to its store of information is to some extent localized (see Ch. 15). The great mass of these results shows that particular parts of the brain are involved in sensory, motor and emotional activities and experiences.

Patients with injury to the visual areas of the cerebral cortex may be unable to recognize and name familiar objects. One, shown a picture of a pair of spectacles, said 'Perhaps it is a bicycle'; shown a sketch of a face, he said 'It seems to be an orange with slashes in it.' Patients with injuries to the right parietal lobe may be unable to recognize faces.[6] This defect, called prosopagnosia, may be limited only to this one type of recognition; other objects are readily identified. So this very important capacity to recognize your fellows, which is characteristic of man as a social animal, depends upon the integrity of that part of the brain. This does not mean that this region by itself is capable of the feat of recognition, but it seems likely that it contains cells that are responsive to particular faces (Ch. 23.iii). However, the nature of memory records in the brain is still uncertain and one of the important matters I will discuss.

Neurologists and neurosurgeons meet a great variety of such defects in the capacity to interpret 'the evidence of the senses'. Other injuries may affect a person's temperament, making him excessively excitable or depressed, easily pleased or the reverse, pugnacious or apathetic and so on through many syndromes extending to total unconsciousness. Later we shall see other examples of the findings of surgeons and neuropsychologists about the location in the brain of areas critical for certain properties such as the power of speech or understanding of language (Ch. 15). I wish to emphasize here the evidence that the actions of the brain are essential for all conscious activities.

Division of the brain by section of the corpus callosum actually divides the consciousness of a person. This large tract of fibres allows communication between the two sides of the cerebral cortex, which have different functions. That on the left has the capacity for language and logical analysis, whereas the right is responsible for recognition of faces and other objects and for musical appreciation. The tract that joins the two is sometimes severed to prevent the spread of epilepsy. The patient is not much disturbed by this in daily life but tests show that he cannot name an object, say a knife, when it is seen only in the left visual field which now communicates only with the dumb right hemisphere. Yet if the person is asked to use the left hand (which is controlled by the right hemisphere) to feel a number of objects, he will pick out a knife. Meanwhile the speaking left brain cannot say what the left hand is holding. There now seem to be two persons, each in some sense conscious. This strange situation emphasizes that conscious mentality is a variable property of nervous tissue.

4. Mentality is not separable from the brain

i. *The mind is not a thing*

Obviously, in the patients discussed in the previous chapter the brain was not working properly. The point for us is that all intellectual and emotional powers require activity in the brain and we are utterly dependent on it. No brain — no mind, no intellect, no nothing. The clinical evidence does not support the idea that there is some entity or spirit that can exist apart from the brain. Nor is it necessary to postulate, as Eccles and some other dualists seem to wish, that our 'minds' constitute some special force acting to control the cells of the brain.[7] It is indisputable that we have consciousness, but must we say we have 'a mind' in the sense of an entity acting upon the world?

Who is to say what is mentality, what is the mind? Is this an empirical question to be answered perhaps by psychologists, or a question of the use of words for the linguist? Some may identify the mind with the soul and call upon the theologian for a definition. This indeed was the position adopted almost unavoidably by many, perhaps most, philosophers of the seventeenth and eighteenth centuries, as part of widespread Christian religious belief. For them, the mind obviously was an agent possessing spiritual powers that were quite independent of the body, in no sense material and yet able in some way to influence the actions of matter.

The problem arises from the need to describe our human condition as conscious persons. In our culture this is usually done by describing two entities — a mind and a body. This technique has an ancient origin, indeed we shall see that it may be a legacy of the very structure of our brains (Ch. 30). This distinction between body and mind comes down to us partly through Descartes and his dictum 'Cogito, ergo sum', and I believe that use of it is responsible for many problems not only in philosophy but in medicine, law, and indeed daily life (Ch. 6.i). It is no longer desirable to use the distinction as a central point of philosophical discussion.

If all mental events are accompanied by physical events there is no need to postulate a distinct entity called 'the mind'. This has been emphasized by many thinkers. As Ayer puts it, 'We do not need to conceive of minds as substances, or indeed as entities of any kind.' And again: 'Like Hume he [William James] sees no reason to assume what is variously called a pure ego, or soul, or mental substance.'[8]

In common speech everyone assumes that he has 'a mind', by which he means a continuous flow of conscious experience. The first part of this book is largely concerned to show how all this mental experience is accompanied by events in the brain. For example, all the information that is available mentally must be somehow recorded in the brain. Again, when one decides to perform some action there are corresponding events in the brain; they begin even before one has made the decision! (Ch. 14). Everyone 'knows' that he controls his actions, and of course so he does, since his mental control is inseparable from the actions of his brain.

My thesis will be that in view of the closeness of this association it is unlikely that wholly different languages are appropriate to describe the mental and the physical. I believe that proper consideration of the nature of persons and their brains and of living systems in general will show that a common terminology can help in the study of all aspects of man. We can profitably use such terms as information, action, choice, aim and even value in connection with physical as well as mental events.

Consciousness is an aspect of the functioning of the brain, not something that can exist apart from it. My brain and body are inseparable from myself. It is an interesting philosophical and linguistic question whether we should say that they are 'the same thing'. I prefer to say that 'mind' is not a 'thing' at all, but that consciousness and mentality are characteristic properties that accompany certain activities of the brain, rather as movement is a characteristic property of legs, or of a wheel, and calculation is of a computer. Searle suggests that consciousness arises as a property of the actions of the neurons as liquidity arises from the molecules of water.[9] These are of course similes like so much of language, devices by which we communicate. The liquidity of water is not a 'thing' apart from the water but a property of it. Similarly, consciousness is a property of some phases of the functioning of the brain. Certainly it is a very peculiar property, being the basis of one's whole 'conscious life'. Discussion continues as to the nature and origin of consciousness. I shall later comment on the strange fact that some brain activities are conscious but others are not. Moreover the property of consciousness is not uniform throughout the brain. As we have seen, in the left hemisphere it is largely concerned with verbal information and logic, in the right with visuo-spatial analysis, but the separation is not completely sharp (Ch. 3).

Consciousness may be connected with the unique capacity of the human brain to form representations, especially of the operations of other people's brains (Ch. 11.iv), but this is speculation. Consciousness is such a dominating feature of one's existence that it is very hard to characterize or analyse it. The classical method of overcoming the difficulty is to speak of oneself as containing an inner *entity* or 'mind'. This solution may be the result of a particular power that we inherit and use from earliest childhood to communicate with each other by using words descriptive of other human beings. This technique of describing the world in terms of human agents leads one to postulate an agent within the agent when one considers oneself. It is indeed very difficult *not* to think in this way. We all experience a continual mental flow, but why should one ascribe it to anything except oneself? Why have an entity within an entity?

Such facts about language are important. Nouns can only be usefully adopted in their appropriate contexts. 'The use of the noun "mind" is dangerously inhabited by the ghosts of old philosophical theories. It is very difficult to resist the idea that the mind is a kind of thing. . .'.[10] This is not to imply that the problems of the mental and material are only linguistic. They are real problems, which can be made clearer if we restrict the use of the words to the right contexts. We do not expect to see a mind or to touch one, so we shall not be right if we try to show that mental events are 'identical' with events in brains, which *can* be seen and touched. On the other hand, mental processes only continue when there is an active brain, and it will be worthwhile pursuing the attempt to find the best way to describe the relationship.

ii. *Correlation of the mental and the physical*

In the extreme case, in the absence of a functioning brain, the mental activities of an individual all cease. Conversely, all mental activities are accompanied by some corresponding cerebral activity. A major difficulty for our discussion is to try to understand what the words 'corresponding activity' are coming to mean, as physiologists gradually discover how the brain performs its operations. They already have enough evidence to show that many of the matters that are the subject of philosophy depend upon the presence of an active brain. Consciousness, perception, language, induction, intention, and indeed emotion, pleasure, and pain can all be shown to be 'correlated' in some way with continued nervous activity. All these will be altered by injury to some part of the brain or modified by electrical stimulation of it. This of course falls far short of telling us how the brain operates in these situations, but it emphasizes that cerebral activity is somehow an essential component of mental activity.

It is tempting to say that events in the brain 'cause' mental events: a formulation used recently by Searle.[11] The conception of a cause is notoriously difficult and ambiguous, but for the scientist it usually implies some sequence of material interaction with expenditure of energy. For this reason I find it undesirable to say that mental events are 'caused' by the brain. The essential point is that *all* mental events are associated with changes in the brain. The best we can do is to find clear statements that describe the relationship between events in the brain and what Honderich calls 'conscious occurrents' (by which he means mental events). As he puts it: 'Any given occurrent obtains in any individual just in case as a matter of lawlike connection one or another of a specific set of physical processes obtains simultaneously in that individual.' This he calls the 'Thesis of Lawlike Correlation'.[12]

This formulation expresses the belief of most physiologists and psychologists. Its detailed interpretation depends upon discovering the 'laws' that are involved, which would mean knowing far more than we yet do about the working of the brain; but there is strong evidence that all mental activity is accompanied by action in the brain, as we shall see in later chapters.

Unfortunately we can only specify the 'set of physical processes' in simple cases. If my finger is pricked with a pin there will be pain, correlated with physical processes in nerve cells in various parts of the spinal cord and brain, which can be described in some detail. Yet even in this case the lawfulness of the 'lawlike connection' is not easy to specify completely. It is well known that in times of stress athletes and soldiers 'do not feel pain', but physiologists can only speculate as to how this inhibition comes about. We are even more ignorant of the variations in the physical accompaniments of a given thought — say about the beauty of a picture, even in one person. Nevertheless the thesis proposes that there are such correlations: most neurophysiologists would agree, and we try to find them. But the 'laws' by which any given brain operates are extremely complex and are changing at least a little all the time as a result of ongoing experience. Your 'lawlike response' to the question 'What is your favourite picture?' is likely to change from time to time. The question 'What is your name?' will be followed by nearly the same brain response every time: but not if it is asked several times in quick succession!

This complexity and adaptability of the brain means that *precise* forecasting of correlations between mental events and physical processes is never possible. Nevertheless, we know enough to be sure that when I recognize a face and then give the name of the owner there will be successive activity in certain parts of the cortex; in fact certain particular 'face cells' will be active and probably particular 'name cells' (Ch. 23.iii). The fundamental point is that all mental events are associated with events in the brain; and it is a continuing task for neuroscientists of all sorts to follow the cerebral events, especially those that accompany our more interesting mental and emotional activities.

iii. *Consciousness depends on the brain*

If damage to the brain has been severe, doctors may make a diagnosis of 'brain death', which for some purposes is regarded as the equivalent to the actual and legal death of the person. The patient's conscious mentality is no longer there. Of course there are many people who believe that this is because the spirit or soul has departed from the body and can persist indefinitely in some other sphere. Most people competent to judge probably find that there is no satisfactory evidence for the action of such disembodied spirits either upon humans or other living creatures or upon tables or other inanimate objects. This is of course not evidence either for or against their 'existence', if entities without detectable properties can be said to exist. If the supposed spirits are free of all dependence on earthly bodies and have no action upon them, then they cannot be like normal conscious mental processes, which are demonstrably *dependent* upon bodies. Furthermore the paradox we are facing arises from the very fact that every person feels that his conscious self *controls* his body. An entity that can no longer control bodies cannot be relevant to our discussion. We conclude therefore that without a brain there is no consciousness or mentality of the type we propose to discuss. Anyone who is not satisfied about this need read no further. There is no more discussion of psychic or paranormal phenomena in the book. It is likely that in the future great discoveries will be made as to *how* the brain is related to consciousness. It is extremely unlikely that future attempts to prove the existence of *independent* spirits will be any more successful than the many failures in the past.

For every individual his own conscious existence is the ultimate reality, beyond any possibility of doubt. The difficulty for each of us is to know how to characterize and name this entity — oneself. Correspondingly, how can we best refer to other people? We can call them plain humans, or persons or minds or souls, each word giving a slightly different emphasis. It is quite clear that one cannot describe oneself or others as 'simply brains'. Yet paradoxically whatever a human person is depends completely on his brain, and if the brain changes greatly, the person (sadly) changes too. Indeed the brain changes daily throughout life as one learns, unless one is too old or has Alzheimer's disease or has lost the hippocampus (Ch. 28).

These are paradoxes that science and philosophy cannot yet completely resolve. Perhaps they never will. The conscious experience of each person remains as the essential entity that is valued as human. It is not for the scientist to lay down the law as to how it should be regarded, but he insists that it only and always accompanies brain action.

5. The brain as an agent. Brain programs

i. *The brain never stops*

Although consciousness and all those other activities require the presence of a brain the reverse is not true. The brain continues to work while we are not conscious or perceiving or intending or speaking or feeling pleasure or pain. This asymmetry seems to suggest that the brain is in some way the source of the enduring mental properties. The brain is a continuously active organ even without any external stimulation. Many years ago Gerard and I showed that a frog's brain continues to show waves of electrical change even when removed from the head of the animal. More important for our discussion is the fact that variations of electrical potential, the electroencephalogram or EEG, can be recorded by electrodes placed on the head even when a person is not conscious, or is asleep. Indeed these 'brain waves' change when one begins to dream. So when we use the word 'brain' we should think not merely of its physical appearance, or even of the nerve cells that it contains, but of its *activities*, as we do other organs, the heart or the stomach.

ii. *Comparison of the brain with a computer*

A reference to a 'brain' is not a statement about a simple visible or tangible object but about a *system* with definite organization, properties and actions, an organization built up partly by heredity and partly by learning, uniquely characteristic of each individual. It is not simply a storehouse of records but a very active organizer, continually at work to initiate and direct the actions of the rest of the body. It is obviously important to find words to describe this incredibly complicated system which does such wonderful things and is so different from any other that is known. Would it help to compare it with a 'machine'? If so, what machine? Comparison with a computer is some help but computers are made of materials quite unlike those of brains. They use some similar principles but also others that are different and in many ways less powerful; in others, obviously more so.

A computer is an engine that can be operated by programs fed to it in an appropriate code. In the brain there is no such clear separation between hardware and software. Each individual is provided by heredity with a brain that already contains certain simple programs, for instance for breathing; it also contains devices that enable it to learn many further, more elaborate programs. Moreover, although the brain transmits information in a digital code of nerve signals (Ch. 12.i) it does not store information by means of simple digits. One of the main current problems of neurophysiology is to discover the units in which the memory record is written in the brain (Chs. 12, 27). It seems that the code consists of various types of units pre-established by heredity. These provide a large set of possibilities among which selection and combination by experience produce actions that are uniquely adapted to meet the needs of that individual. There is thus no clear distinction between hardware and software or syntactics and semantics in the nervous system. For those and other reasons the computer analogy is grossly inadequate to describe the operation of the brain.[13] In trying to deal with these difficult problems we shall nevertheless find the concept of a program useful, as indicating a list of things to be done.

It is not at all easy for those who study the brain to think about how its immense number of cells and nerve fibres direct the action of the body. Even a relatively simple action like the movements of the chest in breathing is regulated by thousands of cells in several parts of the brain. How much more complex must be the system that makes one able to ride a bicycle, or drive a car, or produce a poem or fall in love and decide to propose marriage. Yet each of these actions or conditions involves particular operations of the brain.

iii. *Programs of the brain*

To meet the need for a terminology I propose that we speak of *brain programs*.[14] Although we know only a little about how the millions of nerve cells work together we can vaguely see that their arrangements provide sets of potentialities, the programs that give us all our power of sensing, of feeling or acting; from seeing to suffering, or eating and drinking, or speaking and reasoning. The patterns of nerve cells provide, as it were, a file of programs, some functioning all the time, as in breathing, others brought into action as and when the situation requires.

Rather than talking about 'programs' it would be much better to be able to say in some technical language exactly how the nerve cells work together as we think our thoughts and select our actions. Since this is not yet possible, as a first step we can at least try to define the activities that the cells control more precisely, and this is the point of identifying 'programs'. The programs are previously organized sets of neurons and their connections, among which selection is made to produce mental and cerebral states and actions, as daily life proceeds. There are programs for walking, for reading, for speaking, for fearing or loving, and endless more. All depend upon capacities of the brain, partly inherited and later learned.

The important feature of the concept of programs is that it indicates that living actions are directed towards ends. A program is some form of list of things to be done in order to reach an aim. The word thus has both the sense in which it is used in a theatre or concert hall *and* for the algorithms of computers. Consider that the aim of a computer program might be to control some of the stages of a machine that makes motor cars; a theatre program shows the order of the items in a play. Similarly there are living programs that direct the whole life of a bacterium, or a man, embodied in their genetic material, DNA. In the brain there are programs that allow a person to recognize a face and others associated with weeping and the emotion of sorrow if that face is dead.

Evidently a system that uses programs must have the potentiality for many types of action. Each of its programs selects certain modes of action from a large *repertoire of possibilities*. It is characteristic of living things that they are very complex systems and any individual may act in various ways. Indeed it will be important to decide what meaning can be given to the conception that such a system is 'deterministic'. For the present we shall use the terminology that the brain contains programs, which operate as a person makes selection among the repertoire of possible thoughts and actions. We shall try to clarify the logical status of such programs and to enquire how they are 'instantiated' in the brain.

The brain programs, like those of a computer, indicate the sequence by which decisions are to be arrived at and actions initiated. In this sense they are comparable to the 'software' of computer terminology. But even software has to be recorded in some physical form if it is to be communicated. The essence of programs is that they are coded lists of instructions recorded in some physical form in advance, thus ensuring that the system of which they are part changes its state in such a way that it reaches a particular new state, which is the *aim* of the program. This obviously implies that the instructions are somehow communicated from the past and can be 'read' or 'understood' by a receiving agent that also has the power to put them into action as and when the situation requires. The status of such entities as programs and codes is a unique feature of living systems that has already been discussed (Ch. 2.iii). The organization of the physical system has come to acquire the property of transmitting signals that allow selection of actions from a repertoire, which we call sending instructions that ensure survival. In order to do this, the system of programs must obviously be suited to the conditions that the organism will meet; in this sense it must be a *representation* of the world. I return to this problem again later (Ch. 12).

Speaking of distinct programs is certainly a gross over-simplification of the unity of the ongoing system of action that is exercised in the brain. It is important to realize that it continues even when one is asleep. The combined activity of all its many parts, sleeping or waking, constitutes the essential basis of the continuity of one's whole mental life.

iv. *Initiation of action by the brain*

One very severe difficulty about describing the actions of the brain is to express the fact that they *initiate* action. Many philosophers and neuroscientists have rightly criticized the reflex concept according to which all behaviour is the result of external stimuli activating the nervous system. This is indeed an inadequate basic concept for the description of any life; it is especially evident that higher animals initiate action from within: the Nobel Prize winner Ragnar Granit called his book *The Purposive Brain*.[15]

Yet, so far as is known, there is no overriding central program that selects and supervises all the others. There is indeed down the centre of the brain a set of cells known as the reticular activating system that never come to rest. They rhythmically discharge nerve impulses that initiate the brain waves, which are essential for the action of all other parts. These impulses are fundamental for life, continually sending nerve signals that keep the other parts of the brain going. But the reticular system is not in any sense a supervisor. The selection of which brain program shall operate is made from moment to moment as a result of the combined action of many parts of the brain, influenced of course also by the signals coming from the sense organs. Such a 'democratic' organization is extremely hard to describe. Quite frequently one set of programs will dominate behaviour, as when one is hungry and eats, or becomes angry, or looks at a picture or reads a book, or has sex, or sleeps. Throughout life many different sets of programs emerge sequentially and they interact during a daily round of working, eating and so on.

The various muscular systems of the body are controlled by motor programs, for instance for walking, eating or writing. The brain calls upon whichever motor programs are relevant. It has access to the final motor pathway leading to each muscle. So contraction of the muscles of the arm can be evoked to write a letter, or punch an opponent. This capacity to use the body in various ways provides for the great variety of actions that are characteristic of man. In particular we can do far more things with our hands and voices than any other animal. Details of some of these programs are given later (Ch. 15).

The programs for speaking are especially complex, involving selecting those sounds that serve to express the relations that are to be communicated, as varied as 'the table is one metre long', or 'I love you, darling.' In thinking, presumably, the same parts of the brain are involved without activating the speech muscles. A child learning to write often speaks the words as he writes them; indeed there is evidence for small movements of the speech muscles in some conditions of thinking.

As one proceeds with the business of life one is vaguely conscious of calling upon a series of actions selected from those that might be done. It is difficult to realize how all the succession of thoughts, perceptions and emotions depends upon these specific activities in the brain, as of course, more obviously, do the actions of the arms and legs or tongue. In later chapters I try to show how the programs of the brain include all the multitude that make possible thought, sensation and feeling, as well as action. This is only a way of trying to describe an immensely complicated system, by identifying the actions of its parts. It corresponds well to the experience one has of choosing to do one thing after another all day long. The thoughts that 'pass through one's head' often seem to arise 'by themselves', as dreams clearly do. There is little understanding of what goes on in the brain as we think or dream. Sometimes it is clear that these are fragments of programs for action.

v. *The rhythm of life*

It is necessary to think of the continuity of life as the result of programs that produce recurrent perceptions and actions, such as those of seeing, eating, walking, writing or sleeping. The knowledge now available about the working of the body and brain already provides a vivid picture of this complex web of recurring brain activities, with various time-scales. Some are dependent on rhythms of the glands, such as the pituitary and adrenal. Others depend on the digestion: stomach, intestine, liver and bowel. Many of these internal actions are under the influence of the hypothalamus, a region at the base of the brain (Ch. 32), itself of course influenced by other parts. Other basal forebrain areas are active when we feel and express emotions such as rage or loving sympathy (Ch. 34). Above all are the actions of the cerebral cortex, introducing the major element of control both by initiation and restraint, which the individual person consciously exercises over many of the 'lower' activities. The concept of programs is an attempt to produce order in this array of inter-acting influences. The programs come into play either rhythmically or as demanded by the needs of the moment. Philosophers and neuroscientists could indeed work together to find ways of describing this activity.

If the programs of the brain involve all this, it is obvious that we must do some heavy thinking about the precise meaning to be given to words like 'system', 'coding', 'information' and 'repre-sentation'. If we can define our terms properly it may become possible to give a clear answer to the question 'What's in a brain?' We shall say that it contains *programs* of instructions for actions that may assist in keeping the individual alive, and *information* about features of the world that are relevant to that aim. In order to give content to this statement we shall have to show how the organization of the brain somehow embodies the software of the programs, as in a script. We shall have to define what is meant by saying that the brain contains information and show that the word is used in essentially the same sense as when applied to mental events.

6. Living and knowing

i. *Experience of living as the basis of knowledge*

The joint action of these programs of the brain regulates the activities of all the various parts of the body. This constitutes as it were the program of life as a whole, which is the basis for the individual's experience. The general question we are asking is, how are the experienced mental events related with those in the brain? We have reached the point that the brain is to be regarded as the bearer of a property to be called programmed information, which is essential for the continuance of life. Mental activity certainly involves information or knowledge. Can it be shown that in using this word for both the physical and the mental we are doing more than playing with names?

The fundamental point is that the transmission of information is a unique characteristic of living things, essential for continued life. Mental information or knowledge is the special human form of this property of communication that is characteristic of all self-maintaining creatures. We acquire information by virtue of the fact that we are living systems endowed with these properties of communication and the use of signals.

I therefore propose that we should use this common property of life as a basis for discussion of the nature of the mental information that we call knowledge. For Descartes's 'Cogito, ergo sum' — 'I think therefore I am' — we might substitute the more biological proposition: 'I am certain that I am alive.' This has many advantages as a starting point. First of all it cannot be denied. It would make no sense to say 'I am certain that I am not alive.' Every normal adult human being can agree that he is alive. Animals have life but, presumably, not awareness of life. For us it is a central fact of experience. Descartes postulated two distinct entities in the world, *res cogitans* and *res extensa*, but surely they cannot both be 'things' (*res*). The mind cannot be touched or weighed. Further, by his emphasis on *cogito* he has led us to consider that the 'self' is part of *res cogitans* but not of *res extensa*! This position, adopted by Descartes and those following him, is responsible for the problem that arises when we try to consider whether action is the property of brain or mind. Resolution of this apparent dilemma is essential if we are to form consistent conceptions of persons and agents. Cartesian thinking has assumed that it is useful to keep concepts of body and mind distinct. It is arguable that many difficulties, social as well as academic, have arisen from this distinction. It is the joint task of neuroscience and philosophy to find whether it is possible to bridge the gap, even if we cannot do without the distinction. To achieve this we must insist that the organism is one single whole entity. Our description begins with 'I am certain that I am alive.' We then go back to ask what is involved in being alive, and in knowing one is alive?

ii. *Living precedes thinking*

Living is obviously in a sense more fundamental than thinking. Of course that does not necessarily mean that consideration of life is a more important philosophical task than consideration of thinking. Thought is characteristic of humans, and for this reason Descartes's insistence on *cogito* was correct. But life precedes thought and leads on to it in the history of the individual as it did for the race. What has been discovered about the programs of life in general provides clear insight into the basis of the emergence of brain programs, and so of the thinking that accompanies them. Let us first look at them from the point of view of individual humans: this will lead us to the question of the nature of all life.

iii. *The continuity of experience*

For an individual the essence of life is surely the continuity of experience. I am the same person today as I was yesterday. Following what we have said about the interdependence of the mental and the physical, this continuity of experience clearly involves and implies the presence of a continuing rhythmical pattern of activities provided by the brain, glands and other parts of the body. These determine that the whole organism wakes and is hungry, searches for food and eats it, and if human speaks and listens, and engages in social life. Many of these activities are accompanied by mental life. Indeed the mental counterpart of, say, deciding to eat seems to precede and to 'produce' the action. The person feels 'I chose to eat.' In fact, as we shall see, the brain is active first (Ch. 14), but that does not matter, for it does not alter the fact that the individual's mental event was 'I decided to eat.' Of course he did, because he and his brain are united in the sense that without a brain there would be no 'I' to decide anything. It is essential to be continually aware that mental life is a property inseparable from the brain. We find it hard to undermine the convention of 'dualism' of the physical and mental in spite of analogies such as the liquidity of water or the motion of a wheel (Ch. 4.i). The knowledge that every mental event is accompanied by physical events in the brain at least helps us to come to terms with this dilemma.

So we go on from day to day, doing and feeling, living and experiencing, creating an effective life by use of the programs of the brain. Of course this does not mean that any person does exactly the same things every day. The programs of life are immensely complicated, adaptable, and creative, as we shall see as we try to follow how they operate. Even the most 'stable' individual is in fact continually changing both physically and mentally as the world around changes, providing new food and other materials and new experiences. Nevertheless, paradoxically, each remains 'the same' individual. We shall find the solution to this paradox; what remains the same is not the material physical structure of the body but a non-material entity — the *information* or ordering of its parts. We shall find that we can define this key word satisfactorily, using the facts recently discovered about the nature of living processes (Ch. 7).

Let us first, however, consider that it may be more useful to think about this experience of the continuity of existence than about the particular single chosen experiences and statements that are often the subject of philosophical enquiry. We do not spend our lives going around having 'experiences'. When you enter your kitchen in the morning you do not *see* all the objects in it. You proceed to pick up the kettle and fill it with water without thinking about the *process* of seeing or your 'knowledge' of heat. During daily life we 'see' the things that we need to see in order to do what we want to do. We use our knowledge to conduct life. If an orange is simply sitting in a bowl we pay no attention to it at all, we only 'see' it if our interest is directed to it either from outside or from within. If someone asks 'Do you see that orange?' you may say 'Yes'. If you become hungry you look for one and eat it. The point is that perception cannot be properly considered as a series of isolated events such as are often postulated in philosophical discussion. It is nearly always based upon expectation, somehow elicited or motivated from without or within (Ch. 16). Similarly, the information or knowledge that is gained from perception is essentially a system of expectations about the relations between events, past, present or future. Moreover, perception usually results either in action or in further expectation, even if the action is only to stop looking in that direction.

Perception and the acquisition of knowledge as seen by the biologist is part of the life system of the individual and consists in testing expectations and collecting information about the way things are related so as to assist in the business of living. We now have to investigate the nature of this process of collecting information.

7. Information

i. *Basic concepts*

The programs of life are coded lists of instructions, recorded in advance, which indicate what is to be done to achieve some end. The terms 'programs', 'coding', 'instructions' and 'information' are borrowed from common speech and in that sense are 'only metaphorical'. However, their very familiarity is an asset. We can use them to define the basic properties of both bodily and mental events and they thus provide us with ways of speaking about the fundamental processes of life including 'mind'. These ideas resting upon new discoveries, if properly explored, may even provide a basis for a better use of words in epistemology and metaphysics.

ii. *Order*

The essence of the concepts we propose is that they are related to the *order* or *organization* of living things. Even the simplest organisms are immensely complicated systems, continually active, and changing from moment to moment. By an amazing feat of human discovery and brain-power it is now possible to have some insight into how all this activity is organized. But we shall not let ourselves be deceived: this simple talk of programs and codes only gives the crudest description of the buzzing ferment of change in the simplest cell, still less of what goes on in a human brain. Nevertheless, if used carefully, these words provide for a substantial increase in clarity and precision of thought beyond that which is possible by the use *only* of their subjective connotation.

The concepts we propose to use, then, are concerned with the maintenance of order. Order involves the relation of the parts of living things to each other, which is *maintained by communication*, and, as we have seen, this is an essential basis of the maintenance of life (Ch. 2). This seems to be clear, but in fact the concept of order is full of ambiguities. These have been discussed in detail by Reidl,[16] who comments: 'Indeed it seems to be a general characteristic of order that there will always be arguments about its forms, its limits, and even its existence.' Order is essential for thought, 'the supposed orderly pattern of the outer world agrees [so] strikingly with our own thought patterns [that] (perhaps) what we take for real order is, in truth, only the projection of the fact that our thoughts require order.'

In spite of such difficulties it is meaningful to say that living things are highly ordered, though no one has devised a satisfactory way of measuring their degree of order. Electrical engineers such as Shannon and Weaver measure the amount of information that is passed along a communication channel such as a telephone wire in terms of the control of decisions. One bit of information is the operation needed to decide between two equiprobable events. Such a system works only as applied to situations in which the probability of unit events can be estimated, for instance the words of a language. Attempts to measure living order in this way meet the problem of defining the initial probabilities: should we start with the numbers of atoms or molecules in the body, or cells, or what other units?

Physicists have their own definitions of order, which we cannot adopt in detail, but we can obtain useful ideas by the contrast between living and non-living systems. Unlike all other known things on earth animals and plants defend themselves against the universal tendency to fade away, to merge into the surroundings; in short, they remain alive. The second law of thermodynamics tells us that any isolated system must tend to greater disorder, technically called an 'increase of entropy'. This is the law that says that it is impossible to make a perpetual motion machine. Living systems are not perpetual motion machines; they are not isolated. They continue because they obtain materials and energy from their surroundings, enabling them to do the work of rearranging their parts so as to prevent them from falling into disorder. They are able to do this because they receive from their ancestors a pattern of order, which we identify by saying that it consists of 'information', carried by a code. Living things delay the disorganizing effect of the second law of thermodynamics in this way by the use of inherited information to direct their actions so that they achieve the aim of remaining alive. Our thesis will be that the acquisition of knowledge, which we usually think of as subjective, has developed from this process of accumulation and transfer of information that is essential for all living things.

iii. *Communication of information*

If this way of thinking is to be more than metaphorical we have to consider what is intended in saying that the animals and plants have 'records' of 'information' collected in the past. Clearly these words refer to a form of communication system similar in some ways to that of language, and we must therefore define the technical use of these words. A *system* is some group of material entities enduring through time and influencing one another. At its broadest, *communication* can be considered simply as the transmission of any influence from one part of the system to another part, so producing change. *Communication of information* is a much more complicated concept: it implies a pre-arranged communication channel with transmitter and receiver, using signals and codes. These concepts are only meaningful when applied to self-maintaining systems with aims, and in fact should be limited to living things (or artefacts produced by them).

A code-signal in this sense is a particular physical change passing through a communication system, which produces in some other part a pre-arranged change, which is the 'response' or 'meaning' of the signal. Information is thus the name we give to the capacity of code-signals to produce particular effects in the body. The signs can be *translated*, either into other signs or into actions, normally tending to assist homeostasis, the process of self-maintenance (Ch. 8.ix). Information in this sense is an abstract quality sometimes called semantic information, to be distinguished from the information considered as a measure of uncertainty by the Shannon–Weaver information theory.

iv. *Codes*

The concept of a 'code' comes originally from its use as a 'legal code' for a systematic collection of laws. Hence the essence of a 'code-signal' is that the response to it has been pre-established; it is 'lawful'. In its more restricted sense a code now implies a set of 'code-signs', as in the Morse code or 'genetic code'. I have described 'information' as the essential feature of an enduring system that enables it to remain organized. This means that I propose to use the word 'information' to define a characteristic property of signals and codes that makes possible the collecting and expending of energy to delay the increase of entropy. This power to carry and use conventional signals and code systems is the unique attribute of life, and its implications are fundamental for philosophy: I shall discuss them repeatedly in different ways. To justify this use of information we must identify the features of living things that ensure continuing life. We can then return in Chapter 10 to examine the implications of such a definition of information.

v. *Various living codes*

All organisms, plants and bacteria as well as animals, have such communication channels, through which they send messages in code. We shall obviously have to enquire whether this analogy with language is the best or only way of speaking about these living processes. A code is a set of physical changes that are used in various combinations to evoke specific responses by a receiving agent that is tuned to receive them. The words of speech are the obvious example. Biologists have found a large variety of codes used within cells. The nerves carry signals from the sense organs to the brain and others back to the muscles. Glands send messages by what may be called chemical code-signs such as adrenalin or insulin in the blood, each received and interpreted differently by the various organs. Plants send chemical signals up and down their stems. Bacteria send them from the surface to the inside. The most fundamental code of all is embodied in the units of the hereditary material DNA, which I shall describe in Chapter 8. These chemical molecules provide a language that is common to all organisms and is able to communicate the information that ensures the continuity and variety of life.

The existence of all life depends on these systems for receiving, transmitting and using information. At each stage the process consists in selection from an existing set of possibilities. All 'messages' are made up of selected 'words', whether they are words of human speech or the code-signals in the nerves, or the chemical signals, or the units of the DNA. The messages produce their effects by selecting which actions the organism will take. The information stored in a system is produced by selection among the possible states that it could have, and these states are a memory record of its past history. Each code-signal triggers a specific sequence of responses. The signals and receptors have classical physico-chemical properties but the sequence of response of the whole system *depends on its remote and immediate history* and can only be precisely forecasted if these are known.

Innumerable code-signals of many sorts determine which of the many possible actions the body will take: this is what is meant by saying that they carry 'information'. By their joint effects they select the courses of action that ensure survival. Information is thus carried by physical signs, but is an abstract quality. Similarly the words of speech or of writing are transmitted as physical signs but carry abstract information, useful for humans.

vi. *The origin of living codes*

No other known systems show either this degree of complexity *or* the apparent purposiveness. In this sense we are forced to say that the living things existing today are different from all the rest of nature. One of the great problems for biology is to study the past history of life and to try to discover how this type of organization began. Most scientists hope that it will be possible to show how the properties of 'signalling' and 'coding' arose from physical actions similar to those elsewhere in nature, perhaps along one of the following lines.

Some time after the origin of the earth a wide variety of organic molecules was probably produced, over a period of hundreds of millions of years. Some of these molecules could have associated spontaneously to make larger aggregates (polymers), which were simpler versions of the proteins and nucleotides that are consti-tuents of living things today (Ch. 8). Such polymers might have provided templates for the production of others like themselves, perhaps assisted by inorganic catalysts. Those polymers more efficient in attracting molecules would survive, and so natural selection may have begun.

It has been found by experiment that under the influence of heat suitable mixtures of amino acids assemble themselves to make 'proteinoids' or 'thermal proteins'. Some of these have non-random structures and even enzyme-like properties. Such thermal proteins may have been the origin of polynucleotides and so of the genetic code.[17] Another ingenious suggestion is that the earliest codes took the form of defects in inorganic crystal pat-terns transmitted by repeated crystallization from supersaturated solutions, serving to influence the 'survival' of certain sorts of clay or mud.[18]

The origin of living things by these or any other physical means has not been conclusively shown yet. If it is eventually demon-strated, it will mean that the natural physical processes have given rise to the present immensely complicated living systems, which act with the purpose of ensuring survival.

vii. *The instructions for the control of living*

Study of living codes will obviously involve some technical knowledge. The important general point that will be made is that the organization of the inherited molecular system of the DNA of the nuclei of the cells, which regulates the fundamental opera-tions of living, is closely parallel to human language. Both depend upon the presence of a set of units (a 'code') from which a *selection* is made by a transmitting agent ('choice') in order to send a message ('information' or 'instructions') which when 'decoded' produces 'action' ('control') that is appropriate to maintain the whole system, which is its 'aim' or 'end'. The parallels extend so deeply that they enter into the operation of *parts* of the living system. For instance the immune system and the nervous system also operate by selection from pre-existing codes (Ch. 27.i).

viii. *Living codes preceded human language*

The widespread occurrence of these selective systems requires further discussion by philosophers. In a sense it implies that communication by a sort of language preceded the language of man or of animals. The terminology of linguistics has been developed in relation to our own condition; it seems desirable and not at all inappropriate to use it for the other living systems. Many workers both in the humanities and science still try to reserve terms such as 'information' or 'code' for use only of humans. This has become both impractical and undesirable. The parallels are so close that the biochemist's use of 'genetic code' or 'translation' is irresistible (Ch. 8.v). Similarly, the neuroscientist speaks of the nerve-impulse code in which signals are transmitted along nerve fibres (Ch. 12.i). The important task, for philosophers and all of us, is to clarify the significance of these extraordinary parallels that have recently been revealed. It can hardly be an accident that human language has followed and developed a system that is as old as life itself. However, the extent of the analogy remains uncertain until the systems have been analysed more fully. Both operate by selecting words from a set, but the status of the genetic 'grammar' is as obscure as that of human language.

The pervasive presence of systems of communication by signs and signals has long been explored by students of semiotics.[19] The discoveries of the codes of heredity and the nervous system have extended and justified the idea that codes, signifiers and representations are fundamental features of biological life as well as of culture. The questions of what constitutes a sign, a symbol or a language are certainly controversial. The point I am trying to make in this book is that the recent discoveries of molecular biology and neuroscience add further items to the list of problems that have to be considered by philosophers of language.

ix. *Sources of biological knowledge*

It is fundamentally important to understand as clearly as possible exactly what is implied in these extended uses of language. I shall try to do this with the minimum of technical words, by describing the biologist's view of life.

The work of biologists in the nineteenth and twentieth centuries has gone a long way towards explaining how it is that living things have their very special powers. The answers are not simple. The partial explanation that we can give comes from the work of many different sorts of biologists. Much of what we know comes from the study of evolution by naturalists and geologists, from Darwin onwards. Another important source has been the work of physiologists, which demonstrates how living things are continually interchanging with the environment, maintaining a steady state by the processes known as metabolism and homeostasis. Materials are taken from the environment and combined to make more of the specific substance of each species thus giving the amazing powers of growth and reproduction. Meanwhile, geneticists have shown the importance of variety and how differences between individuals are inherited. Embryologists have analysed the sequence of development from the egg and the importance of both nature and nurture. Biochemists and molecular biologists have been able to define the structure and activities of the enzyme molecules that make all the processes of life possible. Still more remarkable, they have identified the molecules that carry the instructions that are responsible for all these activities of life. The unlikely combination of biochemists with mathematicians, engineers and linguists has produced the new science of cybernetics, which puts all these facts together to provide a view of the control system by a code of information that makes living possible.

8. The maintenance of order. DNA

i. *Control*

This great system of biological knowledge is fundamental to an understanding of the actions of the brain and hence of the nature of knowledge. It is not easy to decide where to begin in order to explain it. Perhaps a good way is to start with one of the most difficult biological concepts — that of *control*. Until recently this word was applied only to human actions: it is now used for various systems that 'control themselves'. Of course those designed by engineers, such as automatic pilots, are only extensions of human control, but in the process of designing them we have learned how to look for the significant features of living things, *which do indeed control themselves*, although each has no single overall controller. The proper regulation of the actions of all the parts of the body follows from the fact that they are made according to instructions provided by the memory record in the DNA. This controls the formation of molecules of protein, which individually and collectively provide the targets and feedback loops that together ensure continuation of life.

ii. *The structure of DNA*

DNA is a very complicated chemical substance whose molecules consist in most animals and plants of two strings wound round each other in a spiral, the famous double helix.[20] The essential feature of the strings is a repeated sequence of four distinct chemical components, the nucleotides: adenine, cytosine, guanine and thymine; we can call them A, C, G and T. The code is provided by the order in which these four occur along the strand. Each set of three, say CCA or GCA, is a code word in the genetic language, which acts in a way I shall explain shortly to produce the molecules, and so the cells and organs, that provide the targets for regulating the whole life of the organism. The DNA molecules are thus very long unbranched threads constituting a linear, four-letter genetic code, written in words of three nucleotides. In a human cell the DNA contains a sequence of about four thousand million (4×10^9) of these nucleotide genetic words. The total length of the strands is more than a metre in each cell, but they are packed by an elaborate system of coiling into the form of the forty-six bodies known as chromosomes. These can be seen with the light microscope and were recognized as the bearers of hereditary characteristics some time before biochemical studies showed the properties of their DNA, and the electron microscope finally revealed the long thin strands.

iii. *The structure of proteins*

Anyone who wants to understand the matter thoroughly should obviously learn more than this about the nature of the genetic code, but we can perhaps proceed with only an outline of its essential features. The controlling action of the DNA depends on making the selections that ensure production of the right proteins. The actions of every living cell depend mainly on the proteins it contains. There are many sorts of protein: the white of an egg, for instance, is a solution of the protein albumin. Albumin is a useful source of nourishment, but other proteins that are much more important are the enzymes, which are the agents that allow 'improbable' chemical activities in the body. For example, enzymes enable the body to 'burn' sugar to give energy. There are thousands of different enzymes, each essential for one special chemical process within the cells.

iv. *Proteins as enzymes*

Proteins consist of long strings of hundreds of chemical units called amino acids, of which there are about twenty different sorts. The special powers of each type of protein depend on the order in which these units are placed on the string. The power of the enzyme is conferred by the fact that the string folds up into a complicated ordered tangle, in which each of the amino acids has a special place. The details of this folding are all-important because it provides chemical nooks and crannies into which different substances fit and are brought close together. This makes them join up easily, just as if they had been heated. An ordinary lump of sugar and oxygen can join together and burn to give out heat, but to make them do this you must first heat the sugar and 'set it alight'. In the body, molecules of sugar and oxygen are brought into close contact by the enzymes and the sugar 'burns' even at body temperature. This is an example of how living things can carry out chemical reactions that a chemist would call improbable, meaning so unlikely that they never happen at that temperature. Sugar does not catch fire spontaneously.

v. *The selective synthesis of proteins*

Living organisms can do these improbable things because they have the right enzyme proteins. The making of each protein is organized by a section of the information in the DNA, or gene, a page in the instruction book, which is first 'transcribed' (as the biochemists say) into a copy written in a slightly different code in molecules called messenger RNA (ribonucleic acid). This transcription is done by special enzymes called RNA polymerases, which move along the stretch of DNA 'reading off' the bases to make the RNA copy molecule. This molecule then moves through the cell to one of the protein-making machines, called ribosomes. These have further special enzymes which 'translate' the information in the RNA to organize the making of a new protein molecule. Each messenger RNA molecule moves through the ribosomes, whose enzymes pick up amino acids one after the other in the right order as indicated by the code, to make the new protein chain. Thus, as the code triplet GAC passes, the ribosome adds the amino acid asparagine to the chain. Next comes GGC, which 'means' glycine; and so on for perhaps 400 amino acids, to make whichever new protein the cell needs. How the 'need' comes to decide which part of the DNA is transcribed is of course a most important point and will be described in Chapter 8.vi.

Notice (once again) how the system proceeds by *selection* from a limited set of twenty amino acids. Each sequence of three nucleotides (say GAC) is the code word that determines which of the twenty amino acids shall be next. Since there are sixty-four possible combinations of the three letters and only twenty amino acids, it follows that there are several code words ('codons') for each amino acid. A code of this sort is said to be degenerate and we shall find that degenerate codes are also used in the nervous system and elsewhere. They provide part of the flexibility that is so characteristic of living control systems.

The details of how this amazing machine for protein synthesis operates are now partly clear. It involves extraordinary mechanical unwinding of the long thin threads of the DNA. It is a process that goes on in any cell of the body whenever new proteins are to be made. In humans the DNA makes some 30,000 different proteins, most of them enzymes, each responsible for a different chemical process.

The processes of life are very complicated. The continuation of even the simplest bacterium is only possible because it has many enzymes, each producing a particular chemical change. In humans and other animals composed of many cells each cell has a complex life and performs some special job for the whole organism. Thus the enzymes of a muscle cell enable it to do work, the enzymes of some pancreas cells make insulin, and so on. The next question therefore is, how is it ensured that each cell has the proper enzymes?

vi. Repression and expression of genes

The DNA that each individual inherits from the parents has to carry the information for all these different cells in the body. Each type of cell uses *some part* of this information: only some of the gene sequences of DNA are used, serving to make the enzymes that are necessary for the functioning of that type of cell. All the rest of the genes are there in the DNA of the nucleus, but are *repressed*. It is rather like the knowledge you have, say of history, which you only bring out if you are asked for it.

Much is known in bacterial cells about how the repression is ensured and how the information is made available by *derepression* and activation. The selection of which enzymes shall be made is an effect of the environment. The bacterial cell is sensitive to its surroundings and has means of transmitting to the DNA the information that, for example, a particular food substance is available. If the cell lacks supplies, the 'need' will set in action the derepression of the relevant part of the DNA. This ensures that the particular enzymes required for the use of that substance are synthesized by the cell. The classic case of this 'induction' of an enzyme is when a culture of the bacteria that live in our intestines are given a new type of sugar, milk sugar or lactose, to feed on. Within minutes after one drinks a glass of milk they will begin to make a special enzyme, β galactosidase, which is necessary for them to be able to use the lactose. They are able to make this enzyme because lactose is one of the various foods available for these bacteria and appropriate mutations have become incorporated in their DNA. Notice also that the whole system depends upon elaborate channels of communication. Signals are sent by the lactose from the surface of the bacteria to the DNA indicating what raw materials are available. Other signals show what provisions are needed by the cell. Much remains to be found out about these signalling systems in bacteria and hardly anything is known of them in higher organisms, where the processes may be different.

vii. Adaptation to environment in bacteria

This selective activation of certain of the genes is the fundamental basis of the process of adaptation to environment, which is an essential part of all living. The DNA carries the information about the various things that the organism can do. By responding suitably to the surroundings each bacterial cell then selects which of the possible proteins it shall make. The particular combination chosen will depend on the surroundings and on the genetic make-up and past history of that particular cell. In this sense it is a novel creative choice, changing from moment to moment and very difficult or impossible to forecast precisely: the organism itself is altering the supply of materials around it. There is no practical way in which the history and state of that particular individual can be precisely defined at any one moment. In order to find it out one would have to change the organism; it is therefore technically indeterminable.

In this process of selection a cell can be said to be using the DNA code for communication about the environment, as we use the words of language. The set of messages from which it can choose is limited to the request to make certain enzymes out of a total of perhaps 2,500 in the case of a bacterium. Its creative powers are limited. Nevertheless they are unique actions by that bacterium, depending upon the repertoire of DNA inherited from its ancestors, or acquired by mutations on the past environment of that individual and on the immediate present conditions. In this sense every action by every living organism *is a unique individual creation*. Even the simplest such action can only be forecasted within statistical limits, determined by the complexity of the system and knowledge of its past history.

viii. *Turnover: continual change of the body*

In organisms composed of many cells, like ourselves, the situation is much more complicated than in bacteria. The body is differentiated into more than 200 types of cell, each with enzymes appropriate to a special function. These cells must all work together for the continued maintenance of life, the process known as metabolism. Food and oxygen are taken in; some of the food is 'burned' to give the energy needed to prevent the increase of entropy. Other parts of the food intake are built into the body. Carbon dioxide and other waste products are removed by the lungs or the kidneys. So there is a continual *turnover* of material: the body is not made of the same stuff from one minute to the next. What endures is not any particular matter but the *organization* of its chemical components and parts in relation to each other. This organization is maintained by the actions directed to achieve survival, which are regulated by the information in the program systems of the individual cells, and of the brain and other tissues, all of them ultimately built according to the instructions inherited in the DNA.

ix. *Homeostasis and selection of enzymes*

It is fundamental to an understanding of life to realize that every creature is in what is technically called a steady state. Things are coming in and going out all the time in a carefully controlled way. This whole process of homeostasis continues in every living cell and every individual, without respite.

So living consists in every organism in making a series of 'selections' or 'choices' by the whole creature and its parts of what to do next. For example, when protein food is eaten, it is broken down into its constituent amino acids and these are carried by the blood to the liver. Here the liver cells must 'decide' whether the amino acids should be used to build more protein, or burned up to give energy. The 'decision' depends upon many factors, such as whether the individual had been taking exercise, whether his tissues are wasted by illness, what hormones are in circulation and so on. The liver cells are provided during their development with a range of enzymes adequate to perform these various tasks. The 'decisions' are taken within the cells, depending upon the abundance or scarcity of the various substances involved and the influence of hormones. These mechanisms for selection are already programmed into the nature of the enzymes, which has been determined by natural selection of appropriate DNA over millions of years. The basic homeostatic mechanisms were evolved long ago and are approximately similar in all mammals and even in other vertebrates. Yet every species has its own characteristic patterns and in each individual the previous experience leaves its mark. For instance, the liver is responsible among its many tasks for the neutralization of toxic substances taken in, such as poisons or alcohol. The liver adjusts its capacity to do this by developing cells with suitable enzymes.

It is an interesting problem to discover how the 'demand' for enzymes to deal with a new situation is met by fresh synthesis. In the daily life of the cell many of the enzymes have the power to regulate their own action by changing their shape; they are said to be 'allosteric'. In one shape there is an active binding site, which attracts the available substrate and converts it to a new product.

Another part of the same molecule takes up the product and this changes the shape of the enzyme molecule, making the binding site inactive. The allosteric enzyme thus constitutes a self-regulatory feedback system: as the product accumulates the number of molecules available to make it decreases. The whole cell functions properly because it has the right number of molecules of each enzyme. These have been produced when the cell was formed, under the instructions of the DNA. The question is, how can such a system adjust itself to meet increased demands or entirely new conditions? The answer lies in the mechanisms of development and adaptation, which must now be discussed.

9. Embryology, adaptation and evolution

i. *Development and adjustment to circumstances*

The many cells of a human being have of course been produced by division of the original fertilized egg cell. We are only now beginning to understand how the DNA of the egg and early embryo is held repressed and is derepressed as each cell develops, some into liver cells, others into bone cells and so on. Current knowledge indicates that the particular position of each developing cell in the embryo decides which parts of the DNA shall be derepressed and activated, and so which enzymes synthesized. Each cell as it develops is therefore *adapting* to its environment among the other cells, though we yet know only little about how the correct enzymes are chosen. Notice that each cell develops in the right way because of the place in the whole system in which it finds itself. The essence of the process is the presence of code sets of instructions in the DNA, acting *within suitable surroundings*. These provide *positional information* as to the direction in which differentiation of the cells should proceed.[21] Much remains to be discovered about this amazing system that produces an embryo with all the 200 or more types of cell in the correct places.

Once this determination has occurred, into skin cells, blood cells, liver cells, muscle cells and so on, it is irreversible. The first determined cells are called stem cells, and often they can continue to divide throughout life, but the products will always make the proteins that are appropriate to that cell type. The stem cells thus retain a *memory* of the differentiation that occurred in the embryo. In some tissues the stem cells continue to be very active; for instance, two million new blood cells are produced every second in an adult human by the blood stem cells in the red marrow of the bones. In other tissues, such as skin or intestine, replacement is slower; in liver slower still; in muscle very slow indeed, and in the brain no new nerve cells are formed at all after birth — but those that are there undergo fundamental changes of shape during learning, as we shall see.

As development of the embryo proceeds, the creature thus becomes increasingly more complicated by virtue of the interactions of its parts among themselves and with the environment. So the system comes to have a continually more elaborate organization for its purpose of living. We can say that the amount of information in it increases throughout life. In a sense a newborn baby contains more information than the egg from which it grew and an adult man contains more still. In the technical sense of information theory it would take more bits of information, that is yes/no answers, to describe a baby than an egg. This increase of information is the result of the creative activities of the organism as an agent, using the programs that it inherited to gather more information and to produce new programs. This capacity for *increase* of informational content is a further example of the improbable actions of living things.

After birth and throughout life nearly all the cells of the body continue to be capable of further adaptation to the particular conditions of the environment. For example, if a person goes to a higher altitude, or loses a lot of blood, certain cells of the kidney respond by making more of a particular hormone protein, erythropoietin. This protein circulates in the blood and stimulates the stem cells to produce more red blood cells in the bone marrow, allowing compensation for the lower amount of oxygen available. Conversely an excess of red cells depresses synthesis of erythropoietin.

The detailed composition and activities of many parts of the body are therefore continually changing in response to circumstances. For instance, the cells of the liver change their enzymes to meet the demands made by whatever food is eaten. Such *adaptational changes* can occur in many tissues: muscles grow with use, bones become stronger, and so on. The capacity for responding in such ways depends upon the composition of each cell and thus ultimately upon the powers of the molecules of which it has been made under instructions from the DNA. This is true also for the most important 'adaptations' of all, those that occur in the brain as the basis of memory. This process of learning is the response to the environment that is particularly characteristic of man. We shall later consider it in detail. For the moment the point is that the DNA code provides the repertoire of possibilities from which the cells of the individual select those that suit the conditions. Next we must enquire how it comes about that the set of actions made possible by the DNA of each individual is appropriate to the circumstances in which it begins its life.

ii. *Genes*

It should be clear even from the bare account given here that the nature of each protein and so its power as an enzyme depends upon the sequence of nucleotides along a particular stretch of DNA. This portion of the DNA is the unit known to the geneticists as a gene. According to the simplest theory (only partly true) each gene produces one enzyme. For example, there is a gene that produces the enzyme that controls the amount of pigment in the iris and so decides whether the eyes shall be brown or blue. Of course genetics is actually much more complicated than this, but for theoretical discussion it may be enough to know that the basic controlling system depends upon the order in which the units A, C, G and T occur. We therefore have to enquire how this order is established and changed and in particular how it comes in a sense to represent the environment in which the individual will live.

The science of genetics was fully developed before the physical nature of genes was discovered. The work of Mendel in the nineteenth century established that hereditary information is passed on as discrete units. Even with no knowledge at all of the physical basis of heredity it became clear that the factors (genes) received from the parents, such as those that make a plant tall or eyes blue, do not merge: when the hereditary factors from male and female come together at fertilization they remain discrete. One factor may dominate (say, brown eyes) but the recessive blue-eye factor remains intact and may appear again in a proportion of the offspring of brown-eyed parents.

It was then realized that these factors lie in the nucleus at the centre of each cell and that they are arranged in a linear order along small threads, the chromosomes, which appear in the nucleus when the cell divides to make two cells. It remained for the biochemists to show that the chromosomes contain DNA and, most important of all, that the nucleotides within the DNA constitute a code, which provides the instructions that make the continuation of life possible by ensuring the production of suitable enzymes.

iii. *Growth and replication*

The motive force that produces the 'adaptation' to environment is the extraordinary tendency of living material to grow, ever striving to produce more like itself. This tendency is indeed 'outside the ordinary', since life itself is 'improbable': yet all living things tend to grow and to divide, thus further multiplying the number of improbable individuals. The central part of this growth and increase is the tendency of the DNA of the chromosomes to be replicated, and so doubled. The DNA strands cannot do this by themselves, but in the presence of the accompanying enzymes and a fresh supply of the nucleotides A, G, C and T new DNA chains are made, using the existing strands as a template to guide the process. Once again we see that the essential qualities of life depend upon the capacities of the *whole* enzyme system of the cell. In this case the enzymes are responsible for increasing the amount of the DNA, whose information (paradoxically) was responsible for producing them.

Replication of the DNA is followed by division of the cell and this happens at very different rates. During development of the embryo the multiplication is strictly controlled so as to make each part of the body grow to the appropriate size. In adult life, cell division still goes on in some tissues that need to be continually renewed because of wear, such as those of the skin and lining of the intestine. Nerve cells on the other hand once fully formed never divide, though they may grow and form new connections (Ch. 26.iv). The influences that control replication of DNA are thus fundamental for ordered life at all ages. Little is known about these influences, but like everything else they ultimately depend on proteins that are themselves synthesized under the influence of the DNA.

iv. *Sexual reproduction*

In the organisms that have sexual reproduction the process of meiosis, or halving, precedes the formation of the eggs or sperms, giving to each of these the parental DNA of either the mother or the father. Therefore when the egg and sperm unite at fertilization the new instructions are not exactly the same as the old but are a fresh set compounded from those of the two parents. This repeated production of new instructions is a large part of the secret of successful adaptation and evolution of organisms.

v. *Mutation*

Variation does not depend only on this sexual recombination. The DNA itself is liable to change in several ways. Whole sections of it may alter their relative positions and this may change their effects. Further variation comes from the fact that the copying is not always exact. All chemical processes are subject to error and may also be influenced by external agents such as ionizing radiation, which may come from various sources, such as an X-ray machine or influences falling upon us from outer space. The 'errors' are known as *mutations*: they involve the introduction of a different nucleotide (A, G, C or T) in place of one that was there before. This of course means that a different amino acid will be added at one point in a particular protein chain, and so a new enzyme may be produced. This innovation may possibly prove to be of advantage at some time in the life of the organism, though it is much more likely to be deleterious. The changes produced by mutation are probably wholly at random; they improve the likelihood of survival only occasionally and by chance. Discussion often centres on this 'random' origin of new features of life and it is true that mutation provides, as it were, the raw material for evolution. But each combination of genes needs to be tried out by the activity of the organism as a whole, *directed by its tendency to take actions that ensure survival. So this striving to find a way to live is the essential agent not only for life itself but also for evolution*. Nature's method for ensuring both survival and change to meet new circumstances is to provide an excess of slightly different types, among which some will survive. The active search by each organism for survival makes use of whatever possibilities are provided by mutation and recombination of genes.

vi. *Natural selection*

So the secret of how the DNA becomes 'adapted to the environment' lies in the continual tendencies to increase, to vary and to strive to survive. An excess of living organisms is continually produced and those that make best use of the available resources pass on their characteristics to their descendants. Here again we meet a process of selection, this time the natural selection familiar to biologists. Every species of animal or plant consists of a number of individuals, each with a slightly different DNA. This means that every characteristic of form or colour, chemistry or behaviour appears in a great variety of different combinations. Among all this variety some individuals will be more likely to survive than others, given the larger number of offspring than parents, and the inevitable shortage of available raw materials. As the result of the process of natural selection the inherited DNA of every individual provides for the formation of a creature able to live under certain conditions. In this sense we can say that the DNA is a *representation* of that environment. The organism that it produces literally re-presents actions appropriate to those conditions.

Every organism is thus said to be *adapted* to its environment. This does not imply that every feature of its structure and chemistry can be considered to have a 'function'. Some biologists and biochemists have emphasized the dangers of looking for the 'adaptive' features of every single type of molecule. Some of the characteristics may be due to 'chance'. To put it another way, we should not assume that organisms are 'perfect'; but they undoubtedly show wonderful capacities for survival.

It is not necessary here to go into the many problems that arise in considering the process of evolutionary change. Organisms are exceedingly complicated systems and their changes proceed in very various ways, which provide many puzzles. There is overwhelming evidence to show that evolutionary change has occurred over millions of years in the past, and continues still from day to day. Nevertheless organisms are also very stable. Systems with such complicated relations to the environment cannot afford to vary much. New types probably tend to survive mainly when a small group is isolated in a somewhat novel or unusual environment. This may be the answer to the debated question as to whether new species appear gradually or, as some hold, suddenly, in jumps, by 'quantum evolution'.[22]

vii. *Progress in evolution*

The long process of evolution has produced repeated changes in nearly all the numerous different types of organism. I myself have made special study of these changes among vertebrates and cephalopod molluscs (squids and octopuses) and I am continually amazed at the variety of special processes by which the thousands of different species remain alive.[23] The fossil record is particularly good in these groups, due to preservation of their bones and shells. The record shows that there has been a sequence of successive changes in which populations have been replaced by others of different form, often themselves descended from the first. For instance, new types of fish have replaced each other rather regularly every sixty million years throughout the history of the group. Moreover, periods of maximum diversity of fishes correspond approximately with the maxima of other animals and plants. The replacements have usually coincided with times of climatic change, a famous example of which is the end of the Mesozoic period sixty-five million years ago, when the reptiles and coiled ammonite molluscs gave way to the mammals on land and the squids and octopuses in the sea.

There is evidence that in each of the later types the processes of homeostasis were more elaborate and more effective than in the earlier, depending on fresh information from the DNA. For instance, the later vertebrates show a much greater variety of types of cell than the earlier. This increased complexity has been associated with the invasion of habitats not previously occupied. The plants and animals needed special mechanisms when they came to colonize the land, and the birds when they began to fly. Again, modern cephalopods have characteristics that enable them to live in all parts of the oceans from the surface of the sea to its greatest depths. Moreover the later members of both vertebrates and cephalopods show more complex brains and so greater capacity for processing information, with a wider choice of programs. This tendency culminates in man, which leads us to regard ourselves as the highest form of living activity. Even allowing for this prejudice the facts of evolutionary change show that there has been an increase, at least in some lines, in the repertoire of homeostatic capacities, an increase in the information available and especially in the power to gain information through the nervous system. These increasing powers provide wider repertoires of possible action and in this sense greater freedom of 'choice' (Ch. 38).

It is hard to find exact measures of such changes of capacity. However the fossil record of the replacements is quite clear. The ornithologist Ernst Mayr expressed the views of most biologists when he said that the record of life from its beginning shows a progression. These changes are the result of the selection of new mutant types under the pressures of over-production and competition. This has led to the success of those organisms whose increased repertoire of possible actions enabled them to colonize new and more 'difficult' environments, that is to say, more remote in composition from the sea in which all life arose. This is the sense in which evolution has been progressive. Life has achieved greater levels of complexity and entered new environments, not by aiming for them, but by virtue simply of the purposeful striving for survival, which is common to all organisms.

10. The languages of life and of the brain

i. *The search for life*

Living entails perpetual creative activity; repeated making of what can be called *choices* and *decisions*. In even the simplest cell the chemical processes must go on continually, but also must continually change. The creature has to adapt itself to the surrounding conditions, which are inevitably altering all the time, not least because its own activities consume the raw material around: it must seek for fresh supplies. In this endeavour we find a series of activities parallel to human actions. In the pursuit of its aim of living, every organism must *search* and *decide* what to do, which way to go to get what it needs. From moment to moment there are several possibilities open to it and the choice between them is made by the information it already contains. Once again I defend the use of such terms, which are usually reserved for human activities. They are valuable both to the biologist and the philosopher because they emphasize that concepts of search, aim, choice and decision can best be considered as parts of the system for support of living. The biologist insists that all organisms have these capacities as agents. They are systems with strange properties of acting purposefully, their purpose being to remain organized.

The extension of these conceptions should help both to express the nature of living and to systematize analysis of thinking, knowing, choosing and deciding, by looking for their functions in life and their origins in its past history. As in all attempts to expand the use of words there is a danger that some part of the original meanings will become lost or obscured. A person's subjective choice between alternatives is obviously enormously wider than the choice of an octopus, which is in turn greater than that of a bacterium. I believe that the gain in generality, opening new views, is worth any loss in precision, which can be compensated where necessary by additional words.

At the beginning of this discussion it was agreed that we should accept that humans have both mental and physical activities and that we should seek for the best way of understanding and describing the relations between them. I believe that this can be found, without adopting the extremes of either crude materialism or crude dualism. Human knowledge, choice and decision are common properties of life that have enlarged recently and probably gradually as the brain became sufficiently complex to allow choices and decisions to be made in relation to many past and present events in the world and in the individual himself. In particular, the success of humans as social creatures may have been due to their capacity to recognize that they share their information with others. This may be the special significance of the evolution of the powers of representation in the brain that allow consciousness of self and of others. We shall pursue this suggestion as we examine the question of the cerebral basis of intentionality (Ch. 11.iv).

In DNA information is embodied (or 'written') in the nucleotide groups that have survived during millions of years of natural selection. In the same way we can say that by organization of the neurons the simpler sort of 'knowledge' had been written in the brain long before man appeared. The 'knowledge' how to breathe, for instance, how to eat and to walk and to mate. More interesting sorts of knowledge, such as how to speak, also have an inherited component though the details of language are learned after birth. All the knowledge acquired must somehow be recorded in the brain during the process of learning. We know that it is there because if the brain is damaged it may be lost. The question of *how* such information is encoded or otherwise recorded is one of the chief problems, which must now be faced.

ii. *Is it sensible to ask 'What's written in the brain?'*

Brains, then, are active agents, continually doing things. Our task is to find how these activities are related to conscious mental activities. First we notice the important fact that whereas the brain is always at work mental activities are interrupted for much of the time while we sleep. They may even stop for days or longer after an accident, and then return, little if any the worse. The obvious conclusion is that mental powers are somehow dependent upon the brain. One's knowledge does not disappear when one is asleep, nor is all of it lost if a person is knocked unconscious, though often the most recent events before the accident cannot be recalled — they had not yet been fully recorded in the brain. Whatever we decide to be the definition of mental activity it is clear that the 'mind' is not an entity that itself contains a lot of information at any one moment.

These simple facts compel us to suppose, as many have in the past, that information is somehow recorded in the brain. Philosophers have rightly pointed out that there are difficulties with this apparently obvious fact. They mainly revolve around the great complexity of human memories and our ignorance about how these are stored in the brain.

Humans have the capacity to rearrange the 'facts' that have been learned so as to show their relations and relevance to many aspects of events in the world with which they seem at first to have no connection. There are many ways of expressing the problem. We may follow the discussion by Dennett of a useful simple example.[24] You will agree that zebras in the wild do not wear overcoats. Yet you have never learned this. Did you perhaps somehow compute it from other information in the brain? If so, when did the computation occur, after the question or before? To put it another way, beliefs are apparently infinitely numerous: there must be a thousand things that one knows about salt. Therefore, as Dennett puts it, 'I generate all but, say, 100,000 of my beliefs by an extrapolation-deducer mechanism.' What sort of mechanism can this be? The 'store' in the brain seems to be something much more than 'writing' in a code. It may be wrong to think that the information in the brain is stored in any 'compiled' or 'coded' or 'propositional' form. Rather we may have to consider it as embodied somehow in the whole organization of the representational system. This is how the child learns, gradually building up a coherent system of brain-working in which all the items are interrelated. Every use of the system, say to identify and name an object, is thus a creative act of discovering new relations (Ch. 30).

It may seem almost impossible to imagine a code that could represent such a lot of information in any known form of machine. We seem to know so much, how can the brain possibly encode it all? In order to begin to solve problems like this it will be necessary to examine further what is implied in ideas of coding and representation. We may then be in a position to ask how far physiology has been able to find evidence about these processes in the brain.

It is abundantly clear that the presence of the brain is necessary for every manifestation of human knowledge and intellectual power. Nevertheless it does not follow that it is satisfactory to say that information is 'written' into the brain and embodied into a 'code'. The process of 'writing' in a code involves selecting from a pre-existing set those symbols that convey the required information and implies all the capacity to recombine these grammatically to give meanings. We have therefore to enquire whether there is evidence of the presence in the brain both of such a set of symbols from which selection is made and of the capacity to use them. What is the alternative? The information is certainly there and must somehow be represented. If it is not written by selecting from a set it must be as it were sculpted into the nervous tissue, so that the brain actually physically represents the world, as a statue represents its model (see Ch. 27.vi). These are among the questions we shall have to discuss when we examine the problems of learning. We shall find that there is good evidence that the nerve cells of the cerebral cortex constitute coded representations even of such complicated things as human faces, but also that in some respects there is a model in the brain that is isomorphic with the world. However we shall have to admit to complete ignorance of how the brain produces grammatical operations.

11. Intentionality

i. *Is Intentionality a uniquely human attribute?*

Many of the problems that arise in the discussion of brains and minds are brought to a focus in the difficult concept of Intentionality. The meaning given to this word seems to vary among philosophers. It was originally used by medieval schoolmen and is still much discussed today.[25] Its modern use derives from the emphasis of the Viennese philosopher Brentano on the fact that beings having conscious intentions can recognize the distinction between their own thoughts and sensory information coming from outside: that is to say, they are self-conscious. Intentionality has been used by some philosophers as the ineliminable mark of the mental. From here some take a short step to the proposition that humans alone have Intentionality and that this is a property of a mind or soul by which humans are distinguished in a mystical or religious sense.

This extension would be repudiated by most philosophers, who fix instead on the fact that intentions are always 'about' something. As Richard Wollheim says: 'The intentionality of a mental phenomenon is its thought content'; and later, 'Total intentionality cannot be captured, and what is captured can be communicated only on the basis of shared intentionality. Yet it is a matter of agreement that we can report intentionality.[26] What one reports is, then, the content of thought at the moment. If the thought is about the future it provides the evidence that humans act with conscious ends in view, which some people take to be the criterion of purposiveness (2.iv). For the neuroscientist the problem of Intentionality is to find how the brain contains representations of possible states of affairs, including future states, correlated with conscious purposes.

The word is printed with a capital 'I' by some philosophers to emphasize that it does not mean only the same as 'intentional' in the usual sense. The criterion of Intentional mental states is that they are about something: as Searle puts it, 'The second intractable feature of the mind is what philosophers and psychologists call "intentionality", the feature by which our mental states are directed at, or about, or refer to, or are of objects or states of affairs in the world other than themselves.[27] Thus to want a piece of bread is Intentional and so is to believe in God. To intend to do something is also Intentional, but obviously from the other examples Intentionality is not the same as intending. If the convention of the capital I is abandoned, the usual sense of the word intention creeps into the discussion. In the careful account of the matter by D. C. Dennett[28] we find the following useful definition: 'Intentional explanations [of a person's behaviour] cite thoughts, desires, beliefs, intentions, rather than chemical reactions, explosions, electric impulses, in explaining the occurrences of human emotions.' Other names used to discuss the behaviour in question are that it is 'purposive' or 'rational' or simply that it is 'action' rather than reaction, and involves an agent. Yet again, philosophers sometimes imply that there is not only a 'physical' but also a logical problem. Dennett says 'intentional phenomena are absolutely irreducible to physical phenomena, that in terms of sentences the claim is that Intentional sentences cannot be reduced or paraphrased into extensional sentences about the physical world'.[29]

It is difficult for the layman or scientist to appreciate the reasons for the great importance that philosophers attach to questions about Intentionality. It is probably connected with the fact that the capacity to describe the content of thought is uniquely human. The neuroscientist will have to agree that we cannot fully explain precisely how the brain stores representations, and computes with them or acts as an 'agent'. Nevertheless we are rapidly acquiring information about these matters. It may well prove that the use of brain language actually helps to solve some of the philosophical problems by finding the neural correlates that are involved, in animals as well as humans. This would indeed turn the tables on Brentano, who revived interest in the medieval concept of Intentionality because he believed that it could not have a physical explanation.

ii. *The characteristic features of Intentionality*

The problem is thus how a person's Intentionality can be related to the activities of his brain. Philosophers are asking us whether we can specify the internal states that relate to the 'objects' upon which the Intentions of wanting and so on are directed. To put it another way: 'Can there be natural Intentional systems?' Such a system would obviously be one with aims and objectives and be equipped with some set of representations of those things that are wanted, hoped for, etc. I have shown already that the brain is just such a system with objectives. We now have to enquire in what sense it contains representations of the world. Once again we return to the problems of coding.

The peculiar feature that defines Intentionality is that it is a property of mental life that refers to entities that are not observable at the time. Intentional thoughts are thus different from other purposive thoughts where the aim is clearly in view. In Chapter 3 we have agreed (I hope) that the actions of all animals can usefully be said to be purposive but that we should not say that an amoeba or a frog acts with intention. To say of a man that he intended to kill someone means that he already had a 'mental picture' of that effect. For the neuroscientist this implies that the person's brain contained some representation of the likely consequence of the act, presumably gathered and deduced from his previous experience.

Similarly all the other examples of Intentional mental events (hopes, belief, etc.) require that the brain contains representations of features of the world that have been learned, allowing appropriate expectations. The most obvious way of finding out whether the brain of an individual contains such anticipatory representations is to ask him.[30] 'Did you intend the shot to kill Smith or only to wound him in the leg?' This makes it seem that Intentional events are the specific property of conscious people using language. It may be indeed that human brains are much better at making such representations than are those of any other animals and this is a question that we shall examine.

To attempt a general definition of Intentionality one might say that it is the state of an individual who is planning or expecting action with reference to some condition of affairs that is not immediately present. We may gain insight into the nature of this state by looking at some possible Intentional states in monkeys.

iii. *Intentional systems of vervet monkeys*

According to our fundamental thesis some brain processes are involved when a person wants or hopes or believes something. Even if philosophers and cognitive scientists are not very interested in these neural processes they can help neuroscientists by showing them what to look for, defining the nature of such Intentional stances. An example is a recent discussion by Dennett of the question whether monkeys are Intentional systems.[31]

The studies of Seyfarth, Cheney and Marker show that:

Vervet monkeys give different alarm calls to different predators. Recordings of the alarms played back when predators were absent caused monkeys to run into the trees for leopard alarms, look up for eagle alarms, and look down for snake alarms. Adults call primarily to leopards, martial eagles, and pythons, but infants give leopard alarms to various mammals, eagle alarms to many birds, and snake alarms to various snake-like objects. Predator classification improves with age and experience.[32]

The question that Dennett asks is 'do they *really* communicate. Do they *mean what they say*?' To answer this he uses the diagnosis of Grice, according to which 'genuine *communication*, speech acts in the strong, human sense of the word, depend upon *at least* three orders of intentionality.' This would involve such a situation as 'Utterer *intends* Audience to *recognize* that Utterer *intends* Audience to produce [a] response'.[33]

How would this apply to the monkeys? Take a situation in which one animal, Tom, gives a leopard alarm call in the presence of another monkey, Sam. Dennett provides a series of

competing intentional interpretations of this behavior, ordered from high to low, from romantic to kill joy. Here is a (relatively) romantic hypothesis (with some variations to test in the final clause): 4th-order. Tom *wants* Sam to *recognize* that Tom *wants* Sam to *believe* that there is a leopard

        there is a carnivore

        there is a four-legged animal

        there is a live animal bigger than a bread-box.

3rd-order. Tom *wants* Sam to *believe* that Tom *wants* Sam to run into the trees' . . .

2nd-order. Tom *wants* Sam to *believe* that there is a leopard he should run into the trees . . .

1st-order. Tom *wants* to cause Sam to run into the trees . . .

0-order. Tom is prone to three flavors of anxiety or arousal: leopard anxiety, eagle anxiety, and snake anxiety. Each has its characteristic symptomatic vocalization. The effects on others of these vocalizations have a happy trend, but it is all just tropism, both in utterer and audience.[34]

This interesting analysis tells us a lot about the attitudes of philosophers as well as vervet monkeys. Dennett unashamedly *wants* to *believe* that the animals have some higher-order Intention. Indeed he goes on to relish further findings that support this view, such as that a *lone* male vervet monkey will on seeing a leopard *silently* seek refuge in the trees. Further, he points out that using the Intentional stance can suggest experiments to test whether monkeys show what we would call rational behaviour, which is an excellent reason for using this stance. Much less usefully, Dennett seems to imply (surprisingly for him) that the higher-order behaviours have no physiological basis. 'The claim that *in principle* a lowest-order story can always be told of any animal behaviour (an entirely physiological story or even an abstemiously behavioristic story of unimaginable complexity) is no longer interesting.'[35] The remark is ambiguous but seems to suggest that he here wishes us to regard him as an out-and-out dualist. What is the point of the denigratory suggestions about physiology? Why speak as he does of 'just tropism'?

iv. *What would be needed to show Intentionality in the brain?*

The various orders of Intentionality imply the presence of increasingly complex representations in the brain. In the zero order it seems to be suggested that Tom has a representation that produces a reaction to the leopard but has no representation of Sam. Surely this is too low an order. A few minutes later Tom may be grooming Sam, he must have representations (and perhaps consciousness?) of him.

In the first order, Tom's wanting to save Sam's life has altruistic implications whose genetic basis we need not discuss here (Ch. 35.ii). It requires representations in Tom's brain of the leopard and of Sam, some system for relating them and of anxiety about the fate of his fellow. This surely need not be more complex than the many examples of parental care for the young. There is no neurological difficulty in extending this to the care of others by social animals.

The second- and higher-order situations involve representations in Tom of the condition of representations within Sam. They involve some capacity by Tom to learn to attribute to Sam the same properties of wanting, etc. as he, Tom, himself possesses. This indeed implies the presence of more elaborate representations than we have yet been able to investigate. It is arguable that it implies a capacity for consciousness of self. Tom has learned a

representation of other vervets fleeing from a leopard. The critical
association with his own fear and flight might be made easier by
their common experience of the situation. This would cover the
second order. The third and fourth orders imply reciprocal associations between representations by Tom of himself and those
within other monkeys. A representation of oneself seems intui-
tively to imply self-consciousness, though it is not obvious why it
should be different from any other representation in the brain.
However, Grice is quite right to use this as the point at which we can
recognize something like the *human* capacity for communication
and possibly of consciousness as discussed already (Ch. 11.iii).

When does a baby reach this 'understanding' of others? May
there be special capacities for this in the human brain, not available to animals? The questions are indeed interesting, in spite of
Dennett's disclaimer. To answer them we need further information about the processes of representation, especially in the
human brain. There is no reason to suppose that these processes
will prove to be inaccessible to investigation. They will certainly
be complex, but they are not 'unimaginable'. It is a great challenge
for neurology to pursue them. This is indeed a frontier of human
knowledge, in several senses.

The general conclusion is that neurologists can suggest the outlines of the representations that mediate the simpler Intentional
processes that are at work when a human being or an animal wants,
believes and so on. The processes are much more complicated than
the 'mere tropisms', which were all that were understood fifty
years ago and should surely now cease to appear in serious discussions of such complicated matters. There is a lack of knowledge
of how the representations are 'manipulated' (what an inadequate
verb!); we do not understand the mechanism of 'thinking'.

The most serious neurological difficulty is to understand the
relations of representations of self with those of other living things.
It is possible that this involves processes that are peculiar to man,
and are the basis of consciousness. I should not myself expect that
there will be found to be any such sharp dichotomy between animal
and human life, though admittedly we are very peculiar animals.

v. *The mechanistic and the purposive*

In later chapters we shall see something of what goes on in the brain
in such Intentional situations. The little that is known can be helpful

in various medical and legal matters. More important for our present discussion is that it helps towards finding a consistent terminology in which to discuss fundamental questions about knowledge, perception, human aims and moral responsibility. It is this last which causes especial difficulty for some philosophers. They express this as the view that, as Dennett puts it, *'the mechanistic displaces the purposive*, and any mechanistic (or causal) explanation of human motions takes priority over, indeed renders false, any explanation in terms of desires, beliefs, intentions.[36] I agree with Dennett that this view is wrong and is due to 'focusing attention on the wrong features of [the] examples'. What is involved here is a confusion between our attitude to other people as fellow human beings and as physical objects. The difficulty disappears once one comes to terms with the fact that the conscious mind and the brain are inextricably connected. There is then no place for conflict between one's attitude to others as persons and as mechanisms. This may not seem obvious at first and is so important that it merits further discussion both here and later.

vi. *The participant attitude*

However much information may be obtained about the brain it is not possible to abandon what Strawson calls the 'participant attitude'. Dennett expresses it thus: 'There is at least one person, namely the one being addressed, if only oneself, with regard to whom the objective attitude cannot be the only kind of attitude that is appropriate to adopt.[37] We are committed to the participant attitude as we are also to induction which is 'original, natural, non-rational (not *ir*rational), in no way something we choose or could give up'.[38]

What such claims amount to is that everyone must admit to having his own mental life and to postulating its existence in others. The first part of this statement at least is obvious and neither part in any way reduces the interest of study of the brain action that accompanies mental life. Nor is it necessary to give overriding priority to the mental and the rational as if they were somehow inconsistent with the physical. This attitude arises from transferring simple ideas about mechanism, such as knee jerks or conditional reflexes, to the explanations to be offered for the complex brain operations that are involved in beliefs and rational thinking. Such an attitude of course leads to the view that 'a piece of behaviour mechanistically explained is what some call a mere happening, not an action'. From here it is a short step to: 'The performing of actions is the restricted privilege of rational beings, persons, conscious agents.'[39] Which is true indeed, but such agents only have their powers because they have brains. Such a statement is not the basis for any pejorative attitude to the mechanical, which is uncalled-for and can only bring confusion. All mental operations are accompanied by cerebral operations; the question is, how can we find out about the latter and best speak of the combination? As Dennett says, there is no evidence for 'an inviolable *terra incognita*, an infinite and non-mechanical mind beyond the grasp of physiologists and psychologists',[40] although, as he points out, the idea of such an area appeals to some people. It is of course the basis of the dualism that Brentano wished to establish when he revived the scholastic concept of Intentionality, using it to distinguish a specifically non-physical state.

Cognitive psychologists are a group who sometimes seem to support the Brentano view. They believe that the only realistic way of describing human behaviour is to use Intentional or mentalistic language and idiom, at least in the present state of knowledge. Of course this is a practice that ordinary people use every day. Indeed it would be absurd to suggest that we should try to substitute descriptions of brain activity for simple statements such as 'he hopes it will not cost more than £100.'

It is not yet clear how far it is reasonable to expect neurology to go. As Fodor puts it in his book *The Language of Thought*, 'If psychology is reducible to neurology, then for every psychological kind predicated there is a co-extensive neurological kind predicated.'[41] This may be an ideal but it is too strong a 'law', at least in the present state of knowledge (see Ch. 4.ii). Present information about the brain is sufficient to help us to speak more precisely about general problems of philosophy and human nature but not to provide substitutes for the daily use of cognitive language.

vii. *Representations and agents*

To find out how the brain operates in Intentional situations it is necessary to analyse what is involved in the process of the formation and use of representations. As Dennett puts it,

What is needed is nothing less than a completely general theory of representation, with which we can explain how words, thoughts, thinkers,
pictures, computers, animals, sentences, mechanisms, states, functions,
nerve impulses and formal models (*inter alia*) can be said to represent
one thing or another.[42]

He adds: 'Having a propositional attitude is being in some computational relation to an internal representation.' Saying 'Aero-
planes fly' involves being able to learn the meaning of 'aeroplane'
and then to operate with that symbol.

There is good evidence that human beings have an innate
capacity to learn languages. This involves much more than
simply learning to associate a given word or other symbol with
the right object (or result) — apes and even octopuses can easily
do that. What the human does is somehow to generalize from the
predicates that he learns so that he can compute an infinite
variety of combinations of the implications of the properties of
the situations he has experienced. You know that zebras don't
wear overcoats but did you compute this implication? If so
when — before the question was posed or afterwards? And how
was it done? These are the sort of questions we have to answer.
What can these representations be and can we find out how the
brain computes with them?

This is where the conception of the brain as an agent becomes
so important and seems not to have been grasped by some philosophers. Fodor stresses that computational processes are distinct
from other processes and considered action is distinct from mere
reactivity. Indeed it is, and the nervous system is not a mere
reactor, it *is* an agent, with an elaborately planned program of
action, by which it continually pursues its aims. The whole concept of representation implies the existence of such an agent. To
quote Dennett again, 'nothing is intrinsically a representation of
anything; something is only a representation for someone; any
representation requires at least one user of the system who is
external to the system. Call such a user an exempt agent.'[43] This
was indeed Hume's problem, but why must the agent be external?
All living things are the users of representations. The arrangement of the nucleotides along the DNA helix of an *amoeba* is a
coded representation, by means of which it is possible for a jelly-
like protein system to continue to exist in water. Life, leading to
human beings, has developed through at least 3,000 million years

the capacity to set up representations and to use them to keep alive. This is the solution to the paradox of how a representation can recognize itself. The essence of living systems is that they are not isolated — they do indeed depend upon an exempt agent, namely their own history. Remember the paradox that the information in the DNA is used by the enzymes, *which are themselves the products of the DNA* (Ch. 9.iii). Dennett considers how the messages in the code of the brain can be regarded as self-recognizing representations. He then gives what he calls 'a side-long glance at DNA'. It is worth much more than a glance, for it shows the secret of the exempt agent we are seeking.

We have seen how the instruction system of the DNA of each species has come in a sense to represent the characteristics of the environment in which the organism will live. These instructions organize the production of enzymes whose actions ensure the active pursuit of life by the individual. In the higher multicellular organisms, such as ourselves, the DNA instructions produce a very active, conscious, seeking individual agent who sets out to pursue the aim of survival by use of the means appropriate to his species. In our own case this largely involves collaboration with others, especially by speech and gesture.

The human DNA provides a brain that is already pre-programmed, as we shall see, for collaboration and for language; perhaps also for much more than this. Each individual inherits also powers of learning, which make possible the setting up of very elaborate representations of the nature of the world around. Each person, as an active agent, uses this store of programs of action and information to conduct his personal and social life.

We can now understand the general features of this whole system of life. What we need to know is how the brain sets up and stores the representations and computes with them. To these major and difficult problems we must now turn. They have not yet been fully solved.

12. Representation and computation in the brain

i. *The nerve impulse code*

What is the coding system with which the brain operates when it performs its remarkable feats? Evidently it is a communication system acting as an agent. It makes computations with entering signals so that these interact with contained representations to produce an output that satisfies some aim of the system. The whole significance of any such communication of information is that it will evoke action by the recipient of the messages. The production of an action can be regarded as decoding of the message that is communicated: it is as it were the 'translation' of its 'meaning' into another language. To investigate the coding system that is used therefore we can start at the *de*coding end and examine the *output* that the nervous system makes. The decoding operations are the translations of the signals that pass along the nerve fibres into actions by the muscles or glands. These produce the acts assisting survival, which are the object of communication within the body.

The nerve fibres, or axons, that carry the signals away from the brain end as little knobs called motor end-plates pressed against the surfaces of the muscle fibres. The signals carried by the nerves are known as nerve impulses and when each arrives at the ends, it cause liberation of a small amount of a special chemical substance (often acetyl choline) known as the transmitter, which has the effect of tending to release the power of the muscle fibre to shorten. These nerve impulses evidently act as the signals that carry messages in this peripheral part of the nervous system. We now know how the nerve impulses are generated. Each nerve fibre is maintained by its enzymes in an electrically charged state, ready to act. The nerve impulse is a wave of discharge of the potential, sweeping along the nerve fibre at speeds up to 100 metres a second. Incidentally this is rather slow compared to the speed of an electric current along a metal wire. Living messages do not travel with the speed of light.

The nerve impulses are perhaps better understood than any other living process, thanks to many workers in the last fifty years, including Edgar Adrian, Herbert Gasser, Bernard Katz, Alan Hodgkin and Andrew Huxley, who all earned Nobel Prizes

for their work.[44] It is known with great precision how the electric
currents are produced by waves of depolarization passing along
the surface membranes of the nerve fibres. There are some details
of which we are still ignorant, but it is fair to say that the method
of propagation of nerve impulses is well understood. Each pulse
is an all-or-nothing event and is followed by a short refractory
period, during which no other impulse can pass. The nerve
impulses in any one nerve fibre are all alike and they follow each
other at short intervals, so that between one and a hundred may
arrive every second at a motor end-plate. In general the strength
of contraction of the muscle varies with the frequency pattern of
arrival of the nerve impulses. The nerve impulses start off in the
motorneuron cells of the spinal cord from which the axon begins,
initiated by influences that we shall have to consider.

These nerve impulses are the simplest units of the code of the
nervous system — those used for messages sent for long distances, for example from the brain to the spinal cord. Many nerve
impulses also pass from cell to cell within the brain: but it does
not follow that all information is coded, stored or transmitted in
this way. We have still not fully discussed what form representations may take there. Moreover a code is not understood simply
by recognizing its units. Clearly the individual nerve impulses are
all alike and do not represent anything. Only by grouping them
appropriately in various ways can they be made to do so. It is
their grouping that is important, just as in the Morse code, or the
sounds that make up speech.

The 'grouping' of the nerve impulses is patterned, both in time
in each nerve fibre and in space among many fibres, to produce
appropriate messages. The fact of spatial distribution makes it
rather difficult to understand the nature of the code. We ordinarily think about a message as being sent along a single channel
such as a telephone wire. The early telegraph messages consisted
of sequences of dots and dashes. In the body, effective messages
consist of sequences of single dots, the nerve impulses, sent along
many separate channels to many separate muscle fibres, which
act as receivers of the message. For example there are ten or more
muscles that move the thumb and each of them consists of thousands of separate little muscle fibres, and each of these receives
the branches of a nerve fibre. The message 'bend the thumb'
involves sequences of nerve impulses in several hundreds of nerve

fibres sent to thousands of muscle fibres. The speed, force and direction of the bending will depend upon the number of nerve fibres activated and the number and frequency-pattern of impulses sent along the various nerve fibres. The speed and force can thus be subtly varied by changing the number of nerve fibres and muscle fibres that are activated. It is characteristic of the nervous system that its messages are distributed in this way both in time in any one channel and in space among many channels. This makes it possible to provide the endless subtle variations of action that are so characteristic of the behaviour of animals and humans.

A great part of our knowledge of the functioning of the brain depends on the study of nerve impulses. Fine wires can be inserted into the brain to record impulses generated within single cells or nerve fibres, or by groups of them. The electrical changes produced by single impulses are small (less than 1/10th volt) but with modern techniques they can be amplified and displayed on a television screen or played by a loudspeaker or analysed and stored in a computer.

Thus we can recognize a *frequency code* of impulses within the nerve fibres and a *place code* or *topological code* depending upon which nerve fibres are activated. These two types of coding also dominate the organization of the central nervous system, though chemical and electrical factors may also be involved there (Ch. 13.iv).

ii. *The logic of the brain*

The foregoing is almost the simplest possible example of how the nerve impulse code works, and it has already been greatly simplified. Imagine the difficulty of trying to understand the coding system by which an image on the retina is turned into nerve impulses in thousands of fibres of the optic nerve. Still worse, what can be the code system by which tens of millions of nerve cells send nerve impulses to each other in the brain? What are the units of the organization in the brain that represent the word 'zebra' or the belief that it wears no overcoat?

Physiologists are only just beginning to see this problem, let alone solve it. So it is no wonder that we cannot understand clearly how information is encoded in the brain! But at least the nature of the problem begins to be apparent, and this is progress.

By the end of the book it should be possible to see the present extent of our knowledge of the subject, and its limitations.

The discovery of nerve impulses in fact tells us a great deal about the nature of the code. It shows that the system involves some form of computation that uses units. Earlier speculations about the nervous system used various ideas about the flow of 'animal spirits' along the nerves and in the brain. Once the nature of the nerve impulses became known it was possible to analyse the logical operations of the brain on the assumption that the essential process was for a nerve cell either to send or not to send a nerve impulse. This simple logical premiss is still the basis for most of the models used to explain nervous actions, though it is only partly true. It assumes that the brain performs computations in something of the same logical sense as does a computer. Unfortunately the analogy cannot be pursued very far. The alternative yes/no operations in the memory units of a computer are performed to answer the questions sent to them in rapid sequence by a central processor. The sequence is organized by the tape of 'software' into which the programmer has inserted the questions for which answers are wanted.

The brain has no central processor. The operations are not performed in logical sequence, but *in parallel*, along thousands or millions of lines acting at once. Somehow this produces answers to the 'questions' that are set by the ongoing life of the individual. The question may come from within, as when one is hungry or thirsty, or from outside, as when it begins to rain and one seeks shelter, or if someone asks 'What time is it?' The questions arise partly in the form of the patterns of nerve impulses that are generated by the sense organs, and partly by the signals arising within the brain itself as indicators of the needs of the moment (see Ch. 16).

Answers are computed by the interaction of the incoming nerve impulses with the coded representations that are already in the brain. This is where our knowledge begins to falter. Physiologists have only preliminary ideas about the nature of those representations: we are beginning to understand their units, but not yet so clearly as biochemists understand the genetic code.

Knowledge is increasing fast. It is clear that the computing is done by the interaction of the nerve impulses within groups of nerve cells, organized into patterns either by heredity or by learning. These groupings of nerve cells provide the programs of possible responses from which, as we have seen, selection is made to produce effective actions (Ch. 5). The trouble is that there is very little knowledge of the actual patterns of connection that provide the representations that are responsible for answering the more difficult questions. Until we know more of these it is misleading to say that we 'understand' the process of representation in the brain.

In order to try to show the extent of what is known I shall first describe the operations of the spinal cord, where the arrangements are relatively simple and well understood. We can then examine some more complex situations involving more interesting human capacities, including language. We cannot show the details of the representations that are active when we speak; but we can at least say something about where they are in the brain.

iii. *Simple representations. Reflexes*

The effect of touching a hot plate is to set up nerve impulses in some thousands of sensory nerve fibres. These signals then cause motorneurons to send impulses to various muscles, which contract and draw the hand away. Much is known about how in this situation the pattern is generated by the motor nerve cells of the spinal cord if they receive a certain pattern of nerve impulses in the sensory nerve fibres coming from the skin. Some sensory nerve fibres are connected directly to the motorneurons, but most of them send fibres to intermediate neurons (interneurons), which receive from several sources, and in turn send signals to the motorneurons. The arrangement of all these interneurons and motorneurons of the spinal cord provides a set of groups representing various actions. Activity in each group produces muscular contractions that are appropriate to a particular pattern of impulses, coming to them either from the hand or descending from the brain. Thus one set of neurons will cause the fingers to grip, another to make them let go, and so on.

The points at which the signals in the incoming fibres reach the nerve cells are the *synapses*. Each motor cell receives hundreds or even thousands of synapses. They release the chemicals called *transmitters*, which serve either to increase or decrease the tendency of the surface membrane of the cell to become electrically depolarized to the point at which it sends impulses along its nerve fibre. The motorneuron therefore sends signals to the muscles only when it receives impulses at a suitable proportion of these synapses. Notice that some of the synapses are inhibitory, that is to say, they tend to stop the motorneuron from sending impulses.

From our point of view it is clear that the arrangement of all these sensory fibres and synapses and nerve cells serves as a representation of the actions that are likely to be effective after contact of the skin with a very hot object. The synapses and cells of the spinal cord perform the operation of electrochemical computation that the appropriate response is to drop the plate; as a result, suitable bursts of nerve impulses are sent along the motor nerve fibres to the muscles to produce this effect. The spinal cord is capable of thus computing an avoidance response, a type essential for survival, without reference to the brain. Moreover the necessary representation does not have to be learned. It has been built into the developmental processes of every individual, instructed by the particular sets of nucleotides in the DNA that have been selected over past ages. Of course signals are also sent to the brain but they probably arrive there after the instruction has already gone out from the spinal cord to drop the plate. The pain that follows involves cerebral events that we shall discuss later.

The signals that go to the brain may also produce modification of the reflex — if they get there in time. A very valuable plate, say of Chinese porcelain, may still be held even if it burns the fingers. Presumably the brain contains complicated patterns of connections that have been learned, and these representations can override the protective reflex; but unfortunately little is known about them, or indeed about the patterns that produce any other intentional actions.

iv. *What study of reflexes can and cannot show*

Knowledge about the coding systems is thus in a very tantalizing state. The code of nerve impulses in peripheral nerves is well understood and their interaction to produce reflexes in the spinal cord has been fully analysed. Most of what is known comes from the study of reflex actions in which the 'stimulus' arises outside the body; we lack information as to how the neurons in the brain interact during the more complicated forms of behaviour and mentality. Complex behaviour has often been ascribed to 'conditioned reflexes' as understood by Pavlov. These could indeed be regarded as based upon representations such as we are considering. However attempts to explain living actions as initiated mainly from outside are bound to miss the main point: the actions of living organisms arise largely from the programs of activity *within* them, modified continually of course by events from outside.

Understanding of the codes of the brain will develop as knowledge accumulates about the rhythmical activities that provide the basis for each day's pattern of action. These arise from the needs of the individual, expressed by the forebrain centres such as the hypothalamus (Ch. 32). There are whole systems of nerve cells, in the reticular system and elsewhere, which never come to rest, and many exciting discoveries are likely to be made before long about these internal activities. They will probably direct investigation of the coding problem away from the study of the input to that of the pattern of the output and the consummatory and reward systems that are satisfied by responses (Ch. 32). The codes and representations will be better understood when the 'values' that they are framed to satisfy are brought into consideration.

There is already a considerable amount of information about the sets of nerve cells in the cortex that provide the units from which the representations are formed. These will be examined later with the study of perception. Before following them it will be useful to examine the evidence that particular parts of the cortex are involved in some of the complex human activities, such as perception of shapes or faces, or uttering or receiving speech. Such powers must involve representations in the brain; if we are to find them we must first seek for evidence of where to look. In the following chapters we shall examine some clues that have been found recently by surgeons, working with psychologists and physiologists, examining conscious patients as well as monkeys.

13. The origin of signals in the cortex

i. *Signals from the human cortex*

To pursue the problem let us consider how trains of nerve impulses are originated in the nerve cells of the brain when it sends signals to initiate actions by the spinal cord, say, bending a finger. Fortunately we can use an example that shows the presence of a nerve impulse code in man. It is possible to study the nerve impulses produced by cells of the motor cortex of human subjects under local anaesthesia while undergoing operations for the cure of epilepsy. Some cells of this part of the brain send their axons direct to the motorneurons of the spinal cord. When the patients were asked to bend a finger some of the cortical nerve cells gave bursts of nerve impulses *before* any contraction could be detected in the muscles. The burst stopped when the fingers were relaxed, but then sometimes other (inhibitory) cells were also seen to discharge. Most of the brain cells studied were connected with the opposite hand, but some with both hands. All of them only sent their signals when the fingers were moved voluntarily. None of them responded to stroking the skin.

ii. *Signals from the cortex of monkeys*

These limited studies do not tell us what happens in the brain when a person decides to bend his fingers! But they do show that part of the process includes the activation of these cells of the motor cortex so that they send impulses down to the spinal cord. It is only rarely possible to make studies of this sort in humans, but many further details about cortical motorneurons have been obtained from monkeys. We are interested in the organism as an agent and therefore take as example the spontaneous action of a monkey who has been trained to move a lever that makes a light appear at a certain place: the animal then gets a drop of fruit juice. An electrode has been inserted in the brain at a previous operation and its tip is close to a cell of the precentral region of the cerebral cortex. Some of the cells of this motor cortex send axons down to the spinal cord, where they activate the spinal motorneurons, whose fibres, as we have seen, carry impulses to the muscles of the hand.

iii. *Synaptic inputs*

The electrode in the brain shows that the cells of the motor cortex send out signals at a low rate of a few a second even when the monkey is at rest. A big burst of impulses begins about a second *before* the hand moves the lever. This does not tell us much about the processes of computation that go on before a decision to act, but at least it shows that patterns of nerve impulses destined for the spinal cord are generated at the output end of the calculation. Much further evidence is available to show that all long-distance signalling in the nervous system goes on in this way. Impulses set up in one nerve cell travel along the axon to its terminal points, the synapses, which are in contact either with another nerve cell or with a muscle fibre or gland cell. In either case, when sufficient nerve impulses arrive at the synaptic end points, chemical stimulants are released and these in turn activate the next nerve cell or a muscle fibre.

The difficult questions begin when we ask what 'decides' whether the cell of the motor cortex is to begin to send its burst of nerve impulses. Obviously this depends on the signals that it has itself received from other cells of the brain, nearby or far away. Nerve cells receive signals through their dendrites (from the Greek for 'tree'), which extend to distances of up to 1 mm at the opposite end of the cell to the axon. The dendrites are covered by synapses, which are the endings of other nerve fibres; up to 60,000 of them for a large cell of the cerebral cortex. This does not mean that each cell receives signals from that great number of sources. Many of the synapses will be the ends of the branches of one incoming fibre. It is not known how many sources in fact contribute to each cortical cell, but it would be safe to say about 100. Some of these inputs will be from nearby cortical cells, others from other parts of the cortex or from other parts of the brain, such as the thalamus or cerebellum or from the reticular activating system.

iv. *Field effects*

As if this were not complicated enough, there may be a further influence in the form of the field effects of local electrical changes of nearby cells, acting directly upon the dendrites, not by nerve impulses arriving through the synapses. Some physiologists believe that slow, graded changes of electrical potential or chemical action serve to 'compute' interaction among neural elements by continuous (analog), not all-or-none (digital) mechanisms. This raises a very fundamental question about the whole operation of the brain. Analog codes of this continuous sort involve units that are in some way isomorphic with what they represent. That is to say, the microstructure of the brain would directly represent certain features of the world as a sort of model. This is a very different situation from representation by selection from a code of arbitrary units, such as we have been considering. The nerve impulses are certainly the units for long-distance communication, but the field effects and local patterns of electrical and/or chemical activity may possibly be factors involved in the computations that initiate the long-distance signals. The extent of such local, graded action is not known. This is a very debated question and much remains to be found out about such direct influences of the local electrical and chemical conditions on neighbouring nerve cells. They certainly exist, but it is not known what part they play.

v. *Selection of patterns of cortico-spinal neurons*

The 'motor cortex' is so called because it is found that electrical stimulation of this region is followed by movements of the limbs. It was supposed for a long time that voluntary actions were actually initiated by the motor cortex. It is now realized that in fact this region of the brain is only sending out the final signals to act — it is far down the chain of the computation that must go on before action begins.

The nerve cells of this motor cortex whose axons pass down to the spinal cord are the largest in the whole brain; they are called the cortico-spinal neurons (CSN). Their control of the motorneurons of the cord is itself a most complicated matter. Each cortico-spinal neuron sends branches to many motorneurons and also to the thalamus and cerebellum. Conversely each motorneuron receives signals from many other cortico-spinal neurons. So the activation of any muscle is the product of selected activity of a particular *pattern* of cortical cells. The presence of these sets from which the selection is made shows the features of redundancy and degeneracy that we have met before (Ch. 8.v). There is not one cortico-spinal neuron for each movement; each CSN usually affects the spinal motorneurons that control the muscles of several joints and vice versa. However, in the hand each CSN often controls only a single muscle.

vi. *Hot points in the cortex*

Nevertheless, in spite of this overlapping, electrical stimulation of the cortex reveals rather localized points from which a particular muscle or group of muscles can be activated. The bending or extension of any joint can be produced from several of these scattered 'hot points'; they are dispersed among the hot points for other joints nearby. So the participation of any finger in an action involves the selection of appropriate members of this set of modules, which is available for the movement of the various joints.

The motor cortex runs down the side of the brain and it has been known for a long time that each part of it sends fibres to a particular region of the body. Especially large parts of the motor cortex are devoted to control of the face, lips and tongue; other large parts control the fingers. Parts of the body that make less delicate movements such as the shoulders or the legs have smaller parts of the motor cortex. This shows again that the nervous system achieves its more delicate operations by the presence of greater numbers of its units — the nerve cells. The coding system used in the necessary computations involves wide spatial distribution of the signals over many neural pathways.

vii. *Inputs to the motor cortex*

In order to take the next step in understanding the code of the brain that is involved in initiating a movement we have to ask how the cortico-spinal neurons are controlled. What makes them start and stop sending nerve impulses, say to the muscles of the tongue to frame a word, or to the fingers to pick up a cup? The answer is not fully known and will certainly prove to be very complicated. We can at least recognize that there are very large inputs to this motor area of the cortex from the region just behind it, known as the 'sensory cortex' and from that in front of it, the 'premotor cortex'. Each 'hot spot' for movement of a particular joint receives nerve fibres from the parts of these neighbouring areas that are concerned with receptors in the skin or muscles around that joint. Other inputs come from the cerebellum and thalamus and other parts of the brain. Much can probably be learned by recording with several electrodes from various sources of input. This might carry us one stage further in the search for the sources of action patterns in the brain. It can be said at present that at this rather low level of the computation by the brain there are some concentrations and canalizations of the wiring patterns. The system has a definite anatomical pattern, though we can only dimly discern it. This does not mean that the actions of the brain are limited only to conduction along certain pathways. The computation system involved is certainly widespread, dynamic and variable. But in every individual who has learned a number of skills the patterns of activity probably tend to flow along certain pathways, which have been called 'assemblies of neurons'.[45] Anatomists, physiologists and psychologists have faith that the system is something like this, but it is vague and there is little detailed evidence about it. Nothing can be said that helps much with the really difficult problem of finding what happens in the brain before one decides to answer a question by saying 'Yes'.

Nevertheless it would be a mistake to be too pessimistic. Study of the brain is proceeding very rapidly in many countries. Whole areas of knowledge are opening up. We shall be able in later chapters to provide further evidence about the organization of the sensory and other areas that send signals to the motor cortex, even though it is not known exactly how they function. Meanwhile we have been able to show that the code of the nervous system involves sending out sequences of nerve impulses from the brain to the spinal cord and from there to the muscles.

These observations of the responses of cells of the precentral motor cortex have given some idea of the pattern of output that is emitted by the cortex as a prelude to a motor action such as bending a finger. This set of nerve impulses, distributed over a number of nerve fibres, each firing at a variable frequency, calls up a faint picture of the earlier activities that had proceeded within the cortex leading to the activation of the cells of the precentral area. Presumably millions of nerve cells in many areas were varying their frequencies of discharge in patterns that bear some relation to the developing intention to move that digit. It is not known how these patterns are organized in time or space, so in that sense we do not understand the code of the brain. Yet, curiously, we can now cite some direct evidence at least about the timing of the cerebral events that accompany such intentional actions in man.

14. Changes in the brain before an intentional action

It has been possible to collect data that tell us quite a lot about the timing of cerebral events in relation to mental phenomena. This is one of the situations in which experiments with humans are actually more revealing than those with animals. We cannot ask a monkey to tell us exactly *when* he intended to move his finger: but Libet and his colleagues have found a way of comparing the times at which events occur in the human brain with those at which mental intentions are reported.

It has been known for some time that electrodes attached to the head will record a slow negative potential shift a second or more *before* a person receives a signal that he expects, and to which he will respond by making a movement. This was first called a 'contingent negative variation' (CNV). Much more interesting is the discovery that a similar readiness potential (RP) occurs before a person makes a *voluntary* action. Libet and his collaborators have now been able to show that this readiness potential change in the brain occurs up to half a second *before a subject mentally decides that he intends to make a movement*. The method is to set volunteer subjects in front of a television screen upon which a spot circulates clockwise at a speed of one revolution every two and a half seconds. The subject is asked simply to decide of his own free will to bend his fingers and to note the position of the spot on the tube at the moment he makes the decision. An electrode attached to his head shows that the readiness potential change in his brain began an average of 350 milliseconds before the time at which he or she reported that they 'wanted' or 'intended' to act. This was also of course long before the time of actual movement of the finger, which was detected by electrodes attached to it.

The readiness potential probably arises from the activity of neurons in the premotor area of the cortex. There may be activities in other parts of the brain at still earlier times before an intended action. No doubt further experiments of this sort will establish in greater detail which parts of the brain are involved in computing the intention to make a movement. The importance of Libet's observations is that they show that the brain is at work *before* a subject's conscious intention to act.

As he says,

Put another way, the brain evidently 'decides' to initiate, or, at the least, prepare to initiate the act at a time before there is any reportable subjective awareness that such a decision has taken place. It is concluded that cerebral initiation even of a spontaneous voluntary act, of the kind studied here, can and usually does begin *unconsciously*.[46]

Although we do not know how the brain computes intentions we now know for certain that it *does* compute them and that the mental events *follow* this cerebral activity. People still sometimes try to dissociate themselves from such discussions by saying 'But it is *I* who make decisions, not my brain.' Knowing that the brain is at work *before* one is conscious of a decision may help us to realize that *it is futile to think of oneself as distinct from one's brain*.

Further evidence shows the complexity of the programming that is involved even in the simplest movements. Electrodes were attached to the head of volunteer subjects and to muscles in various parts of the body, in order to follow the sequence of events that occurs when a subject performs a spontaneous voluntary movement of pointing or punching a target. The sequence was as follows: 1) A negative readiness potential in the brain begins to rise slowly about one second before there is any actual movement. 2) The first action is a 'saccade' movement of the eyes, (see Ch. 24.ii) bringing them to point at the target. 3) At about this time swaying of the body is detected by movement of the platform on which the subject is standing. Such preparatory balancing movements are very important for humans, since the centre of gravity must be kept perpendicularly over the feet. These postural preprograms are organized unconsciously before there are any actual movements of the limbs; evidently very complicated events are then already proceeding in the brain. 4) and 5) Postural movements of the same sort now appear in the muscles of the trunk and legs. 6) Only now do the shoulder muscles begin to raise the arm. 7) A sharply negative aiming brain potential is now super-imposed on the readiness potential. This must be an indication of some further complicated computational events, but we do not know what they may be. 8) The body as a whole may now be rotated. 9) Finally the arm is extended towards the target, about half a second before contact for a punch, and rather longer for a pointing movement. 10) Contact is obtained about two seconds after the earliest readiness potential or rather later for a pointing movement. At the moment of contact a sharply positive 'achievement potential' is recorded. The total duration of the operation is thus 1–1.5 seconds for a punch or 1.5–2 seconds for pointing. 'Only the goal-directed eye and arm movements (2 and 9) are steered consciously, all other processes (1,3–8, and 10) are unconscious co-ordinations, automatised by exercise and modulated by reflexes.'[47]

Studies such as these are useful preliminaries to investigation of the actual programs of the brain. They show at least vaguely the complexity of the processes that must be occurring within it. There is at present no clear indication of how it may become possible to gain more detailed understanding of these processes. Probably it will be achieved only gradually.

15. Some sites of linguistic activity in the brain

It has long been known that injury to certain parts of the cerebral cortex causes the loss of particular mental capacities. After complete loss of the occipital cortex at the back of the brain a person can no longer 'see' in the sense of reading or distinguishing shapes, though he may still be able to tell whether it is light or dark. Chapter 22 provides more detail about the processes that go on when we see. Here we are concerned to show that particular parts of the brain are involved in 'higher' mental activities, such as language. Much evidence about this has come from surgeons who explore the surface of the brain in operations for the relief of epilepsy. Indeed the need for the investigation arises from the fact that each part of the cortex has a different function. Epilepsy is an extremely disabling complaint, which is the result of the presence of a focus of abnormal brain cells whose activities spread through the cortex and produce the fits that are so distressing. If the focus can be found and removed the patient is cured. The site of the focus is identified by its unusual electrical activity, recorded by exploring with fine silver wires on the surface. Before the surgeon can remove the focus he must be sure that he will not deprive the patient of some essential capacity. For instance, removal of any part of the motor cortex, running down the side of the brain, results in paralysis of the muscles of some region of the body (Ch. 13.v). If the epileptic focus is in that strip nothing can be done. It would probably not be worth having a paralysed hand or face, even to be free of epilepsy. Subtle investigation is needed in order to discover what will be the consequence of removing a part of the brain. After the use of local anaesthetics the surgeon can give the cortex a weak electrical stimulus while the patient is still awake and able to answer questions. Very interesting studies of the areas responsible for language have been made in this way by Dr Ojemann and a team of colleagues.[48]

Patients are very anxious to be rid of their epilepsy and are eager to collaborate. Before the operation they are shown by psychologists exactly what tests will be used and how they are to respond. The method is to find whether a weak electrical current applied to various spots on the surface of the brain alters the capacity to answer questions. For instance the stimulus may interfere with the power to name simple objects. Such stimulation produces no pain, indeed the patient does not know when it is applied, but it produces a short pulse of random activity in the cells of a small area under the electrode. This disturbance affects the power to perform whatever task depends on that particular area. A series of pictures is shown on a screen. The patient names them correctly except when the stimulus is applied in certain places. Then, when he is shown a horse, he says 'That is, er, um, you know — I can't say. . .'. A few minutes later, without the stimulus, the name comes at once. The stimulus acts as it were as a temporary removal of one small part of the brain. The discreteness of the effects is very striking. The cortex is a patchwork of columns, each with a different function (Ch. 17.vii).

The two regions where this interference occurs are those where tumours or strokes have long been known to produce 'aphasia', that is, interference with speech. After injury in a more anterior part of the left side of the brain, Broca's area, patients can understand the speech of others but cannot themselves speak coherently; often they talk telegraphically, missing out little words. After larger lesions one or two words may be used over and over again for everything. Indeed Broca's first patient was known in the hospital as 'Monsieur TanTan' because these were the only words he spoke; he used them for everything. So this is the motor area for speech. After damage to another area, further back on the brain, the person cannot understand the speech of others or speak sensibly himself, but the words he produces are all well formed. So this is said to be the sensory, or syntactic, speech area, named after the neurologist Wernicke who described it in 1874.

Stimulation within these areas has produced much further evidence that each part of the cortex has to some extent a unique function. Ojemann and his colleagues found that in bilingual patients stimulation of some points produced errors only in one of the two languages. It was already known that after a stroke only one language may be affected: occasionally a language used for many years is lost and one hardly spoken since childhood reappears.

The localization of function is so precise that particular small areas within the major fields can be found where stimulation impairs only part of the capacity for language, such as naming objects, reading, or identification of phonemes.[49] The pattern of errors can be assigned to various systems. One is the cortical final motor pathway for speech. Stimulation of this stopped all speech and also other facial movements. Stimulation of a different area produced defects in recognition of phonemes (e. g. confusion of the nonsense syllables abma, apma, adma, etc.)

Stimulation of this area was also interesting because it prevented the patients performing tests involving movements of the mouth and face, in which they were required to imitate pictures of lip movements. The authors suggest that this supports the theory that a central mechanism for language depends on sequential motor-phoneme identification. A third system of sites, lying around the previous two, is involved in memory of words heard a short time before. Stimulation at other sites produced difficulty in reading correctly. Further studies have shown that there are electrical changes in these very same brain regions (but not in others nearby) when a patient is asked to name *silently* an object flashed on a screen.[50] The electrical changes begin to be apparent within a few thousandths of a second after the picture has appeared. This is thus evidence of the presence of activity in a *particular* small part of the cortex (but not in other nearby parts) synchronous with a given mental activity.

Of special interest for philosophers is the evidence of patients whose restricted lesions have produced defects of the capacity to use words of specific semantic categories. They may be unable to use or understand concrete words ('blacksmith' or 'macaroni') while recognizing abstract ones such as 'soul' or 'opinion'. Nevertheless they could express themselves well within the limits of their vocabulary. This suggests that there may be quite an elaborate anatomical organization of semantic and perhaps also of syntactic functions.

These studies certainly show that some nervous action related to the use of words in the act of naming is localized in the limited parts of the brain concerned. This does not give evidence about what is going on there, but allows us to hope that we may be literally on the track of the brain-representations we are seeking. The discovery of single nerve cells that respond only to a face (Ch. 23.iii) raises the possibility that neurons may act as code representations of words. This would agree with the way one is apt to lose access to a single word or name.

These observations do not tell us how language is encoded, but they do emphasize that the capacity for it is somehow *there*, in some sense written in the brain. It is no longer possible to say that the idea that speech is encoded in the brain is 'a *mere* metaphor'. It is indeed a metaphor because our way of speaking about this carriage of information is to compare it with our artefact that imitates and enlarges it — namely writing. The problem is how to enlarge the metaphor further by showing how information is written during learning. That means finding the physiological processes that are involved in encoding information in the anatomy of the brain. The processes and the anatomy must be immensely complicated. It is hard to see how progress can be made towards understanding them: probably it will be slow and gradual. It would not be enough to show how some simple experience leaves a record in the brain. Even such simple learning is indeed little understood and will be discussed later. The challenge is to show how the brain acts in typical 'mental' activities and of this, frankly, we as yet know very little. Possible solutions may emerge as we go on in further chapters to study the processes of perception by the various senses.

PART II

Perceiving

We cannot look at perception without considering
co-ordinated movement

(H.-L. Teuber)

16. Perception as a search for information

i. *The problem of perception*

My thesis is that human knowledge can be considered as a special
development of the process of gathering information for life that
is essential in all organisms. This way of thinking is unfamiliar
and perhaps even unwelcome. I hope that it may become clearer
and more acceptable as we see how it helps us to understand
perception.

Ayer begins his chapter called 'The Problem of Perception' by
claiming that the sceptic has here the difficult task of denying that
the naïve realist is on strong ground when he claims that through
sense we have direct access to the nature of objects in the world.[1]
Whatever may be the status of the finer entities of the physicist it
seems at first obvious that what the philosopher Austin called
'moderate-sized specimens of dry goods' are directly perceived.[2]
But the sceptic can raise difficulties with this commonsense view.
He claims that we perceive physical objects not directly but
through the medium of some other entities. Ayer then asks what
these entities can be and discusses the many theories, and the
status of the 'ideas' of Descartes, 'Vorstellungen' ('representations') of Kant, 'sensible qualities' of Berkeley and, more
recently, his own use of 'sense data' and the 'qualia' of Lewis and
Goodman. I shall not try to evaluate these notions, but their
number and variety suggests that it is worth studying the whole
process of perception as fully as we can, in order to find out what
intervenes between events in the outside world and changes

within an organism. As Ayer puts it, we need to examine the status which is assigned to the immediate data of perception. He finally fails to accept the arguments of the sceptic, for his chapter ends: 'Our criteria of reality have in the first instance to be formed in terms of the way things appear to us. We have nothing else to go by.' This seems at first to be a very sensible conclusion but on examination will be found to be far from clear. 'Things' do not usually simply make their appearance — we search for them because we want them, and the motives and sequence of the search very much influence what we find. Moreover it is not clear whether this conclusion is meant to apply to all perception. The word 'appear' suggests that it relates to vision, which is the sense so often singled out for study by philosophers. A more detailed study of the responses of the various other types of sense organ and the associated perceptions helps greatly towards better understanding of this ancient and difficult search for criteria of reality.

ii. *Programs for perception*

It may be that our whole sensory world can properly be considered as a sort of artificial construct useful to provide forecasts for living. Recent investigators give interesting facts about this very question, and they tend to confirm the suspicions of the sceptic. The evidence of physiologists and psychologists suggests that our subjective perceptions of the world are the accompaniments of programs for seeing, hearing and touching.

Most of the perceptions we receive with the senses do not just fall upon us. They are selected by an active search for meaning and significance. When you enter a room during the ordinary course of life you probably 'see' only very few objects. Even the most 'observant' person could not possibly give a list of all the different visible shapes that there are around in every room. What one does is to pick out and attend to those outlines, colours, and surfaces that indicate the presence of *objects* that are of concern because of the ongoing program at the moment. We 'see' the kettle and the cups but not the shadows cast by the chair legs or under the window-sill.

Unfortunately, in most observations about perception made by psychologists and physiologists or considered by philosophers the stimuli are *given* to the human or other organism, not sought out as they usually are in life. But the search and its objectives and its consummation are essential features of 'perception' as it occurs normally as part of the life program of the organism. It is not easy to realize how deeply what we perceive is influenced by a program of expectation. The complexity of perception was summarized by Bartlett in his valuable book *Remembering*: 'Inextricably mixed with [perception] are imaging, valuing and those beginnings of judging which are involved in response to plan, order of arrangement and construction of [the] presented material. It is directed by interest and feeling.'[3]

Every creature has the power to abstract those features that are relevant for its life from all the changes that go on around. The sort of question we should be asking about perception therefore is, how does it come about that the organism makes these selections from the flux of changes? The capacity to produce appropriate responses in reacting to certain features of the pattern of light or sound emitted by some objects must mean that the brain contains some sort of record or representation that matches these patterned signals from the outside world and allows us to identify the object or voice. It is fascinating to consider how this may be done, and there begins to be some evidence about it. It seems as if the brain contains descriptions of all the people and things and sounds and smells that can be recognized. But a better statement would be that each representation is an aggregate of expectations of how to react to these sensory inputs. When someone speaks on the telephone the sound of his voice somehow fits or matches the brain 'description' and you reply 'Hello James.' Obviously this must be a wonderfully complicated process, perhaps of search and matching. It is not known how it works, but there is some evidence about the nature of the record that exists in the brain. Systems of nerve cells must act as what may be called symbols or code signs for particular features or combinations of features of the world around. They act as it were as counterparts or representations for particular visible arrangements of contours or sounds or touches on the skin. The problem for the physiologist is to identify these code signs or representations or whatever we should call them.

Every occasion of perception occurs as part of the pattern of life, whether of an animal or man. Perceptions may sometimes occur unexpectedly, as from treading on a pin or seeing a lightning flash, but more usually they result from some program of search initiated from within or without. We select from the many changes going on around us in the world those that seem relevant to our needs at the moment. In much of vision, as will be described later, we actually create the information about objects in the world, by selection from the complex pattern of electromagnetic radiation. The signals sent to the brain as a result of the selection thus *become* the information that makes one, say, perceive the glass and pick it up and raise it to one's lips. The glass does not send information — it sends reflected electromagnetic waves. The prospective drinker makes this into the information that there is a full glass there ready for him.

iii. *Where is the sender of the message?*

We commonly speak of the 'reception' of information by the senses, forgetting to ask who is sending it. The concept of communication of information implies transmission along a channel from sender to receiver (Ch. 7.iii). The paradox of sensation is that only one agent appears to be involved; how can he be both transmitter and receiver? The paradox is solved as we remember that the senses provide the information for life, which depends upon the maintenance of *order* (Ch. 7.ii). Perception is the active search for the ordered features that we call 'information'. The programs of search by the sense organs are initiated by the needs of the organism, which act as a transmitter, selecting questions for transmission. This is obvious in simple cases: a hungry boy looks around for information as to how he can meet his need; his searching eyes light upon a rosy object on the tree and the signals passing up the optic nerve become the message whose answer is 'apple, pick it'. The features selected thus become the information transmitted in answer to 'questions' asked by the search.

The questions asked are characteristically more complicated in the more complex animals, such as mammals. All animals make some form of search for their livelihood (indeed so do plants), but the 'higher' animals must seek for and find a much more elaborate world than is available to the 'lower', because they exist in conditions that are less directly suited to the support of life (Ch. 9.vii).

Each sensory system will be found easier to understand as we examine how it is used to send coded information in answer to questions that are set by the needs of the organism. All the sense organs provide multiple channels, each carrying signals that answer a different question. There are at least fifteen varieties of touch. Taste is a useful simple example, with its four sorts: sweet, sour, salty and bitter, each providing a different answer as one cautiously licks an unknown food (Ch. 18.i). Hearing and vision provide vastly more channels, but the principle is the same. With all the senses we are actively seeking for the *ordered features* of the world that will help us with life.

One does not usually associate perceptions in man directly with search and action in this way. This is because the peculiar character of the human system of life is indeed the remoteness of the connection, typified by the reader's attention to these very words. Your present perceptions are due to a vague need for information and they will influence action later, by altering your program of life a little. This characteristically human remoteness between much of perception and action is indeed one of the factors responsible for the introduction of these 'entities' that obscure the relationship between an observer and the outside world. Examination of some aspects of the different senses will show that there is a wide range of variation in the separation between perception and action.

Swift action may follow even in a complicated sensory system like that for vision. A sudden flash of light produces a blink, and the observer says 'I saw a flash.' Surely here we can trust the conclusion that there has been an increase in the incident radiation; but even this depends on the situation: he might have been hit on the eye by a boxer. There are difficulties in accepting *all* statements about perception and we can show the nature of the complications that intervene by asking, for each of the various senses, whether the perceptions of change are unexpected or are expected as the result of the situation and of programs of search. These programs are a major source of intervention by the observer, with his expectations of what he is likely to perceive.

These are some of the factors that may affect what we may call the veracity of perception. They are variables not always considered by physiologists or psychologists, who are generally interested in dissecting acts of perception into their components in the sense organs, nerves, cortical centres and so on. Such investigations do indeed provide important clues, as will appear during discussion of the various senses, but I shall try to show that still greater insight is achieved by consideration of whole acts of perception in the context of actions performed as parts of life programs. We shall be bound to conclude that the way things appear to us is never just a consequence of their own nature.[4]

iv. *Input analysis*

The actual changes in the outside world are detected by the *transducers*, sensitive cells such as the rods and cones of the retina, the cells of the lining of the nose, or the hair cells of the cochlea of the ear. Each type of animal has transducers that are appropriate to its environment and mode of life. This already places restrictions on what can be perceived. For instance, the eyes of bees are sensitive to ultraviolet light, which makes the centres of flowers appear to them quite different from their appearance to us. Each species has analysers which reorganize the signals received from the transducers and select among them so that they will report features that are relevant for its life. These input analysers vary greatly in the complexity of the information that they encode. A famous paper on 'What the frog's eye tells the frog's brain' showed that in this animal the analysis performed by the retina reports only a few features of the visual world. The signal given by a small black object acts as a 'fly detector': answer — 'Eat it.' The large dark shadow might be a 'duck detector': answer — 'Jump.' The colour blue indicates water: 'Jump into it.'[5]

The input analysers that are at work in humans must be very complex and they mostly lie beyond the retina, in the brain. They convert the signals from the transducers into signals that indicate the presence of features that are likely to be significant, such as contours, distances and wavelengths. The output from these feature detectors are then somehow combined to indicate the presence of complicated entities, such as faces, tables and chairs, or the written words of language. These re-coded signals are in turn used by the further parts of the central processing system to produce thoughts, decisions and effective action. This is obviously only a vague preliminary account and it will need much further elaboration.

Physiological studies have concentrated largely on the processes of transduction, which are now rather well understood.

Some information is available about the simpler input analysers, for instance for vision. They are nerve cells or groups of them that select certain features from the signals sent by the transducers. An example at low level is provided by the contour detector cells of the visual cortex described in Chapter 23.ii. According to the analysis of cognitive psychologists, it may be that there are also modules for detecting much more elaborate features in the world, like tables or grammatical utterances.[6] Recent work has shown that individual nerve cells can act as representations of complex objects such as a face (Ch. 23.iii). There is evidence that some specific human input-analysers are partly innate and, after practice, may become 'hard-wired' and used consistently as wholes. For example, speech sounds are heard quite differently from non-speech: in a non-speech context the onset of a consonant is heard as a whistle or a glide.

The units recognized by these input modules become compulsive parts of perception. A word is heard as a word even if you focus attention on its acoustic or phonetic features (or indeed on the ink, if it is written). Objects are objects, whether seen or touched. One *has* to make these input computations whenever they are offered. It is impossible to hear speech, in a language that you know, as mere noise, even if you prefer to. Similarly 'you can't help seeing a visual array as consisting of objects distributed in three-dimensional space.'[7]

So it seems that some quite early stages of the input analysis take place by the use of sets of rather restricted modules. As Austin wrote, 'moderate-sized specimens of dry goods' are directly observed. The processes that produce such recognition must be complicated but we now know that much of the information is included in single cells.

It seems that we have no access to the intermediate stages of input processing. As an example of this, tell a person to look at his watch and ask what time it is. 'Nine-fifteen.' 'What shape are the numerals?' Probably he cannot say. Looking at a watch 'means' looking at the time — no other information is recorded, although he must have 'seen' the numerals.

As Fodor puts it, 'input processes are informationally encapsulated, like reflexes.' It makes operational sense that this should be so. These mandatory input modules are necessary for the reliability of perception. It is important that the output of the transducer and analyser should *not* be influenced by complex expectations or beliefs. So 'wishful seeing is avoided by requiring interactions with utilities to occur *after* — not *during* — perceptual integration.'

So Fodor believes that the neural mechanisms subserving input analysis develop according to specific endogenously determined patterns. Input systems constitute a family of modules: 'domain-specific computational systems characterized by informational encapsulation, high speed, restricted access, neural specifity and the rest'.

The physiologist should be happy to believe that this analysis is correct. If it is, it gives him hope that he is on the right track in trying to identify such modules. For all of us it gives a tool with which to deepen our thinking about the early stages of human cognitive processing. It may even be a stepping stone to study of the next stage of analysis, the central processes of thinking, about which no one yet knows anything.

17. The senses in the skin and their cortical centres

i. *Receptor organs in the skin*

Perceptions provided by the skin give good examples of how the nervous system transduces various types of external changes to send coded signals, and how these are then used by the brain.[8] The different receptor organs in the skin provide messages whose information answers various distinct questions. Compare the use that is made by signals from the fingers and from the lips. By feeling with the fingers we can identify objects and perform all sorts of manipulations. Appropriate use of the lips can give information about good food or drink, or all the pleasures of a kiss. Is there any sense in asking which provides the truer information about the world? The individual has learned that the messages coming from these two sources constitute information of quite different sorts, answering different questions and requiring different actions.

There can be said to be three sorts of skin sensation: touch, pain and temperature, and they are widely different. Touch gives information about things in the immediate neighbourhood. Temperature can tell us about the situation, either nearby or further away. Pain is produced by events nearby, but is referred to the skin itself rather than to the external agent. I might perhaps say 'that bee hurt', but the stinging feeling is in my finger.

Each of these three main types of sensation includes several subtypes. There are distinct receptor organs sensitive to light touch, deep pressure, and other forms of mechanical stimulation. The temperature sense is served by separate organs sensitive to hot and cold. Even the sense of pain is not simple but includes signals of immediate fast pain and duller, persistent slow pain (Ch. 19). Altogether the skin contains at least fifteen different types of sense organ, each stimulated by a different external change. The roots of the hairs are surrounded by nerve fibres and are sensitive detectors of movement, especially developed as the whiskers of cats or mice.

In the hairless skin there are many special sense organs. For instance, along the ridges of the skin of the fingers there are various corpuscles, sending different signals depending on the type of contact or movement: some respond to light pressure, others to vibration, others to a sudden prick, and so on. What is felt depends upon the particular combination of the receptors that is activated when that area of skin is used in a given way. The signals sent to the brain by the various combinations of skin receptors then set up actions appropriate to the situation and the stimulus.

Each area of skin has a different set of these sense organs which, with their own connections in the brain, provide for suitable action. Thus the tips of the fingers have many detectors of light touch, which are so connected in the cerebral cortex that they can be used to make fine discrimination of shape. Conversely the skin of the penis or clitoris has hardly any of these detectors and provides little feeling of form, but stimulation of its sense organs and their central connections provides very strong sexual appeal and corresponding action. In animals with whiskers there are especially large cortical areas for touch. The movements that can be detected are so slight that a rat senses the presence of objects by air pressure before there is actual contact. Thus the tactile sense can serve as a 'distance receptor', at least for events not very far away.

A sudden pin-prick seems to provide a simple example of perception, but is not really at all typical in that it falls upon the observer unexpectedly — he does not actively seek it. The response is an immediate withdrawal of the hand or foot that has been pricked (Ch. 12.iii). The nervous pathways involved in this 'flexor reflex' have been fully studied by the classical work of Sherrington.[9] They are laid down by heredity and are little influenced by learning. The connections involved in the flexor reflex are made in the spinal cord and can operate even if the cord is isolated from the brain. There is little doubt about the veracity of the resulting perception. The person who has trodden on a sea urchin has indeed detected a small spiky section of the universe, though he learns nothing about its shape or extent: it might be a sea urchin or a broken bottle. There are many limitations on the reliability and value of the observation; for one thing it is unique and cannot be exactly repeated. Others may tread on other urchins but no one else can have experienced that particular sensation at that moment in exactly the same way. Moreover the reflex and its subjective counterpart are not as invariable as I have suggested. Pathways take signals of pain upwards to the brain and there are descending nerve fibres that can block the flexor reflex, and alter the quality of the pain (Ch. 12.iii).

Altogether the apparently simple 'stimulus response' situation of being pricked by a pin or treading on a sea urchin tells us rather little about the normal functioning of the nervous system. The very conception of a 'stimulus' is itself suspect because it implies something applied to the organism and not sought by it. The value of the pin-prick example is that it is easy to understand. Certain nerve fibres in the skin are provided by heredity with the power to turn a sharp prick into a code of nerve impulses, the process technically known as 'transducing' the stimulus. To allow recognition of shapes other receptor organs in the skin must transduce more complicated mechanical changes into series of nerve impulses in various nerve fibres.

ii. *Scanning by touch*

Most of the important sensations of touch do not just fall upon the skin but are actively sought as part of a program of action. I pick up the pencil that I see and it feels as I expect it to feel. To examine an object by touch in the dark the fingers are moved in directions that are guided by hypotheses about what may be there. This familiar use of the guided sense of touch involves the comparison of the sequence of signals with some model or representation that is already stored in the brain. Recognition of objects by sight also involves a process of sequential scanning, seeking for familiar clues (Ch. 24.i). The movements of the eyes are much faster than those of the fingers, in fact the eye muscles are the fastest in the body. Such scanning procedures emphasize the continuous interplay between action and perception. Indeed perception of a shape by touch *requires* movement by the perceiver. The shape of a complex object moved passively over the fingers cannot be recognized, though the texture may be. The observer needs to compare the program of his own movements with the incoming signals in order to encode them in a meaningful way.

'If I could only move my hand about I should know what the things were.' This was said to Victor Horsley by a patient asked to identify objects placed in his hand three weeks after the arm area of the precentral (motor) cortex had been removed.[10] Movement is certainly necessary for the recognition of three-dimensional objects, though differences of roughness can be detected if the objects are simply pressed against a finger. Simple shapes can also be recognized when presented passively, for instance by tracing them on the skin.

The nerve impulses sent from the skin only become useful information if they occur in sequences that somehow relate to expectation generated by the brain. You wish to telephone and feel in your pocket: 'Yes, this seems to be a 10p coin — I'll try it in the box.' The brain contains some representation of that coin, which has organized the sequence of contacts. The nerve impulses provide 'information' because they serve as answers to 'questions' set by the need of the moment. We could measure the amount of information involved as $\log_2$ of the number of answers needed to identify the coin (Ch. 7.ii). To find out more about the nature of such representations we shall now examine some facts about the cerebral cortex, where these more elaborate processes of coding occur.

iii. *Divisions of the cerebral cortex*

The cerebral cortex is a great sheet of tissue with nerve cells on the outside (hence 'grey matter') and nerve fibres within (white matter). Its whole functioning depends upon the display of activity over this sheet and within and between its parts. The characteristic appearance of the brain is due to the folding of the sheet, allowing an area of no less than 122 dm^2 (half a tennis court) to be packed inside the skull.

Throughout the history of the study of the cerebral cortex there have been persistent attempts to find areas that have particular functions. This tendency has equally often been criticized as 'reductionist' by 'holists', who believe that one should consider the brain as one functioning whole. There is some truth in both these points of view, as will appear from the treatment in the present book. The cerebral cortex certainly does have distinct parts, with different functions; equally certainly there is much interaction between these parts and with the rest of the brain. The nature of the various areas and their interconnections has become more evident recently with the use of new techniques in the work of many anatomists, psychologists, physiologists and surgeons. All the parts of the cortex and the rest of the brain form one interacting community, in which the various centres play different parts in the self-maintaining activity of the whole.

Several different systems are used for naming the parts of the cortex and some mention of them is unavoidable.[11] Indeed some knowledge of the system used to describe the brain is essential for understanding of the philosophical problems involved in cerebral coding. Modern accounts mostly go back to the work of Brodmann who studied the appearance of sections (slices) of the human brain stained to show the cells.[12] He claimed to be able to distinguish no less than fifty areas with distinct patterns of arrangement of the cells. Many later workers were less careful and were unable to repeat Brodmann's analysis. The sceptics who doubted Brodmann included the famous psychologist Karl Lashley, who is much loved by 'holists' for his claim that in some sense all parts of the cortex are equal. Yet recent work shows that Lashley was wrong about this. There are indeed significant differences of structure and function within the cortex. So we go back to Brodmann and everyone still uses the numbers by which he labelled the areas.

He started from the central sulcus, which is a deep groove that can usually be seen down the side of the human brain. The areas behind this groove are predominantly sensory and are given the numbers 1, 2, 3, 5, 7. The areas in front of the sulcus are largely motor and are 4, 6, 8, etc. But this distinction is not absolute; in fact every part of the cortex is in some sense both sensory *and* motor. Nevertheless there is something in the recognition of the two main regions. Signals about the world tend to *come in* to the more posterior parts of the cortex and *go out* from the anterior parts. For instance the 'motor cortex', whose large cells send axons direct to the spinal cord is area 4, lying immediately in front of the central sulcus (Ch. 13). Again, in discussing speech in Chapter 15, it was found that injuries to Broca's area, in the front part of the brain, produce errors in *production* of speech, whereas damage to the more posterior Wernicke's area leads to failures of *comprehension*.

Other systems for naming the major parts of the brain include the anatomical names 'frontal' for the anterior part, 'occipital' for the back and 'parietal' and 'temporal' for the top and sides. The inner surface of the cortex, where the two hemispheres lie side by side, is called the cingulate cortex. It is an important area that receives signals from many parts and sends them to the hippocampus and elsewhere.

Difficulties over naming arise because the folding of the surface of the brain varies greatly in different individuals. There are even worse difficulties in comparing results from different species, such as cats and monkeys, where the brains have different folds. Yet the general arrangement of the areas is similar in all mammals. Perhaps this is a good moment to remember that in other vertebrates the arrangement is quite different. Birds have no true cerebral cortex at all, though they are obviously quite 'intelligent'. But we must leave this tantalizing thought and return to the sense of touch.

iv. *The cortical areas of touch*

Nerve impulses from the skin reach the cortex after passing through several lower centres. Many of the pathways end in the areas 1, 2 and 3 of Brodmann, lying immediately behind the central sulcus and this is known as the first sensory area, S1. Each part of the surface of the body sends signals to a different part of this area, so there is as it were a map of the surface of the body laid out on the brain. The map is distorted, giving much larger areas to the fingers, lips and tongue than to those responsible for the rest of the surface of the body. Thus the capacity for sensory discrimination is refined to different degrees according to the complexity of the actions of each part of the body and hence to the need for information from it. For example, there are few ways in which detailed information from the skin of the back could be used, and indeed everyone knows that it is quite difficult to find where to scratch the mosquito-bite there. But with the skin of the fingertips a person can detect points less than a millimetre apart, or a slow pressure involving denting the surface of the skin by only one thousandth of a millimetre. With these capacities a skilled blind person can read Braille nearly half as fast as sighted people can read with their eyes.

Knowledge about what goes on in these sensory areas for touch comes largely from recording the electrical responses of single cells in the brains of monkeys or cats who have been so trained that their responses show the 'answers' to questions about where they are touched. Many neurons in the postcentral part of this sensory area (known as 3b) respond when single stimuli such as pressure at a point are given to the skin.[13] This may therefore be called the primary touch area and is in a sense comparable to the primary visual area, 17, at the back of the brain (Ch. 23.ii). The actions of the cells of this area 3b produce code-signals for simple stimuli, rather like the simple cells of the visual cortex. In parts further forward, areas 1 and 2, the cells respond only to more complex stimuli, such as movement of a rod in one direction over the skin of a finger or other part of the body.

Some cells of these areas 1 and 2 provide signals only after stimulation of areas of the skin of the arm and body that come into contact with each other when the cat performs a particular action such as licking a paw, or scratching its ear. This tells us a little more about how the brain encodes the information that is needed to compute adequate responses. These areas 1 and 2 receive fibres from 3b, and it seems that their cells are involved in re-coding the simple signals from the 3b cells into larger units. In the areas still further away, known vaguely as S2, still more complex units have been found. For instance, in the parietal area there are cells that only respond when a monkey grasps a straight-edged rod, but not when it grasps a cylinder. For other cells it was the reverse.

There are also cells in these sensory areas that respond to the movement of joints, each giving impulses only when one partic-ular joint is bent in one direction. In area 5 there are cells that respond only when two or more nearby functionally related joints are moved; correspondingly nerve fibres from several parts of the area S1 have been shown to come together in area 5. This convergence may include interaction of signals from the joints with those from the skin. For instance a cell will respond only when the elbow is bent *and* the skin rubbed at the same time.

Proceeding still further backwards from the primary tactile area there are neurons in area 7 whose activities are influenced by vision as well as by touch or movement of the joints. For example a cell may respond when a monkey sees its hand move towards its mouth; if the eyes are covered the cell responds less.

v. *The cortical coding system*

These cortical areas for touch show the principles that are involved in the encoding of incoming signals to the cortex. There are cells that make selection among incoming nerve impulses of those groups that are related to particular actions that are regularly performed. It is not known how far the responses of these cells are determined by heredity or by experience, probably partly by both, as for their visual counterparts (Ch. 29.ii). The selection is made in a hierarchical manner as signals pass from place to place across the cortex. In the primary tactile area 3b the cells respond to simple stimuli. Passing away from here both forwards and backwards the signals are combined among themselves and with those from other receptor systems. It would be a mistake to try to recognize sharply distinct subdivisions within the hierarchy. Probably many combinations and recombinations are involved. It is difficult to imagine how such a system will ever be fully described or conceptualized. It is indeed a fascinating and challenging task.

vi. *Activation of the cortex. The corpus striatum*

This cortical system does not operate alone: it is continually activated by the 'motivational' system that indicates the needs of the individual (Ch. 31). This operates through the corpus striatum and other basal ganglia, which are large masses of neurons at the centre of the brain and are an important part of the whole control system. The corpus striatum receives fibres from the cerebral cortex, especially from the motor areas, and it sends impulses back to these and also to the thalamus. It gains its activation from

the reticular formation, through a system of fibres that use
the monoamine dopamine, and spread widely throughout the
striatum. The striatal neurons have many receptive dendrites and
receive signals from various parts of the cortex. They are not
arranged in any obvious topographical manner but different
groups of them are probably active during the performance of
each individual action. These capacities to activate motor programs are probably learned in childhood and then remain as relatively hard-wired action systems, called into play as required by
the cortex.

Injuries of the striatum produce widespread motor defects,
such as involuntary jerking movements. Parkinson's disease,
involving tremor and difficulty in voluntary movement and
speech is due to a deficiency of dopamine. It can be alleviated by
giving the patient l. dopa, which is a substance needed for the
synthesis of dopamine.

The basal ganglia are thus near the centre of the brain functionally as well as anatomically. They maintain its activity
and monitor its pattern of output. Future knowledge of these
centres will undoubtedly help us to understand the unity of brain
functioning and so to appreciate better the nature of human
personality.[14]

vii. *The columnar organization of the cortex*

In order to describe what is known of the nature of representations in the brain it is necessary to examine some of the details of
the structure of the cortex. The cells of the grey matter are every-
where arranged in columns running at right angles to the surface.
Each column contains about 150 cells, except in the primary
visual cortex, where there are 220. The cells in each column are
not all alike but mostly fall into two types. The pyramidal cells
have axons that leave the column and proceed either to some
other part of the cortex or to another part of the brain or spinal
cord. The stellate cells have axons that end either within the
column or nearby. Each column has a complex internal organization, which it would not be possible to describe briefly, though it
is obviously fundamentally important. The cells are arranged in
six main layers below the surface, with tangential layers of fibres
between them. The cortex therefore has a regular organization
in both the vertical and horizontal directions. This regularity

indicates the profound importance of spatial organization within the nervous system.

The principle of communication by transmitting signals along channels sets strong limitations on the possibilities of organization. The brain is not a continuous mass of tissue whose parts influence each other mainly by processes such as chemical diffusion or gradients of electrical potential, though these are also present. It is a set of units, the nerve cells, which send discrete signals to each other and perhaps interact also by other influences (Ch. 27.vi). In the cerebral cortex the cells are laid out in columns and in the primary sensory areas (and probably also the others) each column is the unit of function or module. We have seen in the primary tactile area 3b that each column responds to a simple stimulus and those in areas further away respond to more complex ones. The same is true in the visual and auditory cortex, as will be described later.

This division into modules, each with its particular function, is a fundamental feature of cortical organization. But it is subject to a very important qualification: each cell in a given column in area 3b will respond to light touch at a particular point on the skin by giving many impulses, but it will also respond to points touched nearby, though less strongly. As a corollary it is obvious that touching any point stimulates cells in many columns, some more strongly than others. So the area of cortex that responds to a given skin stimulus is not sharply circumscribed but may change with various conditions.

These same features of overlap apply to all the other parts of the cortex. They are technically called <u>redundancy and degeneracy</u> of coding. Signals from any point pass to many destinations (redundancy): each point receives signals from many sources (degeneracy). These features of overlap explain much of the power of flexible behaviour in the brain and are probably responsible for the recoveries of function that can appear after damage to cerebral tissues by accident or disease.

viii. *Subjective responses to touch*

So the columns of cells in the 'sensory' part of the cortex constitute distinct modules, each specially sensitive to a particular combination of signals from the skin. Electrical stimulation at any one point on the cortex in a patient under local anaesthesia who is conscious will cause him to report one type of sensation, some-times localized in one place: 'I feel a tingling in the ball of the thumb.' Often it is a vague pricking or 'pins and needles' or a sense of warmth or coldness. The sensation seems 'natural' yet hard to describe. Curiously enough there is usually no report of pain from stimulation of the cortex[15] (but see Ch. 19). Responses of pain produced by damage to the skin are mainly organized at a subcortical level.

These facts show that the cortex contains an elaborate set of modules serving as detectors of events in the skin. Somehow they interact to give 'normal' sensations and to provide the programs by which a search for meaning is initiated. We can follow in some detail the physiological processes that accompany simple mental experiences of touch, but there is no physiological information about the events that are involved in recognition of complex shapes, say of the feel of a fountain pen. This must include comparison of the incoming signals with a stored tactile represen-tation, presumably involving the excitation of certain particular cells or groups of cells similar to those responsible for the recog-nition of faces (Ch. 23.iii).

ix. *Motor programs*

These postcentral and parietal regions are not purely receiving areas. They send descending fibres to other parts of the brain, which can influence the ascending streams of signals at various levels, organizing search movements and providing 'expectation' about what tactile perceptions they will provide. Injuries to the cortical areas produce defects of the capacity to recognize that parts of the body have been touched. The signals sent from the skin enable each person to build a body image, which depends upon the integrity of these parts of the brain. If these areas are damaged by accident or disease the person's image of himself is impaired. In extreme cases a patient may refuse to recognize that one side of the body belongs to him at all. This illustrates clearly the dependence of mentality upon integrity of the brain. Such people have suffered as it were the mental death of part of their person although physically the relevant part is still there. An artist who had suffered a stroke affecting his right parietal area found himself unable, when painting a self portrait to include the right side of his face. So the defect produced by the injury was not one of 'perception' or of 'action' but of both of these; his right hand would not paint that side of his face.

One way to investigate the representations in the parietal areas is to put them temporarily out of action by cooling. A metal plate is inserted over the surface of the brain of a monkey who has been trained to distinguish rough and smooth knobs. When the parietal area of the cortex is cooled the animal makes many mistakes when using the opposite hand. After warming up again the responses become as accurate as before. There are differences in the type of disturbances of functioning with the cooling in different parts of the area.

Obviously a very complicated system is involved, but the evidence from various sources shows that in animals as well as man these parietal areas are essential for the performance of actions involving tactile memories. This of course does not mean that these areas are as it were the sole seat of such memories in the sense of a set of silicon chips or sites on a magnetic tape. We do not yet know enough about memory to say how it is encoded. Probably considerable parts of the brain are involved in the neural system that allows one to recognize a pencil picked up in the dark. It almost certainly takes the form of an active pattern of action initiated by cells of the sensory cortex but involving also down and up interaction with lower motor centres such as the thalamus striatum and cerebellum. The representation that is used for touch must also be somehow related to that for visual recognition of the same object. It is very difficult for the physiologist to understand what form such neural representations may take, using such large parts of the brain. At present we can only say that certain cortical areas are parts of the representation, as is indicated by the reversible failures of tactile memory that are produced by cooling them.

x. *Touch as a substitute for vision*

The use of the sense of touch by blind people has many interesting philosophical as well as practical aspects. Readers using Braille, in which letters are represented by dots, proceed by using hypotheses about grammar and semantics as do those using their eyes. Many questions about the nature of coding and the cerebral processes involved in representation can be approached by comparing the use of the two senses.

Other problems are raised by devices in which the output of a camera system is used to produce patterns of vibration. The Optacon is a television system in which a small hand camera the size of a pen-knife reads lines of text and displays tactile images of them as an array of 144 vibrating stimulators. These are arranged on a curved surface that fits over the tip of the index finger. The blind person follows along the lines of text with the camera and can read up to about ten words a minute. Much better results are given if the machine converts the words to audible speech. The user then only uses the camera for tracking along the lines and can 'read' up to 200 words a minute.

Similar 'electric eyes' have been made to assist movement. The Tactile Vision Substitution System uses a camera on the head and a display of vibrators on the back or abdomen. The interesting question arises whether with such a device a congenitally blind person can acquire a sense of space. Light impinging on the retina gives a percept of external space. Can sensations on the back be similarly externalized and referred to what the camera on the front of the head 'sees'? Reports differ and the question cannot be answered unambiguously for congenitally blind people but asking it serves to focus attention on the problems of perception.

18. Taste and smell

i. *The four qualities of taste*

Taste is the sense that provides a rough test of which foods are good to eat, and so illustrates very well the fundamental value of perception. We use the eye for so many aspects of life that we fail to recognize its 'functions', though we should be terribly handicapped by loss of them. Taste can only be used in one way — to determine the 'value' of food or drink. This is done by special 'taste-buds', little swellings mainly on the tongue. They can distinguish only four qualities: sweet, bitter, sour and salty. Much of what we usually call taste is performed by the nose, smelling the food in the mouth. Tasting usually occurs incidentally, as it were, as we eat. We may of course lick or sip something tentatively but the capacity to taste is essentially an adjunct to the intake of food or drink. The capacity to recognize these four qualities is linked to parts of the brain that produce responses associated with pleasure or distaste, thus preceding particular limited acts of behaviour. We like sugar and salt and swallow them readily. We dislike strong acid or quinine, and make a wry face and spit them out. These are the simpler facts of tasting, but in practice response to substances in the mouth is decided by complicated interactions between signals from the taste-buds and the nose. Such reactions are very much influenced by past experience. It is hard to say how far our chemical senses give 'true' information about the world. Sugar and saccharine are very different chemically but we cannot distinguish between them; nor can a rat.

Taste is obviously a local sense, present only within the mouth in a mammal. Fishes however have taste-buds widely spread over the body, which can detect substances a short distance away. Their nerves enter special lobes of the brain where they activate nerve cells that control movements of turning, to allow the fish to snap up the tasty morsel near its tail. Once again we see how a sense organ provides evidence of a particular pattern in the world that is useful for the life of the animal.

Taste gives no evidence of the shape or form of the substance tasted, but there is perhaps some interaction between taste experienced at successive moments to give 'taste melodies'. The most interesting feature of taste is its influence on selection of foods. Young children or rats spontaneously select from a choice of various foods those that keep them in good health. Sweet and salty substances are in general good for nourishment and bitter ones are bad and often poisonous. The hunger for salt is especially acute and is innate. It leads to taking the right amount but not too much, which can be harmful.

The aversion to bitter things is a response to the substances with unpleasant tastes that have been evolved by many poisonous plants as a protection for themselves. However, some *non*-poisonous, mimic species have found protection by also evolving an unpleasant taste. Mammals have a cortical area for taste and by cautious tasting some animals can learn not to be deceived by the mimic plants that are not truly poisonous.

If an animal or man becomes unwell after eating he acquires a strong 'conditioned aversion' to the taste of that substance. This is a quick and powerful form of learning, occurring after only one trial, and its advantages are obvious. The study of taste strongly emphasizes the homeostatic significance of the sensory systems, which we shall discuss again when examining questions of value.

ii. *Smell*

Responsiveness to smell may have a greater influence on human personality than is generally assumed. It may be that associations made between smells and particular sounds or sights have a profound, if unconscious, influence on the values we attach to their sources. The ability to smell is inborn, but detailed responses to particular odours are very susceptible to learning. Human capacity to recognize some substances is so standard that in coal mines warning can be given of danger by emitting an unpleasant-smelling gas into the ventilator system. Most people recognize the same range of smells, though there are some striking genetic differences: for instance, one person in ten is unable to smell the deadly poisonous gas hydrogen cyanide. The range of scents that can be recognized is very wide, almost infinite, in marked contrast to the limited four qualities of taste. Smell does not always give a good indication of chemical affinity: some substances smell quite different in strong and weak concentrations.

The individual olfactory receptor cells are probably each capable of responding to more than one substance and each substance will stimulate many of the numerous types of olfactory receptor. Once again we see how a combination of redundancy and degeneracy is the secret of coding systems that allow for selection to provide detailed responses to a variety of inputs, the principle that applies throughout the nervous system (and also in the immune system: Ch. 27.i).

The interaction between the signals from these receptors provides a wide potential for encoding responses to smell. On the other hand when the odours are mixed this system makes it hard to discriminate the separate components, though this can often be done by skilled tasters or drinkers. There are various theories as to how discharge of nerve impulses from the many types of receptor in the nose interact to allow recognition of so many distinct odours. An interesting clue is that in a rabbit the spatial distribution of patterns of discharge frequency in cells of the olfactory bulb varies with different odorants. These patterns must provide the code, but physiologists have not broken it. It may be significant that a *spatial* pattern in the brain is involved in the coding of smell, as in the other senses, even though no recognition of spatial patterns is involved.

The diffusibility of odours sets limits on the possibilities of recognizing shapes or melodies by their smell. It is interesting to speculate what the fundamental dimensions of the world would be like for a creature dependent only on chemical sense. There would presumably be some analogies with our space and timz. Judgement of the direction of a source of smell can be made by successive sniffs or by the time difference of arrival of scents at the nostrils.

Many smells are associated with particular emotional and behavioural responses. Most people are repelled by smells such as hydrogen sulphide (bad eggs) and are attracted by sweet flower scents. Bodily odours can produce strong sexual responses, and probably these are to a large extent inborn, though no doubt also subject to later conditioning. Specific substances are often produced by an animal in order to influence others; such substances are known as pheromones. Odours produced by the genital organs often serve as strong sexual excitants. Such scents, including musk, are the basis of many of the perfumes that are found attractive by humans. The odour of the urine of female mice suppresses oestrus in other females but male urine induces it, even at very low concentrations. These odours have great individual specifity. The smell of the urine of a male mouse other than the father will produce abortion during the early days of pregnancy.

The sense of smell differs from either touch or taste in that it can readily be shared. Strictly, a given molecule stimulates only one nose, but a distant source of odour may be detected by many individuals and their response to it is likely to include social activity, for instance in eating, or the response of a herd of deer to the approach of a lion or tiger.

The importance of learning the significance of smells appears in the nervous connections of the nose with the brain. It is now known that smell is connected with the cerebral cortex in the same way as the other senses, via the thalamus. The olfactory area of the cortex is the inner (orbital) region of the frontal lobe, which has long been associated with emotional responses. This is indeed

a region of the brain that plays a fundamental part in manifestations of consciousness and behaviour. Lesions of the medial
zones of the frontal lobes produce 'a sharp decrease in cortical
tone', which 'is absolutely essential for the basic condition of all
forms of conscious activity'.[16] The perception of smell is therefore in this way connected with all our intellectual functions. But
these are very vague statements. As Luria warns, 'the functional
organisation of the frontal lobes is one of the most complex
problems in modern science.'

19. Pain and internal sensations

In studying pain we seem at first to be free of questions of reality:
the pain is perceived by the sufferer as in himself; it is not some
possibly questionable external object or event. Yet even a little
study will show that everyone's pain is variable and will
emphasize how changeable we are: 'The variation of the relationship between pain and injury occupies all positions between
injury with no pain and pain with no injury.'[17] It is indeed hard
to specify 'lawlike correlation' between mental and cerebral
events. After amputation a patient feels pain 'in' a limb that is no
longer there: what sort of reality is that? To find the reality we
must turn to the brain, where there must be some enduring model
or representation of this limb. Examination of the brain has
indeed in a sense been able to find it. Electrical stimulation of the
sensory area S1 for the leg (see Ch. 17.iv) usually produces a
sensation of tingling but no pain. In a person who has had a
painful leg, or an amputation, stimulation of this area *produces
that pain*, indeed he will report pain in the leg also following
stimulation of nearby areas, which are normally concerned with
the arm.[18]

There are many other observations of this sort, and they show
that painful sensations can change the function of the cells of the
brain, probably in many parts, for instance those for reward and
emotion (Ch. 32). Pain may indeed change the whole personality.
The pain following filling a tooth may produce changes such that
pricking some other part of the body ten days later will produce
pain strictly referred to that one tooth that was drilled.

Physiologists have revealed an elaborate 'nociceptive system' of nerve fibres and chemical substances whose function is to produce pains of varying intensity. The system is based on two special sets of nerve fibres that are found in all nerves of the body and serve to send signals indicating that tissues have been damaged. One set, called 'Ad' fibres, send impulses relatively fast when a given small localized area of skin is pricked: they give a quick stinging sensation. The other nociceptors are very thin 'C' nerve fibres, which send slow messages and produce dull, long-lasting pain, referred to a wider area than the tissues actually damaged.

The signals from the nerve fibres proceed to the spinal cord where they may interact with impulses in other nerve fibres that indicate touch or pressure, and also with descending signals from the brain. Such interaction between sensory fibres is the basis for the *variability* that is characteristic of the nociceptive as of all other sensory pathways. From the spinal cord the pain signals are sent on by other nerve fibres to various places in the brain. In particular there are pathways leading to a part of the thalamus (the intra-laminar nuclei) and from there to the cerebral cortex. Relatively little is known about this cortical projection, for the obvious reason that it is difficult to elicit signals of pain without stimulating also nerve fibres for touch and other sensations. Moreover no one likes to elicit pain in another person or animal, and anaesthetics by definition spoil the experiment. These difficulties have been partly overcome by stimulating nerve fibres from the pulp of a tooth, which consist only of the nociceptor classes of Ad and C fibres. Pain is therefore the *only* sensation given by the tooth pulp, as everyone knows from the dentist's chair. Various observations in humans and animals show that after stimulation of a tooth two distinct systems are activated in the cortex. One excites large areas, without the detailed topographical pattern seen for touch, and this wide response is perhaps concerned with the recognition of the painful nature of the stimulus. The other system produces change in single cells in the sensory areas concerned with the skin whose responses may serve to localize the pain.

Enough is known to show that pain is processed by the cortex differently from other sensations. This is indeed only to be expected: pain does not follow a search for the answer to questions, as most perception does. It asks the question itself: 'There is trouble somewhere near here; what is to be done about it?' No doubt many parts of the brain are involved in the search for an answer. The simplest response is a withdrawal from a noxious stimulus — the avoidance reflex, wherever that is possible (Ch. 17.i). When this fails the longer-lasting pain sets up a variable sequence of changes. One effect of pain is an increased alertness, sensory thresholds are lowered and some responses to stimuli are increased.

If the pain continues, the brain has its own capacity to mitigate it by production of the opium-like peptide substances known as enkephalins. There are at least three classes of these, found in different parts of the brain. They are released from the endings of some nerve fibres, including those that carry pain signals to other parts of the brain. The enkephalins act like morphine to reduce the activity of nociceptive pathways. The general biological significance of such action is to mitigate long-lasting pain sufficiently to allow the damaged organism to function adequately while it is recovering.

Pain is valuable because it helps to ensure survival in spite of damage. To do this requires a degree of pain that is adjustable, not an unvarying system of 'automatic relay cells'.[19] Wall points out that this modification of pain occurs at various time-scales: 1) Within milliseconds there is a powerful 'gate-control' of the incoming pain signals. 2) Within minutes the signals of the slow C fibres change the excitability of the various circuits. 3) Within days these C fibres carry chemical influences to and from the damaged areas, which produce further changes, making larger areas sensitive. 4) Within weeks and months there is degeneration of unused fibres and cells in the spinal cord and brain, and sprouting and growth of fibres, producing new patterns of connection. These variations of the brain produced by pain provide a striking example of the adaptability of living tissues. The body continually changes as it calls upon its various programs in the attempt to ensure survival.

Consciousness of internal activities such as those of the intestine or bladder only occurs when they go wrong, and for this there are detectors of fullness and pressure and of pain. They are similar to the slow pain receptors of the skin and they mostly send impulses when there is obstruction and hence stretching of the stomach or other organs such as the gall bladder or ducts from the kidney. Some of these pains certainly have some value for teaching to avoid future recurrence, for example those of the stomach or bowel. It is less clear that any creature could have made use of the pain of a blocked bile duct until surgeons were available to operate on it. However these receptors are certainly useful to humans today for diagnosis.

The intractable pains produced by tumours present a similar problem. Like other aspects of senescence, they may be manifestations of the fact that human ingenuity has recently arranged that we outlive the time-scale upon which natural selection has operated in the past. Yet the existence of these pains can certainly be said to have value for social man today: they motivate the search for methods for the alleviation and cure of cancer and other diseases. The sight of suffering, and the fear that it may afflict oneself, is part of the basis of compassion, which is a valuable asset both to society and for the individuals who compose it. Pain has its positive aspects; anyhow continued life would be impossible without it.

20. The senses of posture and balance

i. *Proprioceptors.   Sensation of self*

There are many receptor organs in the muscles and joints of which we are seldom directly aware but whose signals form an essential background to conscious life. These *proprioceptors* provide information about the position and movements of the head, hands and limbs, which is the essential basis upon which the brain issues commands that lead to purposeful action. Conscious perception is mostly about the state of the outside world and is the basis for relatively slow and deliberate decision as to what would be best to do. The adjustments needed to *produce* the required actions are made unconsciously and very fast, assisted by signals from the proprioceptors.

There are receptors in the muscles that send signals when they are stretched. These signals pass to nerve cells in the spinal cord, which produce contraction of that same muscle. This is the basis of the knee-jerk by which a doctor tests one's reflexes by sharply tapping below the knee. When he does this the extensor muscles are stretched, and the signals from their proprioceptors make them contract, so that the leg kicks up. The signals from the proprioceptors are relayed to the cerebellum, which is a part of the brain largely concerned with unconscious control of the timing and force of movements.

Other receptor organs are placed in the capsules of the joints of the arms and legs and especially the fingers. The signals from these receptors provide the information about the positions from which movements must start, and where they should stop, to produce a given effect. These calculations are of course exceedingly complex and yet precise. They are performed largely in the cerebellum, and much faster than could possibly be followed in consciousness. Imagine the calculations that are involved in getting all the fingers of a violinist or a pianist to start and stop at exactly the right spots! This is a job for a computer that works in the range of thousandths of a second, leaving the conscious cortex to decide about five times a second which notes to play and how loud; which is quite a job in itself.

Paradoxically, although one is not directly conscious of proprioceptor signals, the control of muscular actions plays a very important part in perception. It is clear that searches for meaning are at the basis of much of perception by vision and touch. In these searches the active movements of the eyes or hands are essential, and are programmed by the brain as a search for confirmation of a hypothesis: 'Is it round or square?', 'Are the shapes of the eyes, ears and nose right for it to be Henry?' In order to make such comparisons the brain must have information about the movements that it has ordered to be made during the search. There is evidence that this takes the form of a 'corollary discharge', based on the motor output. This information reaches the somatic sensory cortex (Ch. 17.iv); neurons have been found there that discharge when a monkey makes exploratory movements with hands or arms. They are probably recording the commands that have been issued, rather than being themselves command cells sending control signals for a movement.

ii. *Signals from inside the body*

The receptors systems of the internal organs have special philosophical interest because their actions are continuous but seldom conscious. The operations of the heart, lungs, blood vessels and stomach and intestines all involve elaborate adjustments monitored by receptor organs of whose signals we are never conscious. Receptors signals the need, say, to adjust the blood pressure or to move the food along the intestine. All of this is accomplished without our knowing it and the nerve impulses of the autonomic nervous system, on which these actions depend, are not relayed to the cerebral cortex. This tells us a great deal about the division of functions in the body and the significance of consciousness. The 'conscious mind' relates to dealings with the outside world, which require elaborate analysis in the light of the past, and preparation of future programs of action. We think things over and make plans; there would be no sense in doing this consciously every time that we speed up the heart when we go upstairs, or dilate the blood vessels of the leg muscles to do the work. These things are arranged to happen automatically every time that one has set in motion the action of climbing. Conscious control of the details of these activities would overload the cerebral computer. Past experience does indeed have its effect; repeated use of muscles produces increase of their power and their blood supply. Such 'adaptations' are a form of memory achieved without one's being conscious of it, except in finding that your muscles work better after training.

iii. *Receptors for gravity and movement*

Another large set of sense organs of which we are hardly conscious provides the signals that keep the body the right way up and provides for movements of the eyes to compensate for movement of the head. They are called 'vestibular' because they are placed in a cavity, the vestibule of the ear. These signals are given by sensory hairs similar to those that are involved in hearing. To keep the body upright there are hairs that signal the direction of gravity, being loaded with tiny grains of chalk. As the head moves the hairs bend and this alters the train of signals proceeding from these cells to the brain. There they influence the motor nerve cells so that these produce movements of the muscles of the leg, back and neck to maintain the correct posture.

A second set of hairs detects the turning movements of the head in any direction. These 'angular acceleration detectors' are contained in three 'semicircular canals' set at right angles to each other. When the head moves, the fluid in each canal presses on a

flap, the cupula, attached to the sensory hairs, which then provide the appropriate signals. This information is especially
needed to prevent misinformation from the eyes. Every time that
the head moves the image on the retina moves too and the information from the semicircular canals allows compensation for
this. It is as if the vestibular system says to the brain 'Don't
worry, the world is not going round, we are just turning our
head.' People whose canal system is not working properly report
that the world seems to be continually bobbing up and down as
the head rises and falls when they walk.

So although one is not conscious of the signals from these
canals they are in fact playing an essential part in stabilizing one's
conscious visual life. In trying to understand the biological significance of consciousness it is interesting to realize that the conscious process of seeing is supported by signals of which we are
not ordinarily aware. If, however, the body is rapidly rotated and
then stopped the resulting giddiness is a conscious sensation of
signals arising in the semicircular canals, supplemented by others
from the eyes and muscles. In fact during normal life information
from the eyes is usually enough to keep the body correctly
oriented even in patients whose vestibular organs are not functioning properly. But of course in the dark, or blindfolded, they
cannot keep upright or detect rotation. However, people with
such lesions are lucky at least in one way — they cannot be sea-
sick.

21. Hearing

i. *Sound waves*

The 'information' that we collect through the ears, like that of
other senses, can be shown to be our own version of the changes
that actually occur in the world around. In this case the changes
are minute, rapid wave-like fluctuations of air pressure. The particular arrangements of the mechanism of the ear and brain select
certain patterns of air pressure to encode and so convert into
information. As for the other senses, sound may fall upon us
unasked: one can hardly avoid hearing a clap of thunder, nor can
one reasonably doubt the 'reality' of the noise. For many animals

the localization of sources of sound is of prime importance, whether they are made by predators or prey. Identification of the nature as well as the direction of sounds is of course also important and involves the capacity to recognize temporal patterns of air pressure. This pattern recognition reaches its highest level in the hearing and understanding of human speech.

For most of the day the brain selects for attention from the changes of air pressure that fall upon the ear only those that are relevant to the particular programs that are under way at the time. The sounds for which our human hearing system is especially suited are those of language. The transmission and reception of speech is obviously a process of encoding, indeed it has been a prime source of the use of that concept. There is therefore a special interest for us in examining the encoding process by which the brain transforms the changes of air pressure into the signals that carry the information that leads to understanding the meaning of the words that have been heard.

Perceptions of sound differ from those of other senses in that their significant features are particularly the variations in air pressure with *time*. The whole apparatus of the ear is therefore arranged to respond quickly, and the brain is able to 'make sense' of the temporal patterns of the signals it receives. There are arrangements in the auditory parts of the brain that allow recognition of patterns in time much more subtle than those that can be detected by touch or smell or even by sight.

Sounds that are musical or tone-like are due to regular ('periodic') changes of air pressure. Each note is the result of pressure variation at a particular rate, called its frequency. High notes are due to very fast vibrations of air pressure, such as are produced by the short strings on a piano. Low notes have waves of low frequency, produced by the vibration of long strings. The human ear can detect notes with frequencies between about 30 to 25,000 vibrations a seconds. Vibrations of still lower frequency are 'felt' rather than heard. A cat can go up to about 40,000 and a bat emits notes at up to 100,000, and hears the echoes as these sounds are reflected off a flying insect. These differences in hearing capacity are one more indication that the sense organs of every animal provide it with a range of information appropriate to its way of life.

The human ear and brain both show specific inherited

adaptations for the receipt and analysis of speech sounds. The anatomical and physiological features that are involved must have been developed by evolutionary pressure as speech evolved, perhaps within the last three or four million years.[20] The vowel sounds are mainly periodic tones. Many other sounds are due to irregular fluctuations (aperiodic) and these include the sounds of consonants, clicks and random 'noise'. The loudness of sounds that can be heard varies enormously, over a range of intensity of a million million times, from the faintest whisper to a jet engine or over-amplified rock band. The measure used for loudness is unfortunately a rather complicated scale of decibels (dB, called after Graham Bell). The scale is a logarithmic ratio running from 0, the softest sound audible to a young person, to 140dB, which is the rock band, and is also the threshold for pain. 120dB produces damage if prolonged; 100dB is a full orchestra.

ii. *Ears*

Sounds are of course mainly received by the ear, though they can be picked up by the bones of the head. The curious shape of the human ear has its special significance. It allows for the perception of the direction of sound both side to side and up and down, and is thus suited for the receipt of speech. Other animals, for instance, cats, deer, bats, have ears appropriately modified, and/or movable.

The mechanisms for the receipt and analysis of sounds are complex, and can only be outlined here. Some understanding of them is important for discussion and analysis of the use of the concepts of 'coding' and 'representation'. The fluctuations of air pressure are picked up by the ear-drum and suitably transformed by three little bones, the ear ossicles. These transmit the changes to produce travelling waves along a stretched sheet, the basilar membrane, enclosed in a spirally coiled tube, the cochlea. This basilar membrane is broader at one end than the other and contains a series of transverse fibres of differing length so that it reacts mechanically to the incident sound waves. The wave that travels along as a result of a single note will have a maximum stimulating effect, differently distributed according to the frequency of the note. The actual sensory cells stand upon the basilar membrane and are moved with it. They have hairs in contact with a delicate covering layer, so that with the vibration of the basilar membrane the hairs make minute movements. These are sufficient to change the electrical state of the cell that carries the hairs and thus to initiate or alter the streams of nerve impulses in the nerve fibres of the auditory nerve that lead to the brain. Each hair cell is especially sensitive to a note of particular frequency, though it will also respond to louder sounds of other frequencies. The result is that each fibre of the auditory nerve acts as a filter, giving maximum signals to a given frequency, overlapping those of its neighbours: as usual, we find redundancy and degeneracy. The changing air pressures received at the ear are thus translated into a spatially organized code embodied in the activities of the 30,000 fibres of each auditory nerve. The auditory centres in the brain are arranged to detect significant patterns in these signals and then ultimately to emit the signals that will produce appropriate behavioural responses. There are also nerve fibres going *from* the brain *to* the ear. These probably serve to regulate the sensitivity, so that it is possible to hear both very loud and very soft sounds. There is some evidence that among them there are motor fibres, which make some of the hair cells move, so that the brain causes the cochlea to *emit* sounds as well as to receive them! If this is confirmed it adds interesting possibilities for selective learning.

iii. *Auditory re-coding*

The pathway from the auditory nerve to the cortex involves several intermediate cell stations. At each of these the nerve fibres end and pass their signals to other cells by synaptic transmission. This procedure involves interaction between channels, so each of these changes provides a re-coding of the information carried in the nerve fibres. The centres involved are the cochlear nucleus, superior olive, inferior colliculus and medial geniculate body. In each of these regions the cells retain a spatial arrangement similar to that of the cochlea. It is particularly striking to find this translation of the features of the world into a sequence of *spatially* displayed patterns in a system that must deal with events whose significance is their variation with *time*. This transformation is achieved by the presence, at each of the various levels, of cells that do not respond to steady tones but are activated when the sound *changes* in frequency or amplitude (loudness). Each cell sends signals when it is suitably activated successively to different extents by neighbouring ingoing pathways that encode different frequencies. The spatial organization is obviously well suited to such interaction between neighbours. The effect is to convert patterns of change of frequency into patterns of activity of neurons distributed in space. This is presumably the form in which interaction is possible with coded representations in the cortex.

iv. *Detection of speech*

The human brain is equipped with specific devices for learning language.[21] These are probably based in part on the proper use of inherited cortical neurons particularly responsive to the sounds that are used in phonetic perception of speech. A listener perceives speech in a very different manner from the receipt of non-speech sounds: speech sounds are better received through the right ear, and by the left hemisphere, non-speech sounds the reverse. This is true even of babies only one week old. Babies two or three months old can be shown to be sensitive to the phonetic oppositions that are used in speech, even if these particular contrasts are not used in the language of their parents, and therefore could not have been heard before or after birth. As adults these children will no longer be able to make those particular discriminations. This shows that humans are born with a mechanism capable of selections made in accordance with the particular phonetic structure of the sound, which implies that sounds are encoded into some neuronal units (or modules) that are appropriate for understanding human speech. Later on in life linguistic experience then eliminates the capacities for discrimination that have not been used. This is a clear example of learning from a pre-formed code (Ch. 27) and reminds us of the visual feature detectors of kittens, which disappear if they are not used (Ch. 29.ii).

The equipment for such detection must be very complicated. Phonetic perception occurs when, hearing speech, a listener receives the phonetic message: it consists of lot of meaningless segments but when heard together they constitute the consonants and vowels. These have been ordered by the speaker into strings, and these again organized into larger units, and carried on what is called a prosodic contour of stress and intonation. The segments, both consonants and vowels, are called 'phones', and among the larger units are syllables. In every language certain sounds allow a differentiation of meaning and these are known as phonemes.

Each language uses different distinctions — e.g. the openness of vowels in French (*le, les, lait*), fricatives in English (vine, wine), stress in Russian (*zámok, zamók*), and still greater variations in Oriental languages.

The essence of recognition of speech is the selection of distinguishing contrasting phonetic sounds from the flow of sound, amplification of these and suppression of the insignificant sounds. Thus learning language shows very clear evidence that it is a process of selection and amplification (Ch. 27). A person who has not learned the language simply does not hear the phonemes as distinct. During the early stages of learning there is articulation of the selected sounds as the child deciphers them. This soon disappears, but may reappear with difficult words, or if they have to be written. Thus hearing speech in its early stages involves active *production* of it. Probably this link between action and recognition persists in the dynamic central processes that go on in the brain as an adult listens. He hears what he finds he can say.

v. *Speech detection in the cortex*

The recognition of speech is especially the function of the upper parts of the left temporal region of the cortex (Ch. 15). Patients with lesions of this area cannot distinguish speech sounds. They are not deaf, and can hear other sounds perfectly well. In some cases the injury involves just the capacity to discriminate between similar sounds such as b/p, d/t, s/z, while other differing sounds such as r/m or d/s are easily recognized. Sometimes musical hearing remains intact. This specific effect of lesions of the posterior third of the first temporal gyrus of the left hemisphere shows once again that different parts of the cortex have specific functions. But of course these can only be performed with the co-operation of many other parts of the brain.

vi. *Recognition of meaning*

Linguists and neurophysiologists have made some progress towards understanding how the brain operates this system of communication. The perceived phones are related to the sounds by a 'grammatical' code, which links sound to meaning. The sounds are not truly perceived as discrete entities — it is only their speech meaning that is perceived. Meaning is transmitted by speech much faster than could be achieved by communication of a series of distinct separate sounds. Indeed the vocal tract does not utter the sounds separately. The postures adopted by different parts of the apparatus for articulation of a syllable overlap, technically called co-articulation. The receiver hears the whole syllable not its separate parts. Indeed the resolving power of the ear would not be able to follow all the acoustic segments if they were transmitted in sequence, agrammatically. 'Co-articulation effectively folds information about several successive phonetic signals into a single stretch of sound.'[22]

Even more than this is involved in the complex encoding and decoding of speech. The point for us is that perception of speech is not just the detection of a series of sound waves. The act of reception itself *involves an elaborate re-coding of the sounds according to pre-set suppositions about the words that are being delivered*. If the language is not understood the speech sounds are perceived only as a vague noise. Understanding speech depends upon use of a learned program for recoding, presumably exercised in the auditory cortex.

There are some hints of possible mechanisms for this detection. In cats there are single cells responsive to the rate and direction of frequency change involved in 'miaow' and in monkeys for particular social calls. Evidence for similar speech cells in man is found by the alterations in detection of one sound, say 'ba', that are produced after repeatedly hearing its opponent 'pa'. If such evidence has been correctly interpreted it confirms the evidence already quoted that humans have specific auditory specializations for language. Such detectors extract from the acoustic signal those features that are phonetically relevant. Other more complex mechanisms must be used to extract the segments, syllables and morphemes. Speech is indeed a complicated set of codes.

vii. *Hearing in owls*

The barn owl provides a final example of auditory coding.[23] It is able to pinpoint the source of a very faint sound given by, say, a moving mouse. In the mid-brain of the owl there are 'space neurons' set out as it were on a map, each cell responding to a sound coming only from a particular position in space. Whether the cell will respond is determined by two acoustic parameters, which are provided by the signals given by the cochleas of the two ears. The azimuth (direction) is given by the time difference (Δt) between the arrival of the sound at the two ears. The elevation is given by the difference in intensity (Δi) at the two ears, which is increased by the fact that one ear is higher and larger and shadows the sound. Every fibre of the auditory nerve divides into two branches each leading to a series of four nerve centres, providing for encoding Δt along one path, Δi on the other. The results of these computations are then fed to the mid-brain cells, each of which responds only when both Δt and Δi are appropriate to its position on the map. The nerve impulses from each cell then drive the muscles of the neck so that the head turns to exactly the right position.

An interesting further point is that a young owl has to learn how to use the system, and this experience must be gained during a sensitive period of about one month, shortly after the first flight. If one ear is blocked in an adult owl the map can still be partly readjusted by further experience.

viii. *Summary of auditory encoding*

The sense of hearing thus provides us with useful examples of the process of encoding. The pressure waves falling upon the ear from the sound of 'Hullo' are first transferred by the ear-drum, then by the chain of three ossicles, next by fluid in the cochlear chamber and so into a travelling wave on the basilar membrane. From here they activate the hair cells to modify the trains of nerve impulses in the auditory nerve. These are then in turn re-coded several times before arriving at the auditory cortex. Here there are cells that respond only to certain patterns of these already much transformed versions of the original air waves. This is by no means the end of the process. The cortical cells continually exchange signals among themselves, which represent the patterns that have been learned in the past. Modification of the action of some of the cells by the incoming signals from the ear will produce appropriate outputs towards motor centres. The first response to the sound 'Hullo' may be a sharpening of attention and then, if it is repeated, perhaps a pattern of motor activity by the larynx and muscles of the throat that sends the response 'Yes — is that you, James?'

Notice that the transmitted time-sequence of air pressures which we hear as 'Hullo' is itself an encoded version of the need by James for attention. The time pattern is coded into a space pattern in the brain of the receiver and this is then decoded into another time pattern of sound to give the response that is considered appropriate. Had the receiver detected from the voiced 'Hullo' that it came from an unwelcome visitor the output might be 'Go away.' The decision is made by the person, operating through his nerve cells, as one conscious whole. We understand something about the encoding but as yet very little about the cortical processes involved in recognition and decision how to respond.

ix. *Truth in hearing*

Finally we can ask in what sense the system provides true knowledge of the pattern of variation of air pressures. For a physicist studying these pressures the human would provide strange answers indeed. There would be no detection at all of many frequencies, especially higher ones. Within the medium range the temporal variations most readily detected would not correspond to anything in nature except human beings. A naïve realist would be hard put to it to show that with the immediate data of auditory perception we acquire valid knowledge of reality without any interposing 'ideas' or other such entities.

On the other hand, for detecting the finer details of the information provided by other people hearing is quite amazingly effective.

22. Vision

i. *What is light and what is vision?*

The question' of what intervenes between the world and our knowledge of it has been more debated for vision than for any of the other senses. This is not surprising since, as we shall find, the world we see is largely of our own making. 'There is no light, but we may see light. Light is a sensation, and thus has no physical existence'[24] What a paradox! The very daylight we see is our own creation. What falls on the retina is a flux of electromagnetic radiation, which is absorbed in steps called quanta or photons. The retina sends nerve impulses to the brain indicating the patterns of intensity of reflected radiation, changing in time and space. What the observer perceives, people, trees, houses and the rest, is selected from those patterns by programs learned since birth because of their significance for him. People who have been born blind and are later given sight by an operation find that they can 'see' light, but none of these other things. They may see a confused mass of colours or, as one report, 'I see something but I don't know what.' Later they may learn to see shapes.[25]

ii. *How can visual representations be studied?*

The patterns of possible significant objects and events that reflected light can reveal are different in several ways from those available to the senses of touch, smell and hearing. Visual patterns are very detailed and may be very distant, coming even from the stars. They change in time, but not usually so fast as the patterns of sound pressure. The qualities of colours may be compared with scents, but are perhaps rather less varied. The outstanding significant feature of visual events is the *shape* of the objects they reveal, including particular tiny changes in the features of the faces of our fellows and the detailed shapes of the letters that we read and write. Recognition of shapes is even at the basis of the work of physicists when they are probing into the nature of the atomic world beyond direct perception. The instruments and symbols devised for this purpose would be inconceivable without the sense of sight (nor indeed could they have been made without the sense of touch).

For the extraction of so much information the human visual system makes use of a computational apparatus that is more powerful than any other that is known. It performs feats that cannot yet be approached by man-made robots and computers. It is able to deal with an immense range of natural and artificial forms, seen under a great variety of aspects and changes of illumination. In spite of recent studies by very clever workers in artificial intelligence and neuroscience we still have only rather vague ideas as to how the nervous system performs these feats. The trouble is not merely that we know so little about the nervous system, it is more that we do not have enough understanding of the whole process to know what questions to ask. What is involved in the encoding of a scene into a representation that is carried along the million fibres of the optic nerve and dispersed among millions of nerve cells? Even with computers several times bigger and faster than are now available engineers would not know how to design robots that could match the flexibility involved in the use of the eyes, say while a person cooks a dinner. Part of the reason for this weakness lies in the fact that investigations have largely been limited to the ingoing side of the process, without asking what vision is *for*. In spite of its wonderful powers human vision is a special purpose system, and we can learn from its limitations as well as from its great powers.

iii. *The detection of light*

To allow selection among all the variations of illumination, the retina encodes the patterns of electromagnetic radiation into patterns of nerve impulses in the optic nerves; the first of several stages of visual coding. The very complexity of the processes that we must now follow shows that what we accept simply as seeing or gathering of visual information is only achieved as a result of a long history both of evolution in the past and learning by the individual. The retina itself already makes quite detailed selections. It is more than a simple detector of light, being itself a derivative of the brain and containing many nerve cells. The rods and cones, the actual detectors of radiation, contain pigments that change their chemical structure when illuminated. The rods, containing the pigment rhodopsin, are so sensitive that they can detect the arrival of single photons, which are the smallest possible changes in luminous energy. However, in order that an observer shall see a light, more than a single photon must fall upon the eye, because the cornea and the lens absorb some radiation. Furthermore it probably needs the activity of more than one quantum per rod and the activity of several rods to produce a sensation of light. It is calculated that a person fully adapted to darkness may detect a light corresponding to only 100 photons, which is not very far from the least possible: the human eye is a very good detector. However it can only detect wavelengths between about 400 and 750 nanometers (1nm $= 10^{-9}$m), that is to say between violet and red. Other creatures can do better: bees can see the ultraviolet centres of flowers, which are invisible to us, and some snakes detect infra-red radiation.

The rods and cones have different functions. The rods are the more sensitive to weak light and are much the most numerous:

there are more than 100 million in each eye. They occur over the outer part of the retina and are responsible for detecting movement. Their responses are rather slow, allowing absorption of light to go on for as much as 1/10 of a second, thus increasing their sensitivity. In moonlight only the rods are active, not the cones; no colours can then be seen. In a dim light, thing can be detected most easily when you are not looking directly at them, because you are then using the rods at the periphery of the retina.

The cones are less sensitive to faint light, but are sensitive to colour. There are only six million of them in each eye, mainly concentrated near the centre. Here there is a region, the macula (or 'spot'), with a very high concentration of narrow cones at its centre, making a little pit, the fovea. The 30,000 cones in this pit do nearly all the work of ordinary vision, say in reading. The eye is continually moved so that the image is focused on this small spot. The cones are of three sorts, with pigments especially sensitive to red, green and blue. The pigments have only been isolated recently, finally confirming the three-colour theory first clearly propounded by Thomas Young in 1801.

iv. *Coding by the retina*

When the pigments of the rods and cones absorb radiant energy they change their chemical structure. These pigments are situated in the outer membranes of the cells and as a result of their changes electrical currents are set up, which activate the synaptic connections that the rods and cones make with the nerve cells of the retina. The electrical potentials and nerve impulses that are so produced then interact among the cells *within the retina*, which is thus the first coding system of the visual pathway. The result is the generation of a pattern of nerve impulses in the optic nerve fibres that lead from the ganglion cells of the retina to the brain.

It is important to recognize the nature of the change produced by these retinal events. Certain selected features of the radiant energy falling on the eye have now been *encoded*, that is to say converted into *information*, which can then be communicated to the brain. If radiation of long wavelengths is present, some of the nerve fibres leading from the red-sensitive cones will be active and nerve impulses will be sent along a particular type of nerve fibre. But this is not by itself sufficient to produce recognition of the *colour* red. That involves a complex process of comparing the

discharge in these 'red' nerve fibres with the discharge in others
(Ch. 24.v). What the nerve fibre sends to the brain is only the
information that there has been a change in the intensity of illumination in the red wavelength region on a particular part of the
retina. Some further features may be encoded within the discharge of each fibre of the optic nerve. For instance higher frequency of nerve impulses often indicates greater intensity. The
change is not necessarily from zero to active propagation. Many
nerve fibres send impulses continually and the 'message' they
carry may be indicated by a temporary increase *or* decrease in
firing rate.

The rods and cones and retina are able to signal visual events
that are close together in space and time, and the brain makes
good use of this information. One might expect that the limit of
resolution in space would be set by the diameter of a single cone
($2.0\mu m$; $1\mu m$ or micrometre is one millionth of a metre, that is to
say one thousandth of a millimetre). In fact the eye and the brain
use ingenious techniques of averaging to allow the position of a
line or dot to be recognized ten times more accurately even than
this. Again, the eye and brain can distinguish at least two hundred 'colours' by various combinations of the three receptors.

Resolution in time must be equally important, especially in
estimating the speed of movement of predators or prey, and in
man for speed of reading. A cone response probably covers about
30ms (milliseconds, thousandths of a second) in man; but the
response time of a whole act of visual perception varies greatly
with the task. Interpretation of successive images in a cinema film
exercises the full capacity for resolution in time.

Thus the complicated circuitry of the retina already selects only
some features to pass on in code to the brain by the ganglion cells
and the optic nerve fibres that arise from them. The properties of
these ganglion cells have been especially studied in the retina of
the rabbit. Here most of the ganglion cells send continual trains
of nerve impulses to the brain at between 5 and 60 a second. These
discharges change in frequency when radiant energy falls upon
the rods or cones. Each ganglion cell 'looks at' a certain small
part of the whole scene, its 'visual field', which is usually circular.
Illumination of the centre of the field increases the rate of discharge, whereas a ring of light falling on its outer part stops it.

Illumination of the whole field may therefore produce either increase or decrease or no change in the rate.

All these ganglion cells together send a very elaborate pattern of changes in the rates of discharge. The spatial distribution of these changes over the assembly of nerve fibres constitutes a coded representation of some features of the pattern on the retina, providing the information from which further selection can be made by the brain. Obviously these ganglion cells with their circular fields are good at signalling the presence of white or black spots. In combination they also provide the signals that are used in the brain to detect contours and other features in a manner that we shall now discuss.

23. The visual cortex

i. *Signalling to the brain. The cortical maps.*

The nerve fibres proceeding from the ganglion cells of the retina pass to several different parts of the brain. The information collected by the eyes has to perform other functions besides allowing for recognition of objects in the world. It must for instance regulate the size of the pupil and control the movements of the eyes. Other more subtle actions are the regulation of the rhythms of the glands of the body to suit the patterns of day and night, waking and sleeping. These other functions are performed unconsciously, by nerve fibres passing to special regions of the brain such as the mid-brain, accessory optic nucleus and hypothalamus (Ch. 32.ii). It is important to realize that conscious visual perception is only *part* of the human response to light. Indeed some of these other centres may be involved in the curious unconscious vision known as 'blind sight' (Ch. 24.iv).

The nerve fibres responsible for conscious perception pass through one intermediate centre, the lateral geniculate body of the thalamus, whose cells then send signals to the first visual area of the cerebral cortex. More than half of the whole cortex is devoted to the analysis of the visual scene. This gives some idea of the magnitude of the computational task and of the great opportunities that the flux of radiant energy provides for the extraction of information useful for life. In trying to understand the activities of the visual cortex a major clue is that the nervous pathways from the eyes are so arranged that the points on the retina are represented in their correct relative positions on the surface of the cortex. They are laid out as on a map in this first visual area, V1, placed at the back of the brain. Moreover the representation of the central area of the eye, which does all the work of analysing form, is expanded more than five times on the cortical surface. This expansion is similar to that in the cortical map of the surface of the skin, where the fingers and the tongue and lips are represented by the largest areas (Ch. 17.iv). These facts indicate that the elaborate cortical computations involve dispersal of the signals over a large area. Similarly in an octopus or a squid the signals from the retina are spread over a large area in the optic lobes (Ch. 26.v). The significance of these spatial distributions of nerve signals is not yet fully understood: it suggests that the representation of the world in the brain of any animal is recorded in some form of 'map' that is at least in part isomorphic with the world itself (see Ch. 28.iii). The first visual cortical area of a mammal contains cell systems that begin the analysis of the visual scene. It is interesting that if electrical stimuli are applied to this area by a surgeon during an operation under local anaesthesia the patient reports that he sees only a white flickering light, localized according to the position of the electrode on the cortical map. More complex coding proceeds in further 'representations' of the visual field, as for the senses of touch and hearing. In fact no less than six visual areas (V1–6) are identified by Zeki,[26] and there may be more than that. In each of these areas there is a complete representation of the retina, derived either by projection from the lateral geniculate body or by nerve fibres leading from one area to another. The maps are not all alike; the representation is less localized in the later fields, each point receiving signals from a wide area. The significance of this arrangement seems to be that in each area different evidence is extracted from the signals that are provided by the retina, a process known as feature detection.

ii. *Visual feature detectors in the cortex*

In 1957 Sutherland showed that octopuses distinguish between shapes in terms of their vertical and horizontal extents.[26a] In 1959 I suggested that there are nerve cells tuned to detect vertical and horizontal contours. There was anatomical evidence for such cells in the optic lobes of their brains. It was delightful to see in the same year the evidence of two Harvard physiologists, Dave Hubel and Torsten Wiesel, for the presence of cells with just this function in the brains of cats and monkeys.[27]

The method used by these workers was to record with a fine needle electrode the electrical activities of cells in the first part of the visual cerebral cortex, V1, which receives signals from the eyes via the thalamus. They showed that each nerve cell gave out signals when an outline crossed a part of the visual field at a particular angle. Thus one cell would respond when a line / moved, another only with — , yet another \ and so on. So each cell acts as the code sign indicating that a particular contour has moved. In life this might happen either when something moved in the world around, or as the animal's eyes scanned the scene. Such cells are called *feature detectors*.

In the week when I read the report by Hubel and Wiesel I happened to see a magazine cover with a reproduction of a self-portrait by Van Gogh. I sent it to the Harvard authors, adding 'Van Gogh seems to have broken the code.' The whole picture consists of straight brush strokes, making visual contours such as those encoded by the cortical cells described by Hubel and Wiesel. They replied agreeing enthusiastically, but of course this was only the beginning. We still do not know properly how the human brain puts together the information provided by the feature detectors to give knowledge of the presence of any visual figures, let alone such complicated ones as faces. Their discovery was a great advance, and they certainly deserved the Nobel Prize they received for it in 1983.

Since then much further evidence about feature detectors has been found, for the senses of touch and hearing as well as vision. Indeed, Vernon Mountcastle of Johns Hopkins University had partly anticipated Hubel and Wiesel, showing, in 1957, that the cells of each column in the part of the cortex that deals with touch respond to stimulation of a particular area of skin in a particular way (Ch. 17.iv). In my opinion he should have shared the Nobel Prize with the other two.

Many visual feature detectors are a good deal more complicated than those described. The important point is that we now know that an early stage in the analysis of information by the brain is the activation of numerous separate cells, each indicating that some particular change has occurred. This is a great step towards understanding the coding system of the brain. It is possible that memory records and representations are also somehow made by selection of individual nerve cells, or groups of them, each cell or group indicating that some particular event has occurred in a certain way in the past. I shall later discuss evidence and theories of how this may happen.

It is important from the start to remember that although we talk about responses of single cells, because they are easy to study, in life tens or thousands of cells of each sort are probably activated together. In the cerebral cortex the cells are arranged in columns, and Hubel and Wiesel showed that all the cells in each column are concerned with signalling a contour with a particular orientation. Each column indicates movement of a contour at a slightly different orientation across the field. The columns are arranged in order across the brain, the full 360° being covered every two millimetres.

This first visual area of the cortex (V1) contains individual cells concerned with many aspects of contours, including their shape, direction of movement and distance; and there are also cells responsive to other features such as the wavelength of the incident light. The details of the arrangement and interrelations of these various types of cell in V1 are not known but all the types occur fairly close together in each part of the area. From each point pathways proceed to the other visual areas V2–V6, which may also receive fibres direct from the thalamus. Each of these areas is concerned with analysis of a particular aspect of the visual scene, such as distance and depth in V2 and colour in V4. How all these areas report to each other and interact when the observer recognizes a familiar object remains the great unknown of visual perception.

The great number and variety of the feature detector cells is certainly one of the chief properties of the brain that provides the power of visual analysis. This gives us yet another example of nature's method of performing delicate tasks by selection among large sets of repertoires of possibilities. Change of a given feature in the visual field, say movement of a contour at a particular angle, will affect thousands of different feature detectors. Conversely, each detector while responding mainly to one feature will

respond <u>also</u> to others. So we have again the combination of
<u>redundancy</u> and <u>degeneracy</u> that makes it possible to find exact
'fits' or 'representations'.

It is safe to assume that the human brain also uses a similar
system, in which the information is broken down into numerous
separate features. Direct evidence of human visual feature
detectors comes from study of 'visual gratings'. Some of the
cortical cells are tuned to respond to stimulation by lines spaced
at particular distances apart; we can call them frequency
detectors for gratings. If a person looks at such a grating or
pattern of lines steadily for, say, a minute, his capacity to detect
features of the same spacing in another picture will be temporarily altered. This can best be interpreted as evidence of 'fatigue'
(technically called 'habituation') of the cortical neurons that are
tuned to that frequency. The response of each of these spatial
frequency cells is thus not simply to a contour, but to sets of
contours repeating at a certain particular frequency. Each
neuron is probably tuned to about half an octave. It is suggested
that the brain may be able to recognize patterns by decomposing
the resulting complex waveforms of many cells into simpler components by a type of Fourier transform. The results of the analysis may then be stored and used during recognition to
resynthesize the original pattern.[28] This analysis might possible be
done by a process somehow related to holography; but that is
only speculation; some experimental data agree with such a
suggestion but it remains vague. Such 'holistic' theories of
perception serve as a useful stimulus, calling attention to the
difficulties of the problem. Representations may be somehow
distributed over large networks, each nerve cell providing its
adjustable weight to the total response. In this way the form of a
single visual shape would be encoded over a wide cortical area: its
'address' in the memory is not found by its detailed location as in
a conventional computer memory, but as part of a 'content-
addressable distributed network'.

iii. *Neurons for faces*

A somewhat different interpretation of the action of the cortex is
that features extracted in the earlier stages are combined in the
later, so that at some final place there are cells that respond only
when a particular combination occurs, say the features of a face.

This view early found support from the study of cells far on in the sequence of areas in a monkey's brain, in the infratemporal area, that send out signals only when a monkey's hand appears in the visual field.[29]

Until recently the idea that such cells are the carriers of representations was considered to be simplistic, and they were facetiously called 'grandmother cells' or 'pontifical neurons'. Further work has shown that there are indeed cells in the temporal cortex of monkeys that signal the presence of a particular face, and even whether or not it is gazing at the observer.[30] Head orientation and gaze are signals that play a very important part in human and primate societies as indicators of dominance, rank and threat. It is exceedingly interesting to find that the representations in the brain of these important features include such responses of single cells.

To show this, monkeys were trained to lick a tube of sweetened water at the sight of a human or monkey face, or a picture of one, but not to lick when shown other objects. It was found that nineteen cells in one particular area responded selectively to the sight of a face; this was 9 per cent of all cells examined. Responses were better to real faces than to pictures. Some cells responded especially well to one particular human or monkey face. Nineteen cells were most responsive to the face of one of the experimenters and unresponsive to others. So there *are* cells for the face of your grandmother, and for other people too!

Further interesting facts were that each cell was sensitive to the orientation of the head; many of them responded only when it was facing the monkey, but others more to profile than to full face, and some to both. Some cells were most active with chin tilted up at 45°. A few cells responded only to the back of the head. Some cells stopped responding when the gaze of the eyes being observed was turned away, and this change continued even when only the eyes were viewed by the monkey through a slit.

These cells play a part in providing the information that is needed for a monkey to make appropriate reactions to its fellows. For the present discussion the important point is that individual neurons are able to summarize computations about the visual scene, using information converging from other parts of the cortex. By presenting different parts of the face in isolation the investigators showed that many of the cells had independent sensitivity to various regions of the face. Another whole class of cells was active only when the head *moved* in particular directions. The neurons are evidently acting as the focal points of elaborate computations. It has usually been assumed by theorists that such computations and formation of representations are the emergent property of distributed *groups* of cells, each cell playing only a small part. The existence of cells with such complex powers of summation of information will certainly have to be considered in the analysis of theorists such as that of Marr, which is to be considered in Chapter 25. The discovery is important but is only one step towards analysis of the process of representation in neural networks.

There is at present no information about how these cortical cells come to have their remarkable selective properties. No doubt learning is involved but it is also probable that their *potentialities* are inherited, like those of much simpler feature detectors in the first visual area (Ch. 29.ii). Presumably the capacities of the neurons that are inherited constitute the 'units' out of which selection is made in learning how to conduct an adequate pattern of life.

Direct evidence about the sequence of events in the human brain during vision has recently been obtained by electrodes placed on the head to record the electrical changes in the brain when a person is asked to press a button if he recognizes a picture of a face.[31] The first response is in the occipital cortex, at the back of the head, which is where the V1 area lies, with its simple feature detectors. This occurs after 100 ms, then at 200 ms there is a change in the right temporal cortex, where the 'face' cells are in a monkey, and after 400 ms in the parietal region, which contains the motor cortex. This is still 100 ms before the person presses the button to show that he has recognized the face. When he sees a face that he does not recognize the delays are longer. This sort of analysis begins to show the series of events that goes on in the brain. No doubt in future we shall know more.

There is therefore strong evidence that the process of visual learning involves the inferior temporal area, and also the nearby amygdala and hippocampus. Mishkin has found that the removal of any of these parts of the brain impaired the ability of monkeys to learn visual matching tasks.[32] As he says, it is probable that 'A unique constellation of visual attributes such as size, colour, texture and shape converges on single inferior temporal neurons.'

Capacity to store representations of faces is only one particular talent but it is by no means a minor or unimportant one. These experiments open a whole new world of possibilities for the understanding of the brain. We might go further and speculate that there may be neurons that represent not only physical objects but words and abstract concepts. It is no longer possible to ridicule the idea that there are neurons responsible for representation of the concept of representation!

It is, however, very important not to assume that representations reside only in single units such as these cells. The great computational powers of the brain depend on the presence of large numbers of units operating in parallel, interacting in many directions, not in a hierarchy leading up to a dominant command neuron. We must admit our ignorance of the detailed working of the system, yet the discoveries in the last twenty years of feature detectors and pontifical neurons provide a great step forward by showing some units of the selective actions of the brain.

24. The eye's search for information

i. *Visual perception as an active search*

So far we have not mentioned any connection in the brain between sensory and motor areas. It is clear that the organism must search and act in order to live. Information or knowledge is essential for the formation of programs for decision and action. Perception is an active process of gathering information in order to do something. Of course it does not always seem like that to us. When wandering around an art gallery or even when admiring the girls in a leg show one is not bent on immediate action. The aims of the human search for satisfaction are very devious, as we shall later discuss. We forget to look for these complex motives and so, mistakenly, think of perception as a passive process. The eye is indeed rather like a camera, with its lens and diaphragm. The retina is a plate of light-sensitive points, but *the brain does not record an image like a photograph*. In fact the part of the retina that is used for detailed vision is the tiny area at the centre, the fovea, containing only about 30,000 sensitive cones. As one looks at a picture the eyes are moved continually in a series of jumps, called saccades, scanning the scene with this central area and looking for features of interest (Ch. 24.ii).

What is it then that passes up the optic nerve to the brain? The sensitive cones change their electrical state as the illumination varies on the retina. The nerve cells of the retina, receiving signals from the rods and cones then alter the rhythms of nerve impulses in the fibres of the optic nerve. These impulse patterns in many fibres distributed in space and time provide the raw material from which the brain selects those items that provide useful information about the visual scene. From experiments such as those of Hubel and Wiesel it is known that the presence of a given pattern on the retina, say a line, will activate particular nerve cells in the cortex. Unfortunately there is very little information about the combinations into patterns of the signals in many optic nerve fibres that allow a shape to be recognized. It is technically very difficult to study many nerve fibres at once; and so physiologists have not paid much attention to the problem. Indeed in two large volumes on 'Vision' in a prestigious *Handbook of Sensory Physiology* the problem is only mentioned in detail once, and in the following words: 'little if anything is known as to how the eyes, or rather the perceiver, pieces together from successive oculomotor isomorphs (in cortical area 17), each radically different from its predecessor and successor, a map of immobile egocentric objects.'[33] Since that was written it has become possible to begin to see that the 'isomorphs' are 'put together' because they were not received at random but as part of a program of search for meaning, probably monitored by corollary discharge from the motor systems that are conducting the search.

ii. *Eye movements*

In order to understand the process of seeing, it is necessary to study a further factor — the time element. A great many studies of psychophysics have involved attempts to make the subject 'fixate' his eyes on some point: but in life the eyes are never still. They make very rapid saccade jumps, of both eyes together, with periods of fixation between. The jumps occur about three times a second in reading (with a pause of a second at intervals, often at the end of a line). Information thus reaches the brain in a series of packets, averaging about 1.33 words per fixation in one study of reading. It is obviously important to ask what determines the direction and size of the jumps. This has been investigated by following the actual sequence of eye movements with a technique such as that used by the Russian Yarbus.[34] A very small mirror is attached to the side of the eye and reflected light is transmitted to a photomultiplier and oscilloscope, which thus makes a tracing of the eye movements. The results provide quite revolutionary new ideas about perception. The saccades are found to be of very unequal length. They do not occur in random directions but follow the outlines of the object scanned, say a face. *There must be some plan in the brain that is instructing the eyes where to go.* Many features in a visual scene are ignored. For example, in looking at a face, most of the attention is given to the eyes and mouth. The observer's eyes repeatedly switch back from the outlines of the head or neck to examine these central features. What determines this 'interest'? Clearly there must have been some plan or program in the brain of the viewer, which provided the 'expectation' that movement in these directions would be 'interesting'. The human brain is evidently especially concerned with features of other humans (Ch. 23.iii).

These observations of Yarbus provide specific evidence that what is perceived is in fact *determined by what is already there in the brain*. It is interesting that Yarbus explains his results in subjective terms: 'Eye movements reflect the human thought processes; so the observer's thought may be followed to some extent from records of eye movements.'

If the viewer is actually instructed to look for certain features his plan of eye search will be varied accordingly. This was shown in a further series of studies by Yarbus, in which he recorded the eye movements of subjects as they looked at a picture of a number of people who had been startled by a stranger entering the room. Nearly all the eye movements brought the viewers to examine the people. They looked hardly at all at the furniture, pictures, etc. By dividing the observation into periods of five seconds Yarbus showed how the viewers first studied the visitor's face and his boots then switched to the most obvious person in the room and backwards and forwards between them. Information thus reaches the brain in discrete bits in a search guided by the aim of seeking to understand the relationship between the people shown. At least once in each period attention was directed to the man entering the room. The experimenter next asked the viewers to tell him whether the people were rich or poor, or how they were dressed; accordingly the sequence of their saccades then showed that they were examining the furniture, clothes, pictures, etc. Their program of search had been changed by the experimenter's questions.

iii. *Visual hypotheses*

A person is of course quite unconscious of these continued small scanning movements of the eyes. This gives another important clue to the significance and limitation of consciousness. Looking around, one perceives only at intervals, seeing first one thing and then another. Each perception may or may not set off further active searching: it all depends upon what one is doing and the needs of the moment. There is at present little knowledge about how the signals collected by the eyes at successive jumps are brought together to allow recognition of, say, a face, or whatever is the immediate object of interest. The evidence collected at each saccade is presumably somehow stored, probably not in isolation but as part of an accumulating pattern moving towards confirmation of some hypothesis — for example that the object is a familiar face or word or groups of words. Evidence from studies of reading shows that the amplitude of saccades varies with the linguistic properties of the elements of the *next* part of the text, apparently detected by peripheral vision. This implies that some top–down unconscious cognitive process is at work.

Visual attention has been compared to a spotlight or zoom lens. It can be used over a small area with high resolution or spread over a wide area with some loss of detail. Patients with agnosia (incapacity to recognize) may have to assemble the components slowly before interpretation: 'At first I saw the front part, it looked like a fountain pen. Then it looked like a knife, it was so sharp, but I thought it could not be a knife it was green. Then I saw the spokes.' (It was a bicycle.)[35] Such reports of pathological conditions show how visual search is conducted by testing a series of hypotheses about the context in which the incoming data can be recognized.

iv. *Blind sight*

Studies in which people are given only short visual exposures show that they are influenced by sights that they say they have not seen. Such 'subliminal' influences suggest that the early stages of visual processing involve activation of some outline model or schema, perhaps not resident in the cortex. Indeed patients who have been deprived of the first visual area in the occipital cortex on one side, although they seem to be blind in the opposite eye, yet show what has been called 'blind sight'.[36] When large objects were shown they could *locate* their position and even *recognize* them, as was shown by repeated trials in which they were forced to make decisions: 'Is it an X or an O?' Yet they continued to maintain that they could not 'see' anything and were only guessing to produce such strikingly correct answers. Similar experiments in monkeys show that the mid-brain may be the area that is involved. It has reciprocal connections with the cortex and its own input from the retina. Its activities seem to allow for identification of the position and main features of objects even in the absence of the cortex, but they are not accompanied by consciousness.

These results hint at the great complexity of the visual centres. Scanning the visual scene is the process by which we collect most of our daily visual information. The programs that the eyes and brain have learned can, however, operate very quickly to recognize objects even when these are seen only briefly. Indeed perception of simple visual characteristics of forms, such as orientation of a rectangle, is probably innate: it can be performed by these detectors in an adult without scanning. More complicated stimulus patterns can only be recognized after visual experience, allowing the learning of programs for seeing. The neural basis for these programs is still not well understood but there is much evidence that it depends upon some oculomotor encoding system — a form on the retina sets up a series of sequential visuomotor expectancies to fixate its various parts using a sequence of saccades: 'it is the plan for such active looking-and-testing that is stored over successive fixations, not the myriad details that are glimpsed with each independent fixation.'[37]

v. *Perception of colour*

As we have already noted (Ch. 22.i) it is a paradox that there is no light but that we may see light. Similarly in nature there is no colour but we see colours. How can this paradox be explained?[38] It was proposed by Newton that a colour, say red, is the sensation we receive when a given area predominantly reflects light of, in that case, long wavelength. There are indeed cells in the first visual area of the monkey (V1) each of which responds when reflected light that includes a given wavelength shines into its visual field. Each acts as a detector for the presence of radiation with a particular wavelength. But these cells do not signal colour. This can easily be shown by making light of a mixed wavelength composition to reflect from the differently coloured areas of a picture such as an abstract by Mondrian. A 'red' cell of area V1 of a monkey then always gives some response to *every* part of the picture, because they all reflect some red wavelengths: the cell records them only as differing in brightness. This cell cannot detect which areas are red because it always responds when some long wavelength light is reflected, even if it comes from say, a green area. Similarly, to humans, if the Mondrian picture is illuminated with monochrome light, say red, the different areas appear as having different lightness, they all reflect differing amounts of red light and you cannot tell which are the red areas.

There *are* true colour cells, however, and they lie further on in the cortical sequence, in area V4, receiving their input presumably from the V1 cells. They detect colour by performing an operation of *comparison* between areas that reflect different wavelengths. Red V4 cells respond when, and only when, their visual field contains not only an area of reflected long-wave light but *also* some light of different wavelength, reflected from a neighbouring area. If the entire visual field is illuminated with only one wavelength these cells do not respond at all. They give their response when they receive not only reflected red light but *also* light of some other wavelength with which they compare it. They are able to make their comparisons because they receive signals from very large visual fields. The wavelength-sensitive cells of V1 conversely have very small fields. It is not known how the necessary information reaches V4; perhaps each V4 cell receives signals from many cells of V1, either directly or indirectly. So a red V4 cell will respond to any mixture of wavelengths that is being reflected, providing some long wavelengths are present. This colour constancy is obviously essential if colour is to provide useful clues for behaviour. Green leaves look green both in the early morning, when red wavelengths predominate, and also when reflecting mainly the short wavelengths of the midday sun.

This is an example of how the brain functions to provide useful clues about the nature of the world. The sense organs provide raw data about the changes that are occurring; for instance, as the eyes or fingers move. The primary receiving areas of the cortex, such as V1, contain cells that extract certain basic features, such as distribution of contours or areas reflecting different wavelength. Then further on in the cortex the *relative* distribution of these features is compared, serving to provide clues whose significance can be learned by association with satisfaction of needs; with pleasure or pain. Zeki has shown how this is achieved for cells with wide receptive fields. It may be hoped that further investigation will show how the clues are detected that allow recognition even of faces and other complex features.

vi. *The earliest vision*

If learning to see is so important, we should find out how much a baby can see at birth. Since it cannot tell us, this is difficult, but studies have been made by following the movements of the child's eyes, noting the objects upon which it fixes them and its responses to what it sees, especially by smiling.[39]

The earliest visual activities of the newborn infant seem to involve scanning in the search for contours and outlines. In the first two months the baby moves its eyes a lot, keeping the gaze near areas of maximum contour density. It may be that the 'motivation' of the search is to maintain a maximal firing rate in the visual cortex. Only after this age does a child begin to scan particular patterns. Many investigations have suggested that the human face very early becomes a chief object of attention, though others have maintained that checkerboards or other complex patterns are equally attractive. The careful study by Lewis and his colleagues showed clearly that from twelve weeks infants showed more smiling, fixation and vocalization to photographs of real faces than to cartoons or scrambled faces.[40] Smiling occurs less readily at a face seen upside down![41]

This early attention to faces may be due to the fact that they are such a conspicuous part of the environment of the child. It is possible that the human visual system is genetically programmed for this recognition just as the auditory system is for speech (Ch. 21.iv). Later in life adults discriminate faces more readily than any other objects. Everyone can remember hundreds of faces, in spite of the fact that the differences are very slight. What is more, we use the face as a source of a great deal of important information about the likely behaviour of people around us. No other visual objects are so important, or differ in such subtle ways.

The capacity to recognize faces does not depend upon isolation of single features, say 'large nose', 'wide eyes', but rather on the whole face as seen in a particular social context. We remember the faces of those that we 'know', but not the hundreds we see in the street. A face seen out of usual contex produces a curious feeling. 'I know I have seen that face somewhere.' The technique for remembering faces by social contact is a good indication of the way that the memory works by classifying a complex set of signals in relation to the whole model in the brain (Ch. 30).

A special ability to recognize faces is correlated with the special human powers of facial expression. No other animal has the same capacity to use the complex of muscles around the eyes and mouth. Human social behaviour centres largely round the recognition of the significance of facial expression. It is hardly too much to say that human visual perception is tailored to detect the signals that other humans emit.

It is not yet possible to give any precise account in physiological terms of how the human visual programs are put together. It is likely that in the earliest stages the baby makes use of feature detectors similar to those that have been shown in newborn monkeys and other animals (Ch. 29). But even in these animals physiological analysis has not yet been able to show how these detectors are used to build up useful programs for seeing. We can imagine how this may be done for very simple actions, using the analogy of the octopus (Ch. 26). Up to this level we are able to see that the process consists of selection of possible pathways from a set of alternatives. Marr's analysis, given later (Ch. 25.ii), shows the difficulties involved in study of the process of 'representation' of any complex visual scene, such as a face. It is probable that the process involves the use of a predetermined code set. It seems unlikely that the visual parts of the brain of the human child consist of a wholly undifferentiated mass of tissue in which learning would have to be by 'instruction', where the brain, as it were, takes a direct impression of the world. We shall find reason to suppose that memories are not built in that way. This makes it very important to search for the modules or cell groupings that constitute the set from which a selective process of learning might take place. The existence of such a set presumably determines the limits that define the possibilities of human visual perception.

vii. *The combined actions of the visual areas*

With the conception of vision as an active search we find that the question of which of the many visual centres recognizes the table or the face or other Gestalt has been wrongly phrased. They *all* participate. The cells in each area select different aspects of the incoming information, acting in parallel. Cells in the later stages of the cortical series select those aspects that allow the appropriate response to some current question: 'That is a threatening face — run!' There is no single motor pathway from the visual areas to the motor (precentral) cortex. Each of these areas (except the first) has descending pathways to the thalamus, striatum and mid-brain, and these areas then pass information back up to the cortex. So the mental recognition is the accompaniment of a continual interplay up and down the brain, with the motor output often passing largely to the centres that control the muscles that move the eyes to seek for further information.

These facts are fundamentally important for philosophers. They provide direct evidence that what is perceived is selected largely unconsciously as a result of the history and activity of the perceiver. This was recognized long ago by Helmholtz: 'We let our eyes traverse all the noteworthy points of the object one after another.' So seeing is not passive but an active process directed by definite programs for seeing.[42] These programs are the basis of our visual knowledge, providing hypotheses as to what is likely to come next as we look around the world. This concept makes it all the more desirable to enquire into the question of how the nerve cells and their connections constitute programs and provide representations and expectations. What is it that they do when we report that we see a world of objects with properties, such as tables and measuring instruments, having extension, heaviness and colour? Only if we can answer this can we be said to understand the code of the nervous system.

25. Some theories of vision

i. *How can visual representations best be studied?*

Workers in artificial intelligence (A.I.) and in cognitive psychology have approached these problems of vision from a theoretical point of view. They ask 'What are the functions of vision? What needs to be represented? How should it be represented?'[43] The answers to these questions are far from simple, and workers in A.I. often find it necessary to express them in mathematical form or to test them by computer models. Vision is a very complicated process and sophisticated analysis is needed to investigate it. The studies of these workers are providing the groundwork that will be needed if we are ever to understand the visual centres of the brain. Such work is also the basis of the attempts to make machines that will perform the visual tasks that are needed in order to allow robots to 'see' as they go about their work.

When workers first started to try to make machines that would recognize objects, they were unpleasantly surprised to find that enormous amounts of computation were needed. Moreover, as Sutherland has emphasized, it is very hard to identify the features of images by which objects are recognized.[44] Early attempts to make visual recognizing machines have had to use conventional sequential computers in which data are fed very fast through one central processor. The brain does not work like this: it uses many parallel channels, which exchange information through a very complex communication network. Electrical engineers are now beginning to devise such systems, helped by the great decrease in the cost of logic circuits. Such systems make use of arrangements similar to those of the visual cortex, where there is a series of representations of an image, in each of which the neurons extract a different feature, say contour, colour or ocular disparity. The general plan is that computation between the units of each area can then test hypotheses about the probable nature of the object represented by the image. It is not clear how identification of it is then to be achieved, either by the machine or a brain.

Such difficulties have been among the problems attacked by students of artificial intelligence. The issues involved can be described as largely theoretical and philosophical, and the studies illustrate how these precede and overlap the practical and scientific questions. We may illustrate them by describing some results produced by the group at the Massachusetts Institute of Technology including the late D. Marr, T. Poggio, and M. K. Nisihara. We shall follow the account given by David Marr in his book *Vision* and supplement this by some criticisms and suggestions made by A. Sloman of Sussex University.

ii. *Marr's analysis of vision*

Marr begins by emphasizing that vision like any other complex process has to be understood at different levels. The principles involved in processing the visual information will not immediately appear from studying the actions of individual neurons, any more than the behaviour of the gas in a bottle is best studied by solving thermodynamic equations for the particles in it. To understand an information-processing device such as a computer or the brain, one must study it at several levels. Marr recognizes three. First we must know what has to be done, the goal of the system and the logic of the strategy that is needed to reach it; this he calls the level of computational theory. Then we must find what representation is used and what algorithm or sequence of logical steps is available to process it. Knowing these, we may then perhaps be able to proceed to discover how these are physically realized in the machine or brain. Clearly it would not be sensible to proceed in the reverse direction, although it might be theoretically possible. One could not in practice discover what a computer was doing by examining the state of each of its elements and the same is true of the brain.

The goal of vision research is described by Marr as being to

understand how descriptions of the world may efficiently and reliably be obtained from images of it. [We must ask] what kind of information does the human visual system represent, what kind of computations does it perform to obtain this information and why? How does it represent this information and how are the computations performed and with what algorithms?[45]

Then we can go on and ask about the neural machinery.

The centre of this program of investigation is obviously to discover the nature of representation in the brain. The making of representations is a process that can occur at various levels of complexity. A reflection of oneself in a mirror is literally a 're-presentation'. An artist's picture of a horse re-presents some aspects of the visible shape of the animal, using paint or ink and simplifying the outlines in various ways; that is to say, using a code that the viewer has to learn to recognize. How hard it is to understand the figures in newspaper cartoons in a foreign country! In making representations the brain or computer programmer or those concerned with artificial intelligence use still more abstract code symbols, which have no direct similarity to the object represented. So the making of representations is part of a system of communication; using various sorts of signs. Marr defined it as the making of an explicit statement of selected features of a situation in a formal code.

Information-processing machines make and manipulate representations, using symbols to stand for things and thus capturing certain aspects of reality. The brain reliably derives properties of the world from images of it by making and manipulating symbols. A particular difficulty is the need to obtain constant perceptions in everyday life on the basis of sensations that change continually, for instance as we see objects or people from different angles.

iii. *The sources of changes in an image*

Clearly the symbols that are used and the logical operations performed on them must be very elaborate. The analysis that Marr gives is based on the assumption that vision cannot deliver a complete invariant description of a shape. It does the best possible by making, he suggests, a series of representations. His method of discovering how this may be done is to make first a theoretical analysis of the information that can be derived from the optical properties of surfaces.

The things in the world that give rise to intensity changes in an image are 1) illumination changes, which include shadows, visible light sources, and illumination gradients; 2) Changes in the orientation or distance from the viewer of the visible surfaces; and 3) changes in surface reflectance.[46]

All of these can be thought of as spatially localized, but at different scales. Marr suggests how the visual system extracts from the image what he calls tokens that indicate the physical nature, shape, etc. of the surfaces. The system is obviously too complicated to follow here, but an illustration may show the basis of the procedure: 'One consequence of the cohesiveness of matter is that objects exist in the world and have boundaries. These give rise to the discontinuities in depth or surface orientation with whose detection we are concerned.' He therefore postulates the extraction of 'a set of "place tokens" that roughly correspond to orientated *edge* or *boundary* segments or to points of *discontinuity* in their orientations, to *bars* (roughly parallel edge pairs) or to their *terminations*, or to *blobs* — roughly, doubly terminated bars'. He calls these place tokens 'primitives' and with them, he suggests, is constructed what he calls the 'raw primal sketch'.

iv. *A sequence of sketches*

Without going into details, it is clear that the eyes and brain could extract data such as these 'primitives', to provide what Marr calls a 'raw primal sketch'. The sketch is then supposed to be refined by operation upon it with processes of selection, grouping and discrimination to form tokens, 'lines, curves, larger blobs, groups and small patches to the extent allowed by the inherent structure of the image'.

The primal sketch is obviously not an analysis that yields sufficient detail to identify objects in the world. The next question is, how is this primal sketch used to make a representation of an object that is invariant and independent of the position of the viewer? Marr suggests that it is done in two stages, first by what he calls a 2½D sketch and then a fully three-dimensional (3D) representation. The 2½D sketch uses the orientation of surfaces, as outlined in the primal sketch, their distances from the viewer, their depth, colour, and other features. This sketch is still viewer-orientated and cannot by itself allow recognition of objects, which indeed are not specifically isolated in this sketch. What is an 'object' anyway? How does the analysis of the visual image proceed to isolate objects, particularly since they vary in appearance with the angle of view? The fully 3D representation obviously requires further information and is made by using hints derived from the 2½D sketch to give access to the memory store and allow isolation and identification of 'objects'. This is of course the most elaborate operation of all and there is really very little information as to how it is achieved.

Construction of the full 3D representation thus essentially involves additional information from memory of relevant facts that are common to all objects, for example that they are rigid and continuous in spite of stereoscopic changes. The secret of the whole process is the use of information about the valid constraints that are imposed by the ways the world behaves. As we shall see later, there is evidence that a child has to learn these constraints and so to acquire a program for seeing that interprets images by deduction with the aid of these assumptions. They obviously include the 'entities' that 'intervene' in vision as philosophers suggest (Ch. 16.i). In fact Marr's analysis of the computational theory of vision brings out and clarifies the nature of the philosophical problems that are involved.

v. *Modular design principles*

An important element in the analysis has been the separation of the visual process into a series of pieces or *modules*. The elaborate computation involved is split up and implemented as a series of parts, 'as nearly independent of each other as the overall task allows'. This *principle of modular design* has obvious advantages. It avoids the danger that a small change in one place will have many consequences elsewhere. This would have the result that 'the process as a whole [would be] difficult to de-bug or improve, whether by human designer or in the course of natural evolution'. Analysis of cortical function also begins to show evidence of modular design, with separate areas serving to carry out distinct subroutines (Ch. 16.iv).

vi. *Supplements to Marr's analysis*

It would be impossible here to summarize the many technical enquiries made by workers in A.I. into the process of vision. Sloman has recently made a brave attempt in his article 'Image interpretation: the way ahead?' He also lists the relevant literature. His analysis is in many ways on the same lines as Marr's: it is

primarily top–down: attempting to derive structure from functions and constraints. Analysis of function involves studying the purposes for which vision can be used and the circumstances in which it can achieve those purposes. Such things as required action times, error-rates, type of degradation in various circumstances (e.g. occluded objects, poor lighting, mists, blizzards, loss of one eye, rapid motion etc.) can be thought of as more detailed specification of function.[47]

Obviously this approach is very much in line with the emphasis on function throughout the present book.

The attention to these practical constraints leads Sloman to doubt whether the approach advocated by Marr can be adequate. For example, he questions whether the production of full descriptions can be the central process of vision. How could such descriptions be used by the brain in the short times available when we are seeking to match our stored representations? The descriptions cannot be wholly geometrical, as he shows with the example of three well-known visual illusions. The Necker cube illusion is wholly geometrical, but

The face/vase figure includes both geometrical ambiguities concerning relative depth and also abstract ambiguities of grouping: what 'goes with' what. But when you look at the duck–rabbit picture the flips feel just as visual, though the change is not geometrical. Instead you see different *functional* components (eyes, ears, etc.) and even more importantly the *direction the animal is facing* changes . . . The duck or rabbit is seen as *looking* in one direction or another. Here 'front', 'back' and 'looking' are not *just* arbitrary labels, but imply links to elaborate systems of concepts relating to the representation of something as an *agent*, capable of moving, of taking in information, of making decisions etc.[48]

This quotation illustrates the complexity of the processes that will have to be taken into account if we are ever to know what is involved when one says 'I see a rabbit.' At present there is no information as to how the geometrical information coming from the retina is combined with the stored information that is involved in making these interpretations. It is worth quoting Sloman again:

The suggestion that vision involves much more than the production of descriptions of three-dimensional structures . . . conforms with the common-sense view that we can *see* a person looking happy, sad, puzzled etc. Seeing into the mind of another, seeing an object supporting another, seeing a box as a three-dimensional structure with invisible four sides, may all therefore use the same powerful representations and inference mechanisms as seeing a line as straight or curved, seeing one shape as containing another, etc.[49]

vii. *A system of descriptions*

One possible system that avoids many of these difficulties could use what Sloman calls 'an "active" multi-processor representation'. This would involve 'a large number of independent processes all simultaneously attempting to analyse these structures in a variety of different ways and offering their results to other sub-systems'. This reads surprisingly like a description of the activities of the many visual areas of the cerebral cortex. The representation would then be 'not in terms of some sort of static database or network of descriptions, but in terms of a pattern of processing in a large number of different sorts of processes'. As Sloman adds: 'It is not going to be easy to build working models.'

viii. *Some possible primitive descriptions*

There seems to be much agreement that the system must depend upon the use of sets of modules, each capable of recognizing certain 'primitives'. Marr tried to make do with a small set of generalized cylinders as primitives, but this is probably too simple. Sloman suggests that 'We seem to need a vocabulary of many sorts of scene fragments.' He goes on to list no less than twenty-six possibles, including surface patches, concave and convex curves, corners, furrows, rods, holes, gaps, etc. Also 'process fragments' such as folding, coming apart, entering, flowing, splashing.

In fact we simply do not know what 'primitives' are used, nor how they are represented in the brain, nor whether they are innate or acquired. The feature detector neurons discussed in Chapter 23 are perhaps very primitive primitives and they seem to be innate but capable of improvement by use. Are there also rather more complex primitives wired into the brain by heredity — for example, 'face primitives'? It seems unlikely that such a complicated visual system can be organized entirely after birth. There are many hints that the brain at birth is far from being a blank sheet. It is almost certainly provided with equipment for making representations that are useful for human life. It cannot be an accident that certain parts of the brain have specialized functions, for instance recognition of faces or indeed speech.

ix. *Cognitive friendliness of the world*

Some of the built-in capacities probably depend upon assumptions about what Sloman calls the 'cognitive friendliness' of the environment. Examples are, assuming that surfaces are rigid, or continuous, or have clear boundaries. The assumptions may involve intermodal processing, such as the expectation that an object will feel solid after visual perception of it. The capacities are apparent from the first months of life and may be innate, as is the ability from birth to reach for an 'object' seen. Perceptual constraints are built into the information-processing system that is appropriate to each species. These invariants of a higher order are linked to the physical properties of the world and operate irrespective of the modality in which information is received. In general we assume that there are only certain limited variations of the features of a scene. Moreover, in sub-optimal viewing, features should degrade in a reasonable manner (though strange figures may 'appear' in a mist!) Such assumptions that are so useful for vision may of course become restrictions in the search for the 'true' nature of the world. Too great a reliance on the 'cognitive friendliness' of the world would limit our understanding of it.

x. *Does the picture organize the details?*

These selected quotations from Marr and Sloman can give only a faint idea of the problems of vision as they appear to workers in A.I. At least they show some of the conditions that have to be fulfilled to allow useful vision. It remains unknown how these conditions are met in the brain. If David Marr had lived he might have helped us further along the way to finding an answer to this question. It may still take some time, probably many decades. At present we have evidence that vision is a process operated by many channels in parallel. There is some understanding of the stages of encoding that occur in the retina, lateral geniculate body and primary visual cortex (V1). The encoding in the cortex involves the activation of numerous modules, each composed of groups of cells mapped on the surface, and each representing the occurrence of some change in the light intensity at some place in the visual field and perhaps also at some time in the sequential process of scanning. It is now known that in later stages of the visual cortex there are cells that represent complex situations such as the presence of a threatening face.

These are all hard physiological facts but they leave us uncertain how to put them together to describe what goes on in the brain to allow the cells to make these computations, still less how they are used in daily life. The clue may be to ask once again 'What is vision for?' The whole process is the search for information that may answer a question asked, so that to a large extent *we know already what we are going to see.* For example, some patients with visual agnosia who seem to be unable to name things do quite well if given hints (Ch. 3). This suggests that we should stop trying to analyse how the 'picture' of a face is built up by the modules in the cortex. Rather we may use a top–down approach to find how what is already there provides a hypothesis that is confirmed by consultation at the lower levels.

This sounds vague physiologically and so it is. But it agrees with the ideas of those practitioners of A.I. who are trying to develop systems of parallel processing that may be similar to the operations of the brain. They may be called the New Connectionists.[50] They start from the assumption that cognitive theorists are wrong to suppose that mental processes are analogous to computer processes, in the sense that they employ manipulation of formal symbols in a series of stages in a logical manner. This seems a good criticism, if for no better reason than that such procedures take too many steps and are highly implausible and profoundly unbiological. Instead the New Connectionists depend upon computations that follow various analogies of processes of interaction between a number of elements to reach a particular statistical steady state. One model is 'simulated annealing', the computational analogy of alternately 'warming' and 'cooling' structures to get them to settle into the best combinations. This may not be so far-fetched if we remember that in a visual search the best solution may be that which the brain already 'knows' and is 'looking for'. Once again we meet the overriding influence on the brain processes of the needs of the organism. Such approaches have the great advantage that they deal statistically with large numbers of distributed units (which need not all be alike). The 'solution' or disambiguation' is achieved globally by interaction between many units, and it is limited by some pattern that is at least in part already there. All of these are features that we imagine to exist in the brain: the baby may be born with systems already tuned to recognize the relevant features of a face. Moreover such global solutions could be reached within the limits of milli-seconds, which can hardly be long enough for elaborate serial synaptic actions in a logical network. Nevertheless the analogy is very remote and uncomfortably vague. Anyhow it does not tell us what the brain state is to which the system settles in (say) recognition of a face. But it suggests the possibility that in looking first at the striate cortex we may be starting at the wrong end. Perhaps it is the monkey's hand cells or face cells or other 'pontifical neurons' that organize the activities of neurons 'lower down'. Incidentally this is not the way Dennett and others look at it; they regard the New Connectionist approach as being bottom–up; which only shows the state of uncertainty and informality of the subject.

   Physiologists would probably mostly reject suggestions such as those of the New Connectionists. But it is interesting that these workers in A.I. who are trying to understand the more complex processes in the brain feel the need to consider such analog solutions. They are acutely aware of the weakness of attempts to compare brain activities with those of a digital computer. Thomas Poggio (a collaborator of David Marr) writes

neurons are complex devices, very different from the single digital switches as portrayed by McCulloch and Pitts (1943) type of threshold neurons. It is especially difficult to imagine how networks of neurons may solve the equations involved in visual algorithms in a way similar to digital computers. We suggest an analogue model of computation in electrical or chemical networks for a large class of visual problems, that maps more easily with biologically plausible mechanisms.[51]

Such views become more plausible as recent studies of the pharmacology of the brain show that synaptic transmission is not a matter of single chemical messengers; the action of many synapses is modulated by neuropeptides, purines and other agents. Ideas about the operation of the brain are likely to change considerably in the years to come.

xi. *Rotation of mental images*

Other investigations of cognitive psychologists, through not dealing with the nervous system directly, nevertheless provide further valuable insights into the nature of representations in the brain. They have been able to show that some mental processes seem to be analogical, for example that mental rotation of an object is related to physical rotation.[52] To show this, subjects were presented with a solid object seen from one angle and asked to find out which of the two symmetrical solids in a mirror corresponded to it. The time taken to answer was found to be proportional to the angle of rotation needed to make a fit. This suggests that the solution of the problem involved some actual rotation of a process in the brain rather than an algebraic computation, the time for which would presumably not change in this way. Similar results have been obtained by asking subjects to compare the sizes of imagined objects or the lengths of imagined trajectories. Evidently these calculations involve something that is similar to an actual physical manipulation of the object. The corollary may be that the representation of a visual object is to some extent a model isomorphic with what is represented, though it is difficult to see what this might mean in neural terms. It may be that, rather than rotating the representation, the brain applies to it some analog of rotation chosen from a kit of transformations that is available for exploring spatial relations. These suggestions of the analogical character of brain representations may be encouraging for those who favour 'holistic' theories of cerebral activity. The rotations could be achieved if the 'image' was holographic (Ch. 27.vii).

PART III

Learning

26. Memory

i. *Gaining new information*

Memory is a concept so close to the centre of our being that in a sense it includes all other philosophical ideas. The very existence and continuity of each personality depends upon memory. It is no surprise therefore to find that memory is also the central concept of biology: the continued maintenance of life is made possible only by a memory record that each individual organism receives in the DNA. This situation is described by saying that the DNA provides information, written in a code, which enables the performance of activities that have provided for survival in the past and are therefore likely to be adequate in the future (Ch. 8).

The inherited genetic record may seem at first to be something very different from the subjective experiences that we commonly call memories. The philosopher may wish to dismiss the comparison as 'only metaphorical', but I am aiming to show that making sharp distinctions between the languages of subjective and objective description loses the advantages that both viewpoints can bring to understanding of our nature. Neural memories, like the memory of the DNA, can be considered as coded stores of information that are needed to allow decisions as to what it is best to do for survival in the light of past experience. Neural memories have the special advantage that they are set up rapidly to correspond to conditions in the immediate past. The efficacy of the DNA memory is guaranteed only by the fact that it has provided for survival under conditions that occurred in the past, some of them long ago.

Subjective memories are the counterpart (if that is the word!) of some of the new programs that are set up in the human brain by learning after birth. They vary from the programs that enable one to speak or to read, to memories of individual events and places. All are potentially useful. My vague memory of the geography of Scarborough, which I have not visited for sixty years, provides information that might help if I went there again. More practically, the programs that I have acquired for speaking, writing and reading are fundamental to my life every day. And so on for all the knowledge and programs that we use. As situations arise or questions are asked, whether from outside or from inside oneself, we call upon the file of information that has been somehow written into the brain.

The fundamental problem is the nature of the plasticity of the nervous tissue; how does it come to be able to change with use so as to be more effective in the future? This organized plasticity is the basis of our 'cognitive' memories as well as the simpler learning of motor skills by animals or humans. Neither human nor animal memories precisely reconstruct the past or plan the future. Their function is to provide information that will allow effective creative responses to situations as they arise. As Richard Wollheim puts it 'event memory is a forward-directed phenomenon, so that an event occurs, and then at a later moment, or when I centrally remember it, it thereby exerts an influence over me.'[1]

It is often said that knowledge about memory is still very scant and that it is 'the next frontier of biology'. Nevertheless we are beginning to understand the physiological changes that take place during learning. What is so difficult is to know *where* in the human brain these changes take place. This is part of the question of the nature of representation in the brain, which has already been discussed. I have long held that the best basis for further attack on the problem is the thesis that learning involves selection from a large set of possibilities.[2]

This view has now been supported by others such as Changeux, and Edelman and Mountcastle.[3] We then have to find this set from which selection is made, and to ask how far it limits the possibility of making memory records. This brings us directly to face the very old philosophical problem of the *tabula rasa*: 'Is the mind at birth a blank sheet?' 'Can *anything* be written on a baby's brain?' Fortunately psychologists and physiologists have recently provided data that enable us to answer both questions in the negative. The problem is thus to find the nature and extent of the limitations imposed heredity.

ii. *The inherited capacity to learn*

The biological purpose of the brain memory is that it shall provide instructions in the light of recent experiences, more up-to-date than the genetic memory. The genes provide in the brain a system that is *capable of learning in certain specific ways* from experience, after the child is born. Many organs of the body similarly inherit the power to adapt to the conditions that are experienced (Ch. 9.i). Muscles and bones becomes stronger with use, more red blood cells are formed at high altitudes, and so on. Each of these capacities for adaptation depends upon the presence of particular enzyme systems, which are produced under the control of relevant sequences in the DNA code. Similarly, the power to set up records in the brain also depends upon particular properties of the nerve cells, provided by the DNA. As Edelman puts it, we learn to classify events by a 'selective system in which a large pre-existing set of variants of neural networks formed during embryonic life . . . are later selected for and against during the worldly life of the animal.'[4]

The question is, therefore, what are these properties of the nerve cells and pathways and how do they come to allow learning of new programs that will be useful for survival? Here we do indeed approach the 'frontiers' of biological knowledge. Only a little is known about the relevant properties of the assemblies of nerve cells, but yet enough to show some hints of what is already written there at birth.

iii. *Plasticity of the brain*

There is much evidence that the strength of the connections in the brain depends upon use and can be rapidly changed. The regions where the nerve endings come into contact with each other to make synapses are known as the neuropil or nerve felt. The fibres make an extremely fine network, like a carpet, in which immense numbers of the minute active nerve endings of incoming axons and outgoing dendrites are mingled. Here therefore are many possible points of contact. Whether any pairs of these fine fibres are functionally connected up to make active synaptic junctions probably always depends on how much they have been used.

The beautiful work of Kandel and his colleagues on the sea slug or sea hare, *Aplysia*, shows in some detail how changes in connection between a few large neurons occur in the processes known as habituation and sensitization of a reflex, which are very simple forms of learning.[5] These workers have been able to show that the actual chemical changes in the cells during habituation involve exhaustion of the simple ion calcium, which is needed to make the synapse between two cells work. The channels that admit calcium through the membrane become closed so that the reflex response no longer occurs; it is 'habituated'.

Reflexes that have become habituated may remain ineffective for hours or days, but they can be reactivated by a stimulus given somewhere else on the body; this is called *sensitization*. Kandel has shown that in *Aplysia* the sensitization works by activating another, parallel, channel, leading to a smaller cell, which secretes the substance serotonin at the synapses that it makes with the cell that has run out of calcium. When this happens, the calcium channels are reopened, calcium enters and the original reflex is restored. So, if you allow us to call these processes of habituation and sensitization forms of learning, we can say that we understand the chemistry of the memory of *Aplysia*. Notice that it depends on a change in the connections of certain specific cells, using a simple chemical, *not* on the production of any elaborate specific chemical molecule.

iv. *Evidence of changes in the brain*

It is much more difficult to study detailed changes in the connections of the complex brains of higher animals, which are of course those that interest us most. Fortunately one area of the brain that is certainly known to be related to memory formation in man has also provided the best evidence of capacity for physiological and anatomical change. The hippocampus can be regarded as a region lying as it were between the cerebral cortex and 'lower' brain centres. It is part of a complex system of circuits linking the various cortical areas with the hypothalamus and other parts that control the needs of the ongoing life of the individual. Its place in the organization of this circuit will be considered later (Ch. 28). Here we are concerned with the fact that, following electrical stimulation of the nerve fibres that pass from the cortex to the cells of the hippocampus, these latter become more readily excitable. This changed state decreases only gradually and can still be detected even after several days.

This is good evidence for capacity to change with use, although the crude electrical stimulation activates many fibres, in abnormal patterns of time and space. Study with the electron microscope after stimulation shows increased size of the fibres in the neuropil. This may include both the ingoing (presynaptic) and outgoing (postsynaptic) fibres.[6] There is also evidence of the converse change. The spines on the pyramidal cells of the visual cortex of mice become reduced if the animals are kept in the dark.[7] The spines are the receiving (postsynaptic) agents of many cortical neurons, and it is suggested that changes of their size and shape would rapidly alter transmission through the neurons.

Any long-lasting change in the nervous system presumably involves the synthesis of new proteins. It is therefore no surprise to learn that learning is inhibited if animals are given injections that block protein synthesis. Changes in nucleotides, especially RNA (ribonucleic acid), are also to be expected during learning, and have been found for instance in particular parts of chicken brains. Many people have suggested that there may be specific 'nervous memory molecules', on the analogy of DNA. This is most unlikely. The particular responses of the brain are a result of the pattern of connections in it, not of the presence of memory chemicals. However it is certain that there are enzymes, proteins, peptides and other molecules that are peculiar to the nervous system and are necessary for the changes of synaptic connection.[8]

Striking evidence of the plasticity of the brain has come from song-birds. In canaries there are areas that enlarge in each spring in the males, and are larger in those individuals that sing well. Females do not have these centres but they can be induced to form by injection of the male hormone testosterone: the female bird then begins to sing. The dendritic fields are found to be increased in these induced song areas. This effect of a hormone injection on the growth of certain particular neurons raises the possibility of producing comparable effects in mammals and man. It is indeed claimed that some memory defects of elderly people can be ameliorated by various drug treatments.

v. *Learned programs in the octopus*

The octopus has proved to be a very suitable animal for the study of memory processes more complex than those of *Aplysia* but in some ways simpler than in mammals.[9] Its learning consists in selection between possible alternative actions and this involves a complicated set of activities. An octopus can be taught that one object, say a vertical rectangle or a rough ball, is 'bad', by giving shocks when the animal touches it. Conversely a horizontal rectangle or smooth ball becomes 'good' if touching it is rewarded with a piece of food. The octopus performs these discriminations correctly after only a few experiences. Such memory records are certainly likely to be useful in its life. As it sits in its home among the rocks the arms of an octopus will come into contact with many objects and it cannot transfer them all to its mouth for testing. Similarly it would certainly not pay to venture from home to attack every object that appears. Such dangers are avoided by the presence in the brain of parts that can acquire memories of things that have proved to be good to eat — whether seen or touched. Once thoroughly learned such discriminations are retained at least for several weeks or even months, which is a large part of the total lifetime of an octopus (about one year).

It follows from this that the animal must have 'feature detectors' such as those already discussed, which are able to distinguish these objects. Indeed there is anatomical evidence that there are cells in the optic lobes of an octopus similar to the contour detectors described by Hubel and Wiesel in mammals (Ch. 23.ii). Since the octopus can be taught that say a horizontal shape means food and a vertical means shock, the detector cells for both directions must have had possible connections both with the cells that make the animal attack and with those that restrain it (training is possible in either direction). After training, the activation of the detectors for 'vertical' will restrain the animal, and those for 'horizontal' will allow it to attack. So the learning consists in the *elimination* of the inappropriate response in each case and probably also *strengthening* of the channel that is 'correct'.

In exactly the same way there must be feature detectors in the nerves of the suckers of the arms for the degree of roughness of objects; incidentally, also, detectors for chemical properties, which the octopus can use for discrimination, as shown by M. J. and J. Wells.[10] In this case too the feature detectors must be capable of connection *either* with the system that makes the arms take an object, *or* with that which rejects it. Learning again consists in altering the probabilities, so that activation of either type of detector then ensures the biologically appropriate response.

The situation is obviously much more complicated in learning by mammals. However, the evidence of previous chapters clearly shows that the sensory areas of the mammalian brain contain modules that detect particular features. Each of these modules, whether composed of one cell or many, must have several potential outputs that could connect with other pathways, and so ultimately with motorneurons that produce action. Learning must consist in selection in some way among this vast set of possibilities. The problem is thus essentially anatomical. Which are the channels that become changed to establish the memory record?

vi. *The memory system has many parts*

A further clue from the octopus is that the whole process of memorizing involves the operation of several regions of the brain, each playing a different part in making the memory record. The animal has two distinct memory systems each consisting of a set of four lobes, one set concerned with visual memory and the other with tactile memory. In this animal therefore we can actually identify the parts of two separate but similar neural memory mechanisms. Experiments have shown that the two are almost completely distinct, so that by small operations it is possible to remove the visual memory and leave that for touch, or vice versa. Notice that removing the memories does not deprive the animal of the relevant senses. After certain operations on the visual memory the octopus can still 'see', though it cannot learn a new visual program: indeed after the operation it attacks *all* objects that appear, in spite of receiving shocks. Similarly an animal deprived of the touch memory draws in *every* stone, or other object that it touches, and tries to eat it.

The details of the working of the four parts of each memory system are complicated; memorizing is not a simple process. One of the four lobes in each system is concerned with bringing signals from the eyes or the arms together with taste signals from the lips. Such connections are obviously necessary if any animal is to learn which objects provide food. Another important part of the mechanism ensures that signals from the sense organs, for instance those of one arm, are spread about so that the octopus does not have to learn everything eight times over. This function of *generalization* must also be a feature of all learning systems. A simple example from ourselves: what a person learns with one eye or hand can be performed with the other. The term generalization actually covers much wider experiences than these, for instance the capacity to recognize objects seen from different angles or of different size.

Another part of each system in an octopus brings in nerve fibres from all parts of the body, which we believe carry signals of 'pain', such as would be given by an electric shock. This lobe lies on top of the brain and is called the vertical lobe. It is easy to remove it by a small operation and after this has been done an animal comes out to attack every object that it sees, in spite of receiving shocks. Such behaviour is no recipe for survival.

Yet another feature of these four lobes in each memory system is that they are connected to form circuits in which the signals can circulate. This led me to suggest as long ago as 1938 that such re-exciting circuits might serve to keep a record of what has occurred.[11] Dynamic circuits of this sort are hardly likely to provide a permanent memory, but they may be the basis of short-term memories, which are set up immediately after the event and maintain associations until the long-term memory has been printed. There is much evidence for these two sorts of memory. For instance it is well known that after an accident or sudden shock people cannot recall events that occurred shortly beforehand. Similarly, giving shocks to an octopus shortly after training prevents the establishment of memory records. Such shocks would disturb the self-re-exciting circuits. The basis of long-term memory must surely be a physical change in the nervous system, since it can remain, in man, for a hundred years or more.

Analysis of the brain of an octopus emphasizes that even their simple memory has a complex physical basis. It is not surprising that the much more powerful memory systems of vertebrates and man are proving so difficult to study.

27. Memory as a process of selection

i. *The memories of natural selection and immunity*

Learning in the nervous system by selection of responses is one of many ways in which tissues become changed by experience so that the survival of organisms is ensured. Muscles, bones and glands all show alteration with use. Survival depends on having systems that are variable and opportunistic, not rigidly planned and deterministic: this flexibility is the secret of successful life. I believe that at least some of the difficulty in understanding memory may disappear if we follow the idea that the marvellous accuracy of nervous connections is achieved by selection and elimination under the influence of experience. This will tell us what features to look for in the brain.

The multitude of detailed fits between organisms and their environment have been achieved by natural selection. This depends first upon the presence of a large number of individuals who are not all alike, next upon selection of some of these by the action of the environment and thirdly by increase of the number of those that have been selected. So if memory works in a similar way, we should look in the nervous system first for the presence of numerous varied units; secondly we should find how the environment makes selection among them, and finally see how the effects of those chosen are amplified.

A similar process is seen in the production of antibodies by the immune system of the body. A very good exposition of the similarity between neural and immunological memory is given by Edelman,[12] himself a distinguished immunologist.

ii. *Multiplicity in the brain*

The analogies of natural selection and immunology do not of course prove that the neural memory works in the same way, but they may stimulate us to look for the relevant units in the brain. One of the most striking things about the nervous system is the enormous number of cells and pathways. There are nearly a thousand million nerve cells in the human cerebral cortex (44×10^9). The cerebellum contains even more (10^{11}). Each cortical cell may receive up to 50,000 synapses (though these do not all come from different sources). Each of the 10 million Purkinje cells of the cerebellum has some 60,000 synaptic points (spines) and no less than 250,000 parallel fibres pass near to each cell and could provide synaptic points of communication. So the number of possible pathways is quite staggeringly large in the cerebral cortex, where there may be as many as 10^{15} synaptic points, and also in the cerebellum, both of which have been suspected to be involved with memory. This multitude is exactly what is needed for a selective system. For it to work there must be numerous possibilities, all slightly different. Such multiplicity is not at all necessary in the non-learning parts of the brain. There are relatively few cells in such regions as the hypothalamus, although these have functions that are in a sense more important than memory, such as regulating the need for food, warmth, sex and much else (Ch. 32). In a squid the whole jet propulsion system is worked by just *two* nerve cells; but the learning part of the squid's brain has many millions, as has that of an octopus. Multiplicity is a prime clue to the nature of memory.

iii. *Overlapping activities in the brain*

It is also known that there is a great *variety* in the properties of the cells of the cerebral cortex. In the first visual area there are some 425×10^6 minicolumns of cells, each mainly responsive to a particular visual contour or other feature.

This must mean something like 360 different columns of cells for each few degrees of the visual field. But contour is only one of many variables. Some cells respond when the contour is of indefinite length, others only if it is short. Other cells of this area recognize the disparity between what is seen with two eyes, and so signal distance and length. Still others respond to particular wavelengths as a basis for colour vision, and so on. There are certainly plenty of feature detectors. How does this repertoire arise; is it the basis for processes of selection and amplification to provide the programs of action that we are calling memories?

We have considered in the octopus how selection *must* occur somewhere along the line in the pathways leading from feature detectors to motor neurons. That is an example of learning of programs that provide appropriate responses to very simple features such as a contour or degree of roughness. Can the same principle be applied to more interesting examples of learning? Certainly the nervous system shows the features of overlap or degeneracy, which provide the flexibility that is needed.

In studying vision it is found that a young kitten is provided by heredity with cortical cells responsive to particular contours, *but at first they are not very precise.* Each cell responds maximally to a contour of one angle, but also to others that are similar. As a corollary, every contour produces some response in many cells. Moreover, in the young animal, each cell quickly habituates, or fatigues, when repeatedly stimulated. These characteristics are not defects: they are the features of redundancy and degeneracy that are needed for a selective memory system. In the columns of the primary visual system (V1) there are many neurons with maximum sensitivity for any one contour (redundancy); conversely each contour is coded into many cells, because each cortical cell is not sharply tuned but responds to a range of contours (degeneracy).

With normal visual experience some of the cells will become more sharply tuned and reliable. Presumably they are now being used as parts of the kitten's power to operate among the objects of its environment. In kittens raised with limited visual experience, say of *either* vertical *or* horizontal contours, only the relevant type of cell will mature in this way: the unused neurons cease to be excitable.

iv. *Selection by competition and co-operation in synaptogenesis*

This and other evidence shows that selection of which of the initial neurons and pathways shall survive depends upon use. Further, it has been shown that pathways may either compete or co-operate in the selection. In very young monkeys the cells at a certain depth in the first visual area of the cortex receive signals from both eyes. Later there is a segregation into columns of cells, each responsive only to stimulation from one eye. If one eye is kept covered it will be found that nearly all the cells soon become connected with the uncovered eye. Evidently the axons coming from the eyes compete to form connections and the effect of the nervous impulses is to increase the number and efficacy of synapses. Conversely those that are not active disappear.

The effects of co-operation are shown by other cells of the visual cortex which are normally driven maximally only by input from both eyes together. If the eyes have been covered *separately*, on alternate days, these binocular cells fail to develop:

synaptogenesis only occurs if the impulses arrive at the cells synchronously. It has even been possible to show in kittens that the binocular cells will only develop if the separation between use of the two eyes is less than ten seconds. This principle of *associative synaptogenesis* is probably fundamental. It allows for the development of cells that record the regular combinations in which events occur and so to build representations of the world in the brain such as 'face cells' (Ch. 23.iii). We shall see more detail of how this may occur in the formation of a cognitive map by the hippocampus (Ch. 28).

v. *Recovery after injury*

It is probable that processes similar to those in development continue throughout life. There is much evidence that there are many latent or little-used pathways in the brain. For example each pyramidal tract neuron (PTN) of the motor cortex of a monkey influences many motorneurons of the spinal cord; thus it may influence the contraction of many muscles (Ch. 13). In normal functioning probably most of these possible influences are held inhibited, but some of them may come into play when special movements are attempted. In exceptional circumstances, as after an injury or stroke, connections that were not previously used may become developed. This power of learning even in adult life is very important as a basis for the recovery that can gradually take place after such damage.

The phenomenon is probably parallel to the learning of all motor skills. Among the original multitude of more or less haphazard movements the correct ones are recognised as such by means of the sensory information they feed back to the central nervous system, and this information is later used in selecting the correct movements in further training.[13]

This quotation, emphasizing selection, is by a distinguished neuroscientist who studied his own recovery after a stroke. He stressed the great effectiveness of effort and use of the brain to produce the new movements.

vi. *Holistic theories of brain function*

This may be a good point to consider the dangers of the whole enterprise of looking for units. In the history of this subject there have been repeated efforts to treat perception and memory in terms of the operation of whole masses of nervous tissue rather than of the individual cells or groups of cells. This is a healthy reaction is so far as large numbers of cells undoubtedly work together even in a simple response, such as when an octopus decides to attack a vertical rectangle; many times more cells are involved in human recognition of a face. It is very difficult to find ways to describe the operation of such complex systems. Indeed searching for new mathematical tools for this purpose provides a major aim for theorists. Some more subtle 'holistic' theories look for explanations of complex behaviour in terms that do not depend only upon signalling by the transmission of nerve impulses (Ch. 12.i). Nerve cells produce electrical currents and electrical fields of various sorts that we have hardly considered (Ch. 13.iv). These may influence other nerve cells nearby, or even at some distance away. Furthermore, neurons produce various chemical substances and these may diffuse and act upon other neurons, not necessarily at synaptic junctions.

These local influences certainly exist and it is uncertain whether and how they may modify the theories we have been considering. Most physiologists would probably argue that these influences are local and that they do not fundamentally change the picture: it is not popular to consider that the brain is a sort of homogeneous soup or jelly, traversed by fields and gradients. It may yet turn out that this scepticism is unwise. It may be a product of the fascination that physiologists have felt for their microelectrodes over recent decades. At present there is a growing interest in the variety of small peptide molecules, such as enkephalin and 'substance P', that are released by nerve cells.[14] Further knowledge about the diffusion of the effects of these substances may produce an altered picture, perhaps of groups of nerve cells united by chemical or electric fields as well as by nerve impulses.

vii. *Holographic memory*

A different approach has been to consider electrical interactions between nerve cells in terms of interference waves.[15]

This theory is difficult to explain shortly: it depends upon the analogy of holographic photography, discovered by Dennis Gabor. By using special lighting by laser beams it is possible to make a photographic plate of a scene which, though unrecognizable to the unaided eye, allows the whole scene to be reproduced when an appropriate beam of light is shone through any small part of the plate! The representation of all parts of the scene is therefore distributed over every part of the plate. The analogy seemed especially appealing in the light of some work by the famous physiologist Karl Lashley (see Ch. 17.iii). He thought he had proved that memory in a rat for running a maze was distributed all over its cortex and that the memory was retained so long as any small part was intact. This concept of non-localization of memory records has been steadily losing its hold as surgeons, physiologists and psychologists have explored the functions of the human cortex, with conclusions that have already been discussed. In a few cases quite specific memories have been awakened or suppressed in humans during electrical stimulation of particular points on the cortex.

However, it would be a mistake to interpret these results as demonstrating that each item of memory is to be found pigeonholed in a few cells of the brain. As has been emphasized, we do not understand how representations of complex situations are encoded. It may yet prove that local electrical and chemical processes in addition to those of nerve impulses and synapses are involved. Some such effects may be holographic. It will be exciting to find out.

28. The hippocampus and memory

i. *Human memory and the hippocampus*

People who have lost the part of their brain known as the hippocampus are quite unable to establish new memories, even of what happened a few minutes ago; yet they retain some old memories, including how to speak. This region is perhaps the part of the brain that has been most definitely shown to be involved in the making of memory records (see Ch. 26.iv). The famous patient H. M. entered the Montreal Neurological Clinic for an operation to cure his epileptic fits. The fits were shown to originate in his temporal lobes, which include the hippocampus, and these were therefore removed. When he recovered from the operation he found that he could not remember things that he had done even a few minutes before: tell him something new and he forgot it at once. He could not recognize a doctor or nurse he had seen a few minutes earlier and he was quite unable to remember his way around any rooms or streets that he had not known before the operation. This condition has continued without essential change for eleven years, during which H. M. has willingly colaborated with Dr Brenda Milner and her colleagues, providing valuable information from his unique condition.[16] The operation will never be performed again, but other clinical evidence supports the conclusion that the hippocampus is essential for normal human memorizing.

ii. *Theories of hippocampal functioning*

Theories of two different types have been advanced to explain the memory functions of the hippocampus. It was pointed out by Papez[17] that this lobe is a part of a so-called limbic circuit, which includes parts of the brain that have been described as concerned with 'emotion'. This would therefore be a place at which signals from the outside world are brought into relation with those from within that indicate the needs and and rewards of the individual itself, and this theory in various forms has been widely quoted. More recent work has shown that the connections of these circuits are different from those originally proposed by Papez, and much more complicated. Indeed there are several routes by which such conjunctions may take place, not necessarily by passing through the hippocampus. A more detailed hypothesis has been proposed by John O'Keefe and Lynn Nadel to explain the function of the hippocampus in maze learning by rats, and they apply their ideas also to human learning.[18] Their detailed and scholarly review provides some of the best insights into the philosophical and scientific difficulties involved in study of the problem of 'writing in the brain'. The system they propose is complicated but worth describing in some detail. It will serve to show the way in which problems of representation in the brain can be approached.

iii. *Place memory in the hippocampus*

The theory is that the hippocampus is so organized as to allow learning of behaviour related to *place*, which they call 'locale memory'. The inputs that come together in the hippocampus build what O'Keefe and Nadel call a cognitive map of the environment.

This map is then used to orientate the rat as it learns to run a maze.

For these studies the authors used implanted electrodes to detect the signals that are given by single neurons as a rat runs the maze for a food reward. Various cues are provided in the surroundings, such as a light, a fan, a buzzer and a white plate. The authors call this a 'neuroethological study' of the behaviour of the animal, as it might be in a normal environment. They found that each nerve cell of the hippocampus discharged impulses when the rat was in a particular position in relation to various cues: the cells were *place coded*: they had become detectors of certain particular relations between features of the environment.

Reduced to very simple terms, the hippocampus can be considered as a set of numerous parallel strings, each of three neurons. The first neuron of each string receives signals from various cortical receptor systems, visual, auditory, etc. These cells thus come to be coded versions of the *combinations* in which the external signals occur. Each cell receives its input *mainly* from one source, say visual, but also receives from various others. Each string of cells is thus concerned with signals indicating the presence of one feature when it is combined with signals from others. For example, one cell will respond when a light-bulb is seen at a particular angle at the moment when a buzzer sounds. Another cell will respond when the bulb is at a different angle, a third when there is no buzzer, and so on. The huge number of cells available makes possible the encoding of many combinations in this way. So each cell becomes a code sign for the relations between parts of the world. One cell may stand for 'bulb is to the right of fan as you approach from the corner near the buzzer', and so on for hundreds of relations that have been experienced as the rat moves in the maze.

The second members of each string serve to represent various combinations of the combinations of signals that are encoded in the first cells, whose axons they receive through their copious dendrites. The cells of one string also receive fibres from neighbouring strings. Each cell here also responds *mainly* to one feature, as signalled to it by one of the first cells, but also receives signals from neighbours.

Throughout the assembly of strings strict topographical relations are conserved. They thus constitute a map, in which each cell represents mainly one feature *in its relation to other features*. The third cells of each string include two types:

one type, the place unit, is built up from the convergence of excitatory inputs, all tending to fire the unit [when the animal is] in a particular place. The other type is a misplace unit whose field is constructed from primarily inhibitory inputs, which prevent the units from firing in those parts of the environment outside the place field.[19]

The first stage is thus

involved in organising the environmental inputs . . . into a schema required by the mapping system [and] combining of simple stimuli into complex stimulus configurations as well as a representation of the angle with which they conjointly impinge upon the animal. The second stage . . . represents places in the environment and the connections between those places. The final stage continues the map and includes a misplace system, which signals the presence of something new in a place or the absence of something old.[20]

The map is learned during the process of exploration, which is a characteristic activity of rats, and indeed of all mammals. Neurons indicating places that have been the source of food or other reward will of course be so marked, by association with appropriate signals. The later neurons of the hippocampus, place cells and misplace cells, send axons to various other regions and through these their influence can reach to the brain-stem nuclei, which organize motor programs. These are the pathways by which the hippocampus alters the direction of movement.

iv. *Activation of the hippocampus and its brain waves*

The activity of the whole individual is regulated by the reticular activating system, whose influence on the hippocampus is seen in the special form of the EEG, known as theta waves, originating in the septum. The theta waves sweep across the cells of the hippocampus, inhibiting most of them but leaving a few that are active in each phase of the wave. This means that at each moment certain cells only are open to receive excitation: thus the synaptic changes associated with particular situations will occur in a certain order.

The generation of waves is linked to the movement of the animals: this is the link by which the map is produced during exploration and used to find a goal. During exploration the synaptic changes of cells associated with particular situations will occur in a certain order. As a result these cells come to be more easily activated, so as to constitute the course on the map, which can be read again in the same order. During search for a goal a special high-frequency theta is found. This shifts the focus of excitation from the place cells corresponding to the position at the start of the movement to the cells whose co-ordinates fit the direction and distance of the next place in the sequence. If the destination then proves to be correct the process is repeated with the next cells and so on until either the goal is reached or misplace cells are encountered: in either case movement is then stopped, and if necessary the search can be resumed.

v. *A hungry rat in a maze*

Let us follow an imaginary hungry rat. As he begins to move, the septum issues theta waves to scan the hippocampus. The cells corresponding to his position will be at a low threshold and become active; so also will the cells corresponding to the position of past feeding (because the rat is hungry). The relative position of these two points and some other visible or audible feature allows determination of the general direction of movement that will reach the goal. The signals issuing from the hippocampus then direct the motor systems of the brain stem so that the animal moves in the right general direction, even if it does not take the shortest way through the maze. It is finding the *general direction* that is important. The rat does not have to learn exactly what turn to make at each point of the maze; there is flexibility in the way it proceeds to its goal.

It has long been known that animals, like humans, show such flexibility; they continue to reach the goal even if some conditions in the maze are changed. The learned skill is not a particular sequence of movements; the goal can still be found if the animal itself has to use new movements, say because it has lost a limb. It will get there somehow, using the map to show the right direction.

vi. *Cognitive maps*

The experimental data to support this theory came from experiments with rats, but O'Keefe and Nadel show in their book how the theory of cognitive maps may be extended to human memory. In the spatial map that we have been considering representations of objects experienced in the environment are ordered within a framework generating unitary space. However, the central property of the locale system is its ability to order representations in a structural context. The development of objective spatial orientations is not the only possible use for such a system . . . mapping structures can represent verbal as well as non-verbal information . . . [this is the] form of memory concerned with the representation of experiences within a specific context.[21]

vii. *Theories of space*

No doubt these views on mammalian memory will be modified and improved: for criticism of them see Miller.[22] They suggest possible approaches to several old philosophical problems. O'Keefe and Nadel emphasize that the hippocampus provides human beings with a unitary spatial framework, present innately. They contrast this Kantian type of absolute space, which is *a priori* and Euclidean, with the relative or egocentric space built up by experience and so *a posteriori*, as advocated by Poincaré and Piaget and many others who are impressed by our capacity to conceive of non-Euclidean space. The great advantage of the cognitive map system from our present point of view is that it suggests how inputs from various sources can be combined to form representations, units of higher order than the simple feature detectors. The 'place cells' of the hippocampus can be considered as such higher-order representations, and the routes are representations of a higher order again, chosen from the relations between those units that offer rewards or avoid punishments. Moreover, we can see from the scheme how the appropriate selections come to be made when an animal or human is motivated to make explorations. These ideas can be extended to the rest of the cortex.

viii. *The unified map of experience*

The entire cerebral cortex is made up of columns, containing pyramidal cells that are fundamentally like those of the hippocampus. They all have extensive dendrite trees, through which pass many input fibres, capable of making the necessary synaptic contacts with the dendritic spines by associative synaptogenesis. We have seen that there is evidence that in many parts of the cortex the cells are concerned with particular activities. For instance the recognition of faces and hands in the parietal and inferior temporal areas, production of speech in Broca's area, performance of motor skills in the precentral area, colour vision in the visual area V4, and so on. It seems likely that memory records concerning these activities are largely stored within the relevant area. They cannot usually be reawakened by electrical stimulation of the area, but Penfield occasionally found spots that evoked short sequences of recollection, although stimulation at a point is a very crude procedure.[23] We can imagine that the memory records in these areas are complicated sets of relations between thousands of nerve cells, depending to some extent on the actual topographical relations between the cells. The numerous cases in which topographical relations are preserved in the cortex strongly suggest that many sorts of information are stored in some kind of map.

It is also significant that these different areas are not isolated and independent. There is overlap between areas, anatomically and functionally, just as there is between the cells within any area (see e.g. Ch. 17.iv). The system is one unitary whole, driven by a central reticular system and organized to support the life of the individual and provide his central concept of identity.

It may be helpful to consider the whole human memory system as one large map organized around certain co-ordinates. The most general of these are perhaps the systems that record the internal needs of the individual himself. Early external information is about the mother, and then about other human beings, who continue to be important reference features throughout life. Some facts about space and time may be implicit in the map from the start; perhaps we *must* perceive the world in those terms.

The advantage of a good general map is that new information can be added to it in an appropriate place and later retrieved by reference to some of the features that are already there. Everyone has evidence that recall depends upon the use of some such technique: 'Where have I seen that face?', 'What was I doing when I last saw my keys?' The concept of the memory as a unified map of experience will cover these and much more important items. O'Keefe and Nadel have provided at least a plausible theory of how the brain provides just such a map.

Probably representations in the brain do not consist only or mainly of separate records for each type of object or sound that can be recognized. Indeed the memory store should not really be considered as a 'record' at all: it is a *program for acting* in a particular way when a given situation occurs in the future. The store of information is not a set of distinct bits labelled by column and row, as in the memory of a computer. In a computer there is a separate engine, the central processor, which consults the memory: there is no separate processor in the brain. The 'consultation' is a property of the whole engine, but there is still no hard evidence about how the system is organized nor how we gain access to facts remembered.

Finding the right answer depends somehow on finding the right subject, the facts about large classes of events being as it were stored together. Access may be first to a class and then to details. A memory system of this sort is said to be 'content addressed'. All faces or all houses are recognized by a few features and then further examined and identified by the details of this face or that house. But this is only a rough idea. The problem is indeed baffling especially for complex memory systems such as our own: some clues can be obtained from simpler animals such as the octopus.

29. Memory and development

i. *The earliest memories*

At first the child does not know how to find the candle with his gaze. From this I conclude that the interpretation even of some of the simplest and, for the human child, most important visual images must be translated by him and are not given in advance by inherent organisation without preceding experience.[24]

Some of the clearest evidence about the nature of memory changes comes from study of the earliest stages of development. These include the period when programs that ensure perceptual competence are first developing, long before the advent of what we usually refer to as 'my earliest memories'. These very early stages have been of interest throughout the history of philosophical and psychological enquiry. Research with babies is inevitably difficult: Haith has pointed out: 'verbal report is unavailable, discriminative response indicators are severely limited, and direct neuroanatomical investigation is impossible. Even so research on visual perception in the early weeks of life has made both methodologic and conceptual progress'. He goes on to comment that 'special intrigue accompanies the attempt to represent the perceptual world of an organism whose status we once shared, but can no longer remember, whose impressions of the visual world must, in some sense, be like our own yet still quite different'.[25]

ii. *Memory in kittens*

Studies of the development of animals do not present quite such difficulties.[26] After some controversy it is now agreed that kittens are born with at least 25 per cent of the cells of the primary visual cortex specified as feature detectors for particular contours, as has already been discussed (Ch. 27.iii). The same has been shown for young monkeys and lambs and is probably true of human babies. In normal kittens as development proceeds the proportion of cells so specified increases rapidly, they become more specific and fatigue less quickly. If kittens are kept in the dark the proportion of specific cells decreases. If visual experience is limited by keeping a kitten exposed to either vertical or horizontal lines, then only the cells detecting that direction will develop; the unused ones will disappear. Recordings by electrodes from the cells of the visual cortex of a kitten whose vision has been limited in this way show responses mainly to contours with the orientation of the lines running in the direction that the animal had experienced. Moreover, kittens who had seen only vertical lines would only pay attention to a stick if it was moving up and down; those kept with horizontal lines, the reverse. It is important to note that these effects happen rapidly. Exposure to stripes of a particular orientation for *one hour* is enough to bias the response of the cortical cells studied twenty-four hours later. But the effect is not seen if the cells are tested *immediately* after stimulation. This is a most interesting demonstration that the establishment of a long-term memory takes time (Ch. 26.vi). If the experiment is done with one eye of the animal closed and it is then killed and the brain studied, there can be seen to be a greater density of synapses in the cortex on the side that had received the stimulation. So this form of learning seems to involve the making of new connections and the loss of those that are not used. There is still some question as to how far they can reappear if a normal environment is restored.

iii. *Critical periods in development*

The need for visual experience is especially seen if the animal is deprived of normal vision during a *critical period*. The plasticity is maximal in a kitten at one month and declines until no longer present after three months. A kitten kept in the dark for six weeks shows few orientation cells. Six hours of vision leads after one day to nearly normal orientation sensitivity. However, if the kitten is returned to the dark, receptive field properties degenerate and once lost can no longer be recovered. There are similar critical periods during human development. Pediatricians have been able to use knowledge of this sort in identifying and correcting tendencies to squint and other visual abnormalities. Kittens deprived of normal vision by closing one eye during the sensitive period can show recovery of vision if this eye is later opened. The recovery is better if the closure occurred in the early part of the sensitive period (four to six weeks) and is helped by closure of the previously opened eye. Similar effects are known in children. The use of a patch for as little as a week can produce changes in vision. All these facts show how rapidly experience selects among the possibilities open to the young nervous system.

30. Summary of some essential features of memory systems

Setting up a memory record in the nervous system depends upon the possibilities of alteration of the connections between neurons. In very simple animals such as the sea slug *Aplysia* this may involve changing the responsiveness of conduction through a single cell. In more complex animals such as an octopus the code set from which selection is made includes a greater number of receptors and feature detectors, and of possible responses. Setting up effective memories then involves a complex system of centres, each playing a different part in the process. One centre allows for interaction of incoming signals from receptors from the outside world with others from inside that indicate whether the animal's resulting action has been rewarding and should be repeated, or not. The system is so designed as to reduce the probability of the use of unwanted pathways and increase those that are advantageous. Another part of the system in an octopus serves to depress the overall tendency to act, allowing only the selected pathways to operate.

Many millions of neurons are involved even in the simple visual and tactile memories of an octopus. The memory systems of higher animals, including our own, seem to operate on similar principles but are immensely more complex. Selection is now among responses to an essentially infinite variety of possible *combinations* between the signals of feature detectors. These detectors are originally provided by heredity and are developed by use, or atrophied by disuse. For any given environmental feature there are many detectors (redundancy); moreover each detector is often not sharply tuned but responds also to neighbouring features (degeneracy). The result is to write into the brain a representation of the environment; not in the sense of a picture but as a pattern of connections that produces behaviour appropriate to each environmental situation.

Lesions in various parts of the human brain show that there are several different types of memory. Recognition of faces is impaired by lesions in one area, of speech in another, of motor skills in the precentral area, and so on. Some of the most striking failures of memory occur after damage to the hippocampus. These defects may be due to the fact that the hippocampus serves to allow learning of behaviour related to place. Its cells receive signals from various cortical receptor systems, and come to act as coded representations of the combinations in which signals of locality occur. The hippocampus thus acts as what O'Keefe and Nadel call a cognitive map of the environment (Ch. 28.vi).

The activation of the memory in the hippocampus or any other part of the brain comes from the reticular activating system of the brain stem. There is evidence that the EEG initiates the theta waves, which are characteristic of the hippocampus. These waves scan the map and give an animal or man the general direction in which to proceed towards a goal. This theory suggests that the human brain is provided innately with a unitary Kantian framework of absolute space.

A similar type of hypothesis will begin to explain how inputs from various sources are combined to form group units acting as representations of higher order than the simple feature detectors. The whole memory system may constitute one large map, organized around certain co-ordinates, such as facts about place and time, the needs of the individual and especially the characteristics of other humans. New features are placed appropriately on the map and retrieved by their relationship to features already there. Human learning involves selection from a vast set of possibilities, but with limitations that ensure effective life — for instance in learning language. The system of connections that results from learning operates to a large extent as a single whole, comprising the knowledge and life pattern of the individual.

This unity of the brain system corresponds to the subjective unity of the mind and personality. Moreover it strongly emphasizes the importance for epistemology of considering the whole of life of each individual, his capabilities, wants and needs. His knowledge and capacity for reasoning are part of the whole program for living. Every philosopher's theory of knowledge or metaphysics, however abstract, is influenced by the whole life system of the individual who propounds it, and the culture of which he is part. The joint problem for the philosopher and scientist is to find better ways to describe this life system.

PART IV

Valuing

31. Wants, needs and values

i. *A naturalistic fallacy?*

The idea that study of the brain and other biological subjects is useful for philosophy has been resisted more strongly in relation to questions of value than in any other aspect of human thinking and behaviour. Nevertheless there are insistent reasons for further consideration of the processes of valuing. Recent studies have shown that the achievement of satisfaction of various sorts of need is accompanied by activity in specific parts of the brain. The neural systems that ensure satisfaction of physical needs, such as for food, are obviously directed towards self-maintenance: we judge this to be a 'good' aim and its converse as 'bad'. More interesting neural systems are now known that are associated with general conditions of happiness or depression. This raises the further question as to whether and how all our considerations of value may be connected with the various brain mechanisms that ensure the continuation of life. It will be necessary to discuss what meaning should be attached to such words as 'associated' or 'connected' in this context, but undoubtedly these facts about the brain introduce new factors into discussions of the alleged 'fallacy' of naturalism.

It is particularly interesting that neuroscientists now realize that these basal forebrain areas, such as the hypothalamus, septum and striatum, are at the centre of the action system of the brain. Though they are relatively small they provide both the targets at which activity is directed and the motors by which action is initiated. We thus begin to have the outlines of knowledge of the nervous apparatus that is involved during the mental process of valuing.

The difficulty of understanding the relationship between the mental and the physical is especially acute when we think about values. One's pleasures or pains, loves or hates are essentially parts of oneself and it is hard to think of them as necessary accompaniments of events in the brain. A certain resistance to the thought is probably the basis for the concerns of antinaturalists, who fear that attention to the brain may somehow 'reduce' the beliefs and values that they rightly consider to be of fundamental human importance. No sensible neuroscientist would wish for any such reduction. On the contrary, he would claim that knowledge about these basal areas of the brain has already contributed substantially to an *increase* in human welfare and happiness. For example, psychiatry, though far from perfect, at least provides a partial understanding of some of the major causes of human misery, and has found means to alleviate them. Still more important is the positive contribution that knowledge of the brain can make to our appreciation of the place that ethical and aesthetic values have in human life (Chs. 35–7).

The resistance to allowing people to search for reasons for their values has a long history. It may have sprung originally from the anxiety of princes, priests and other authorities to impose standards allegedly coming from a superhuman source. The modern philosophical version of the argument had a more academic origin when in 1903 the Cambridge philosopher G. E. Moore proposed the concept of a 'naturalistic fallacy'.[1] He described this in various ways, the most direct being 'that good is good and that is the end of the matter'.

It is interesting that there is evidence that Moore himself later wished to qualify his views. His literary remains include an uncompleted draft of a possible preface written in 1920 or 1921 for a second edition of *Principia Ethica*.[2] In it he writes that what he really meant was that Good is simple in the sense of being indefinable or unanalysable. Good, he wrote, is not identical with any natural property with which it is the business of the natural sciences or psychology to deal. But he seemed to be uncertain of this formulation and perhaps confused by the distinction between what we may call specific or limited and more general assessments of value, which recurs throughout discussions of the subject.

For the biologist also it is clear that there are both specific and more general needs and satisfactions, each with associated cerebral activities. In some simple situations the valuations 'good' and 'bad' are prompted at least in part by the reward systems that promote the support of life; for instance, the taste-buds and associated nerve centres indicate sweetness or bitterness (Ch. 18). It may be that the more general concept of goodness refers to the *general* system for self-maintenance and the activation of systems that indicate a condition of satisfaction with life. The decision that the promotion of one's life is Good is indeed arbitrary, though it would seem perverse for a living thing to deny it. Certainly there are parts of the brain that are in action when we experience pleasure, success, or well-being — that life is going well. Such a view of ethical concepts as relating to human life would agree with Mackie's general definition of the concept of 'good' as that which satisfies the requirements or wants or interests of the kind of thing in question.[3]

Philosophers still argue actively about naturalism today. The discussions emphasize that 'naturalism' can have various meanings, all of them 'imprecise'.[4] The question of naturalism evidently turns at least partly on the problem of how man's nature compares with that of other creatures and in what sense he transcends the others. Obviously, the biologist must have something to say about this. Indeed in a sense it is a discussion about the extent and limits of biology. Few people will doubt that the cultural values embodied in custom, religion and law are unique human products, with at most only faint analogies among animals. Yet the making of all valuations and commendations must itself be accompanied by activities in the brain. We may find some help in understanding the nature of valuation by study of the information that is available about the central brain regions that are involved in converting needs into action. These are also systems that provide the set points or targets at which action is aimed. Valuations are obviously related to goals subjectively, and so they are in the brain.

ii. *Personal values and public values*

A large part of the difficulty that we feel in the subject is that 'valuing' covers a very large range of human activities. Moreover, values lie, or should lie, at the base of most public social life: we have a duty to examine our values. As Honderich puts it. 'Every political philosophy, ideology and party creed should begin from an explicit response to the question of what well-being there ought to be, and, whether as means to an end, what distress.'[5] Besides the simple cases, such as valuing food or comfort, there are all the difficult ones involved under the subjects of ethics and aesthetics.

Thinking about the various sorts of value raises questions about how values are determined. Do they in any sense have one single source? Why do we use the word 'good' in so many contexts? Is it possible to say why we consider strawberries are good? In what sense is it for the same reason as we think that kind or courageous actions are good — or a Beethoven sonata, or a picture by Picasso? The biologist believes that he can give at least partly satisfactory answers to some of these questions. The insistence of the simpler sorts of need, for instance for food and drink, is produced by well-known events in the brain, and satisfaction of such needs is accompanied by further brain processes. Examination of these systems of reward may illuminate the question of the value of valuing in general. It is especially significant that there are areas in the brain whose stimulation provides satisfaction and reward independent of any particular simple bodily need (Ch. 32.iv). Achievement of this general condition of satisfaction is probably the basis for the more sophisticated types of valuation that are involved in aesthetic appreciation and love of knowledge and truth. The capacity of the human brain for complex intellectual and intelligent computations is backed up by the development of emotional powers that allow appreciation of the results of such activities. For this there may well be special developments of the human basal forebrain centres, as well as the cortex, allowing us to recognize and value our achievements. So we use the word 'good' for the successful performance of many characteristic human actions.

iii. *Valuing and acting*

To find out what an animal or man wants and values one observes what he does: valuing is preliminary to action; broadly speaking, we do what we want to do and what we need to do for survival. So it should be no surprise to find that the parts of the brain that set the standards or aims that ensure the continuation of life are closely related to those that initiate action. This certainly applies to those parts that deal with simple needs. Less is known about aesthetic satisfaction, but a person who values music or pictures that he judges are good will take action to satisfy his 'taste' (Ch. 37).

In common use, the conception of 'wanting' something is mental. It is an ancient philosophical problem whether wanting is a causal factor in action. This will of course depend upon one's interpretation of the difficult notion of causation. In an attempt to make the problem more precise Davidson has written: 'Whenever someone does something for a reason he can be characterized as a) having some sort of pro-attitude toward actions of a certain kind, and b) believing (or knowing, perceiving, noticing, remembering) that his action is of that kind.'[6] This is a useful formulation. The basis of 'pro-attitudes' may well be in states of those parts of the brain that tend to make us hungry, thirsty, sleepy, sexy, angry, loving, happy, depressed and so on. These include the hypothalamus, septum and other basal forebrain areas, which we shall describe. The influences under heading b) are those that have been acquired by learning, especially in the cortex.

Admittedly we know only little about the brain activities in either category, but the formulation at least allows us to give a rough description of what goes on in the brain to accompany the sensation of wanting; with any 'pro-attitude' there must be some particular action in the brain. In this sense wants can be causes, as we individually feel them to be. I am myself unwilling to speak of mental events as 'causing' physical events, or the reverse, for reasons already discussed (Ch. 4.ii) For me it is more interesting to discover what processes in the brain accompany the experience of wanting.

It would be satisfactory if we could define these processes precisely. Fortunately there is some evidence about the nature of those in the hypothalamus. The intractable problems involved in identifying the cortical events that accompany 'pro-attitudes', such as believing and the rest, have already been discussed. As Davidson puts it, they include 'moral views, aesthetic principles, social conventions and public and private goals and values . . . the word "attitude" does yeoman service here, for it must cover not only permanent character traits . . . but also the most passing fancy . . .'.

The complement of wanting is satisfaction. The feelings of

pleasure and reward that arise with consummation of wants and needs are, like all mental processes, the accompaniment of nervous activities. Something is now known about the nature of the neural processes that are involved; they go on in areas close to those that also take part in the generation of wants and needs and of the actions that satisfy them. These various operations that mediate homeostasis are thus all linked together in the central parts running along the axis of the brain. They include the reticular system, the brain-stem nuclei, the hypothalamus, reticular nuclei of the thalamus and the striatum, septum and other basal ganglia of the forebrain. All of these are involved in what may loosely be called the emotional life of the individual and this implies that they are also involved in his valuations and his actions.

32. The hypothalamus

i. *Targets for survival*

Human valuations extend from those connected with satisfaction of simple physical requirements, such as for food, to the need to satisfy the highest spiritual and aesthetic aims. It is these last, I suppose, that are especially labelled 'non-natural'. I hope to show that it is not necessary or desirable to make this sharp separation. The general aim of living is to preserve the distinctive organization of oneself and one's kind. A great variety of experiences and provisions are needed for this end, and should be valued. Human life depends upon language, art and all the complications of culture as much as on food — it would ultimately collapse without them.

The very simple general thesis we have been following is that the brain is so constructed that it continually allows for programs of action that help to maintain life, varied in response to circumstances. In order to achieve this aim of continuity, preventing the dissolution of the living organization, the programs have to cater for a very wide variety of needs. Let us look at some of them: first some of the simple ones. There must be enough oxygen, food of many sorts and water; the body must be neither too hot nor too cold. There must be the right amount of sugar in the blood, the right amounts of calcium, sodium, potassium, phosphate and so on. The brain contains neural systems that monitor the levels of these substances and many more. The target systems that do this are largely in the hypothalamus, a small lobe at the base of the brain, whose cells detect whether there is too much or too little of each of these things and set off actions by muscles or glands that correct the error. These target systems determine that in childhood we grow up to the right size and weight and then remain there for the rest of life in spite of the tons of food eaten and gallons drunk. These are the systems that set the standards for the cruder physical activities of our life. Moreover, to ensure the continuity of human life by reproduction the brain also contains the elaborate systems that insist upon sexual activity and demand the care of the young.

The human hypothalamus weighs about four grams; only 0.3 per cent of the whole brain. Yet it sends and receives signals to and from probably more other brain areas than does any other part. It is the centre of the brain both physically and by its connections. It receives direct connections from the areas all around it and via these from almost all other parts, including the cerebral cortex (via the hippocampus). With this central position the hypothalamic neurons are indeed well placed to organize the aims of the whole body.

From the hypothalamic cells nerve fibres proceed to many other areas, including those from which they receive them. They also control the body by chemical means: the signal substances that they produce (called releasing factors) are main regulators of the multiple actions of the pituitary gland, which lies just below the hypothalamus. The hormones of the pituitary gland in turn control the thyroid gland, the adrenal and the sex glands; and the hormones produced by these in their turn influence every cell in the body, including those of the hypothalamus itself. The balance of interactions of so many factors is indeed difficult to comprehend. Yet it is this balance that regulates our basic moods and desires, though these are moderated by higher cortical intellectual activities: there are pathways by which the cortex may influence the hypothalamus. The temperament and actions of the individual are certainly the product of a very complicated set of influences — as we all know from experience. A particular influence from either heredity or upbringing or environmental conditions may alter the whole balance and produce swings of mood such as those of schizophrenia.

As a final turn of complexity, all the different parts of the hypothalamus itself are interconnected. Thus hypothalamic cells that are controlling the thyroid gland or the adrenal themselves directly influence the neurons controlling sex, and so on. Who can expect to make accurate forecasts of the behaviour of such a system? The study will require the best efforts of theorists and mathematicians.

ii. *Goal-directed activities*

This complicated network of influences constitutes the agency or motivator that moves an animal or man to action and determines our mental moods. Each separate part of it influences desire and behaviour in one direction or another, according to the needs of the moment and the external conditions. Much of daily life follows an internally produced rhythm in which the hypothalamus acts as a master clock. The timing is entrained from the changes of day and night by the eyes, through the special tract from the retina to the hypothalamus (Ch. 23.i). This is quite distinct from the main optic tract, which serves the conscious process of vision. Daily rhythms cease after injury to a particular part of the hypothalamus of a rat (the supra-chiasmatic nucleus).

iii. *Positive valuing: seeking satisfaction*

Many varied effects have been recorded after stimulating or removing parts of the hypothalamus. Electrical stimulation of the lateral hypothalamus has been reported to produce various sorts of goal-directed behaviour; eating, drinking, mating and even killing. A rat with electrodes planted in certain places will learn to press a lever that delivers a stimulus to this part of the brain. This is so rewarding that the animal will press repeatedly for hours on end, to the neglect of eating and drinking.[7]

Various areas of the brain are involved in this self-stimulation. Many of them lie along the course of the fibres running forwards in the medial forebrain bundle from the substantia nigra or the hypothalamus to the striatum. These pathways use the mono-amine transmitter dopamine. Conversely, with electrodes in certain other regions a rat will carefully *avoid* any action that produces stimulation of these fibres or neurons. These latter regions are called the mid-brain raphe nuclei and the fibres proceeding from them use acetyl choline and the amine serotonin (5HT); they will be considered later.

The effects of these various chemical transmitters are to activate or restrain the activities of the neurons in areas that activate the cortex, lying further forward and including the striatum, septum and other basal ganglia, whose interactions with the cortex are associated with continued consciousness and the selection of programs of action.

iv. *Neural activities in satisfaction*

The signals produced by stimulating some of the fibres of the medial forebrain bundle are thus 'interpreted' by the striatum and related centres as indicating 'satisfaction'. There is evidence that activity in such areas in man is the neural accompaniment of feelings of pleasure. Electrical stimuli are sometimes applied by surgeons to the basal ganglia during operations performed for the relief of pain. The patient may report that while the current was turned on he experienced feelings of pleasure, sometimes of a sexual nature.

In Chapter 17 we have described the striatum as the area controlling motor actions, in co-operation with the cerebral cortex.[8] It is significant that the striatum is also a region whose activities accompany sensations of satisfaction. This and other basal forebrain areas such as the septum and amygdala evidently play a central part in the whole life system. They ensure that the actions of the individuals are monitored to select those that are satisfactory. These are the parts of the brain that are active as we decide that some cortical activity is 'good'. They thus act as the monitors for the more complex parts of the life system that depends on the cortex, as the lower hypothalamic centres do for feeding and other simpler activities. This is obviously a very elaborate system and is still little understood. It seems likely that action in these areas accompanies the feelings of satisfaction, joy, hope, and pleasure that we experience in even more complex conditions of social and intellectual and aesthetic activities. The difficult question of whether the physical events in these areas should be said to 'cause' the satisfaction is relevant but need not be separately discussed here (see Ch. 31.iii).

The actions of the basal forebrain areas are fundamental in

determining the whole 'operating tendency' of a person; in subjective terms, his desires and moods. The relations between these areas and other parts of the brain are no doubt greatly influenced by learning, especially during childhood. Unfortunately little is known in detail about this relationship, but many traits of character and personality presumably depend upon the particular connections established by these 'reward centres', especially in relation to parents and siblings. One cannot emphasize too strongly that human 'needs' are for emotional and social satisfaction as much as for food and sex.

v. *Negative valuing*

Stimulation by electrodes at sites not far from these for positive reward serves to generate discomfort or pain. Rats will quickly learn to take actions that avoid such 'aversive' stimulation. As already mentioned, one of these pathways uses the amine serotonin, another is a set of 'periventricular' fibres (around the central canal of the brain) which have acetyl choline as transmitter. Animals in which either of these pathways has been blocked by antagonistic drugs will no longer learn to avoid aversive stimulation.

These punishment systems are probably as important as the positive-reward pathways. Drugs that inhibit the action of acetyl choline are found to prevent learning by rats. Moreover, failure to achieve a positive reward can act as a negative stimulus, and vice versa. The two systems work together to produce the balance of exploration and restraint that proves appropriate in a given life situation. Again, the painful effects of childhood experiences may leave their mark as inhibition by the negative reward centres of the capacity to relate to others in adult life, either sexually or socially. We have seen evidence in Chapter 19 that pain quickly produces actual changes in the connections in the brain. These facts should be remembered every time that one punishes a child. Frustrations and disappointments may all leave their scars.

The operations of the positive- and negative-reward centres obviously lie at the base of the psychological and emotional conditions of life. It is a pity that Freud did not live to learn of these facts, which provide the physical basis that he hoped would be found for developmental psychology. It is not appropriate to try to spell out here how the life pattern of each individual may be built up from childhood. It involves the learned combinations of experiences registered in the cortex and emotional experiences from the reward centres. There is immense scope for developments by psychologists and philosophers. As Richard Wollheim says, 'All value originates in the projection of archaic bliss, of love satisfied.'[9]

The great variety of the results that have been reported leaves no doubt that the hypothalamus and related forebrain centres are deeply involved in initiation of searching activities by men and animals and in their termination by satisfaction. These areas with their reward systems are fundamental for the direction of all activities and also for the memories that are left of them. The systems for arousal, reward and memory are all linked. Firstly, they are active as one selects the goals for action, say to find food. Secondly, they steer the course as one seeks the goal and then when the end is achieved their signals accompany the feeling of satisfaction. Finally the signals pass to areas that serve to print memory records of the routes of successful search and to eliminate unsuccessful ones (Ch. 27). Single cells in these reward centres send nerve impulses when a monkey sees an object that is associated with food, but not when he sees other objects.

Such experiments, and the rewarding results of self-stimulation, show that activity of the nerve cells in some of these pathways is sufficient to generate feelings of satisfaction. This activity is also generated by drugs, such as alcohol and tobacco, that we use (and abuse) to provide pleasure. These drugs imitate the actions of the various transmitter systems that operate in these pathways; they activate the reward systems and/or depress the punishment ones: morphine, heroin, nicotine, alcohol, ether, lacquer thinner, marijuana and codein all produce hedonic effects of well-being and relieve feelings of not being liked.[10] Even more complex effects are produced by the very powerful psychosomatic drugs such as lysergic acid (LSD). These act by influencing synaptic transmission in many parts of the brain as well as the basal ganglia, producing exaggerated sensations of strange forms, sometimes terrifying, sometimes of great beauty. Quite small doses can produce effects lasting for weeks or months, which is another example of nervous plasticity and a pointer to the danger of all these drugs.

These findings have obvious philosophical implications. They show the physical correlates in the brain for at least some of the simpler wants and satisfactions with which we are all familiar. It should be no surprise to find that there are such correlations; but we must beware of considering them too simply. Neither animals nor humans are automata directed by unvarying set-point controls. The mechanisms concerned contain many parts besides the hypothalamus. Complexity and variability are among the secrets that enable us to perform subtle and varied actions, suited to the circumstances. We may examine the systems concerned in the relatively simple examples of control of temperature and of eating and drinking.

33. Some examples of regulation

i. *Temperature control*

Wanting to keep warm or cool may not seem to be instances of value judgements with deep philosophical implications: but they show how the properties of conscious and unconscious processes can be systematically considered. In regulation of temperature these processes work together to give great stability, but at the price of a complex set of operations. Like all homeostatic controls they include a variety of mechanisms, from the nerves of the skin that make you shiver to the cerebral cortex when you decide to buy an electric fire or migrate to the Mediterranean.

The human body maintains an average temperature of 38.4°C, with small diurnal changes, falling to 38.0°C in the early hours of every morning. The set-point is determined by receptor cells in the anterior part of the hypothalamus (pre-optic area), which are activated when the blood temperature rises or falls outside narrow limits. The level at which the temperature is set is determined by the DNA of the genes, which give these receptor neurons the properties that have been proved by natural selection to be appropriate to regulate the human body temperature. The signals from these cells are not consciously felt: they initiate the actions that correct variations of blood temperature, by producing sweating, shivering and increased metabolism of fat from the liver. The conscious sensations of heat and cold are provided by sensory cells in the skin. The nerve impulses that these receptors generate activate the highest nerve centres of the cerebral cortex, initiating programs of action, such as lighting the fire, which tend to prevent further rise or fall *before* there has been any substantial change in body temperature. These conscious actions have been learned, whereas the unconscious responses from the hypothalamus are innate. The cortical temperature sense gives only *relative* values of external conditions. Familiar experiments with the hands in hot and cold water soon convince us that the skin gives poor indications of absolute temperature: the skin receptors are designed to give information that things are getting hotter or colder. The thermostat in the hypothalamus, on the other hand, is an instrument that signals departure from an absolute level of 38.4°C — but not to consciousness.

The automatic and behavioural mechanisms usually work together, but one can substitute for the other. If the pre-optic area of a rat is removed the body temperature, in a room at 16°C, drops from the normal 38.3°C to 23.0°C or less. But the rat can be trained to press a lever that turns on an electric fire if it feels cold. By pressing this lever the rat then keeps itself to within 0.75°C of normal, at least for some hours. This shows that the 'satisfaction' of being warm does not depend on the temperature-regulating centre itself, which had been removed from these rats. It suggests the important point that satisfaction and well-being are properties of some *general* 'satisfaction system', not of the particular parts of the homeostat. This is confirmed by further experiments in which these same rats were given levers for *either* heat control *or* self-stimulation. They preferred the latter and allowed their temperature to drop by many degrees, neglecting the lever that gave warmth. So the properties of the 'satisfaction' system are evidently available for association with various conditions. Some such independent satisfaction system presumably operates to provide the 'rewards' by which we learn to conform to human values much more elaborate than those that we are now considering.

ii. *The control of eating and drinking*

The interaction of conscious and unconscious processes can be seen equally well in the control of eating and drinking. Here we are more clearly dealing with questions of wanting and choice, which seem to be less involved in the regulation of temperature: obtaining food may involve action by the whole body, perhaps an elaborate process of exploration. The lateral hypothalamus is an area deeply concerned both with activity and with feeding. In cats from which the lateral hypothalamus has been removed all spontaneous behaviour at first stops. 'The animal is somnolent, akinetic and cataleptic. It will not eat and may die of inanition.'[11] Some recovery may take place, but the animal remains more like a machine than a normal cat, responding only when stimulated. It will take food, but stops eating before it has eaten enough. Conversely, animals with electrodes implanted in the lateral hypothalamus can be stimulated to eat excessively. A nearby area of the ventro-medial hypothalamus seems to have exactly the opposite effects; it prevents or stops feeding. So these are distinct centres providing for the initiation of eating and its termination by satiety.

The situation is actually much more complicated than this. The lateral hypothalamus is not so much a centre as a pathway, through which fibres proceed up and down. The lack of activity after removing it may be due to the development of an excessive inhibition because of interruption of these pathways. Ascending fibres of the reticular formation are the basis of the general activation of the cerebral cortex and hippocampus. The particular conditions that direct activity to feeding are determined by the metabolic needs, which are signalled by the ventro-median hypothalamus. The start of a meal is the result of a hunger signal from this region, accompanied by the familiar stomach contractions and sensations. The presence and smell of food itself stimulates the eating. The satiation may be due to the reduction of the hunger signals, and there are also other complex influences.

The balances between the various amine transmitter substances, dopamine, serotonin and noradrenalin, may be responsible for changes in the activity of the animal or person. Some of the nerve fibres using these transmitters have a very wide distribution. Thus there is a set of cells, known as the locus coeruleus or blue nucleus, in the medulla oblongata at the hind end of the brain, whose fibres spread out to all parts of the cerebral cortex and cerebellum. It is not known precisely what these cells do, but a rat from which the locus coeruleus has been removed can no longer be readily trained to run a maze for a food reward. So it may be that these fibres bring signals to the cortex (and the hypothalamus) indicating that an action has resulted in food. The regulation of feeding is thus dependent on events both above and below the hypothalamus, which acts as it were as a central point at which influences converge.

Regulation of drinking is similarly complex. There are cells in the hypothalamus that are sensitive to salt concentration. They can be stimulated by introducing drops of salty water into the brain of a goat — which immediately lowers its head and drinks from a bowl of water. Conversely, animals deficient in salt will drink salty water in preference to fresh. There is also a set of receptors sensitive to the volume of blood, lying in a different part of the brain, the subfornical organ. They are stimulated by a substance that is released by the kidney when there is a deficiency of blood (angiotensin II).

The general point is that the self-maintaining, homeostatic properties of the body are produced by the interaction of *many* factors, acting at different levels. The metabolism of the cells uses up the available materials in the blood, whose change then stimulates the brain to direct activity to a search for food or water, and so on indefinitely.

34. Emotional responses

The systems for ensuring self-maintenance (homeostasis) are not limited to those for physical functions such as feeding. In front of the hypothalamus and striatum, and connected with them, are areas that are especially involved in production of mental and physical conditions, such as rage and aggression, or loving care. These responses are largely social and may be characterized as 'emotional'. The areas concerned, including the amygdala, may collectively be called the basal forebrain areas, lying anatomically and functionally below the cerebral cortex. They involve performance of elaborate actions and are even more complicated and variable than the systems for eating and drinking. The details of their operations are only now beginning to be understood.

It was shown many years ago that after removing much of the cortex and forebrain of a cat, but leaving the amygdala, the animal shows a picture that is called 'sham rage'. On the slightest stimulus it bares its teeth and hunches its back and the hairs stand up as when it fights a dog. We cannot say whether this can correctly be called 'sham' rage, but clearly any stimulus now touches off a program that a cat may use when threatened.

Conversely, electrodes in other centres have been found to switch off aggression. A monkey that is dominant within its group can be prevented from attacking others if the weaker individual is trained to press a lever which activates electrodes placed in the brain of the aggressor. It has even been claimed that the attack of a bull can be stopped in this way. As so often, it is important to avoid the conclusion that single centres are involved. One experiment on the aggression of rats against mice showed that there were six such forebrain areas: three tended to increase the aggression and three to restrain it. Moreover, all of these would normally be under the influence of the cerebral cortex, not to mention that of the environmental stimuli.

These areas all exchange fibres with the cerebral cortex and the reticular activating system in both directions, and are involved in determination of the course of action of the individual at appropriate moments. These cell systems are active during the sequences of mental and physical changes that occur when an emotion is aroused. When a person is attacked he becomes angry and defends himself. Again, if a woman sees a man hitting a child her visual areas act with the basal forebrain areas as she shows the visible and mental signs of anger at the aggressor and compassion for the child. The capacity for such responses is obviously useful for life. They are part of homeostasis in its wider sense.

The action of these 'emotional' areas is not limited to such particular events: they are probably at work throughout the day. They play a large part in determining the temperament, mood and behaviour of the individual. Understanding of the whole system of reward centres and emotional centres in the brain has increased with the discovery that they use various amine transmitter substances such as dopamine and noradrenalin and also peptides such as enkephalin and various opioids. The changes of mood produced by drugs of all sorts such as heroin, alcohol, or even coffee or tea are almost certainly produced through influencing these systems. Use of such stimulants has good and bad effects on mankind and further knowledge is obviously desirable. It is satisfactory that we begin to understand how drugs produce their effects. From our present point of view these provide familiar situations that illustrate the relations of the physical and the mental.

Aberrations of the metabolism of the transmitter substances in these areas may be involved in conditions such as schizophrenia, and these may be ameliorated by drugs that influence the amines or peptides. Conversely it is often suggested that conditions of depression in humans may be themselves induced by unfavourable circumstances or unhappy personal conditions. This may indeed be possible: conditions in other parts of the brain or in the environment may alter the aminergic or other systems and so produce aberrations. In such a complex system it is very difficult to disentangle causes and effects. As before we see that in dealing with living systems it is difficult to identify lawlike sequences of behaviour.

There can be no doubt that humans possess such systems that provoke us to rage and aggression as well as others that make us tender and loving. It is surely relevant to moral judgements that there are obviously large variations both between people and within a given individual in the intensity of the actions of these parts of the brain and the control of them by higher centres. Of course it will be objected that all this is nothing new: it is obvious that people have desires and tendencies, peaceful or aggressive. 'Man is placed under the sovereign mastery of pleasure and pain', as the founder of University College, London, Jeremy Bentham, put it. But I think that the discovery of the existence of these systems that can be triggered into action introduces new factors into old questions about determinism and moral responsibility. Moreover, for our discussion the point is that it gives a new urgency to the need for philosophical and sociological discussions about them. For instance, both physicians and judges are hampered in their treatment of individuals by the persistence of attitudes that ignore these factors that influence behaviour. To give one simple example, it must often be relevant to judgement that 62 per cent of violent crimes by women are committed in the five days before menstruation and only 2 per cent shortly after it.

35. Ethics

i. *Ethical values*

Some of the most severe strictures of antinaturalists are directed at attempts to provide 'natural' standards for social behaviour. If we have established that there is a case for saying that some valuing has a natural basis, the question then is how to relate the use of such evaluative words as 'good' to ethical judgements. We have seen that some of the simpler sorts of valuing involve particular operations of the brain. Many people have argued forcefully that there are no similar objective moral values. Must we then suppose that there is no connection between these different sorts of valuing? Mackie, who holds that 'There are no objective values', later says 'it would be most implausible to give to the word "good" in moral uses a sense quite unconnected with its sense or senses in other contexts.'[12] Perhaps the biologist can help to find the common factor.

The simpler values that we have been dealing with are all provided with some kind of set-points, incorporated in the brain and at least partly inherited. It is much less easy to find set-points to direct the search for guide-lines as to what we ought to do in relation to each other. Clearly the varied customs and laws by which social behaviour is governed are the product of centuries of custom and tradition. They have to be learned afresh by every individual. Yet in following customs we use programs operated by the brain. We have seen something already of the brain activities involved in language, recognition of faces, loving, hating and enjoying. It is certain that the brain is involved in all the other attitudes lying behind social organization, including commanding and obeying, believing, worshipping, and many more. All of these things are parts of the system by which human life is lived.

Granted that the details of social behaviour are inherited culturally, are there any 'facts' that may help in determining social value? The biologist's contribution may be, firstly, to show the specific propensities that make culture possible. Language is an obvious example. We have repeatedly seen evidence that human beings are pre-programmed for this form of communication, which is the basis of all culture.

Secondly, the very existence of social life depends upon capacity to interact in orderly social ways, although this capacity is evidently not limited to man. Such restraint must have a basis in specific cerebral activities; it involves the development of positive altruistic attitudes, and the acceptance of restrictions on one's own behaviour. Individuals of social species undoubtedly perform actions that promote the survival of others and the propensity to do so must involve particular cerebral action, as does the tendency for a mother to cherish her young. In that case the hormone condition of the female influences her brain, and something is known of the details of this. Obviously not all social behaviour is conditioned by hormones in this way, but the example shows how the operation of a particular part of the brain can profoundly influence the mutual response of individuals. There is little evidence about the brain activities that are at work to allow two or more individuals to sit quietly together for discussion, but it is an important human characteristic, clearly less developed in apes. The special development of such powers may have been a prime secret of human success: language would be of little use among groups that lacked the power of attention.

ii. *Altruism*

Discussion of the possible biological basis of altruism arouses as much controversy as other forms of ethical naturalism. In particular, people do not like the suggestion that their acts of giving are related to the prospect of reciprocal reward. It is an important paradox that knowledge of the brain *confirms* this prejudice. If the propensity to act altruistically is part of one's brain programs, whether inherited or acquired, then such acts are indeed free gifts of one's human nature; not necessarily anticipating immediate reciprocity. The hints that we are creatures endowed with generous brain tendencies is not 'reductive'; such knowledge *enlarges* one's view of human nature.

The theory of natural selection implies that the patterns of action of individuals of a species have been selected because they tend to promote the propagation of the genes of the individual. How then can altruism have been evolved? It may be defined as taking action that promotes the homeostasis of another individual at the cost of reducing one's own chance of leaving offspring. Obviously actions that help relatives who carry one's own genes will be selected; this has been called kin selection.[13] But there are many examples of behaviour that helps distant relatives or even members of another species.

Whether genes for altruism will spread in a population depends upon the cost–benefit ratio of the actions involved. It is 'worth' expending energy on grooming another member of the species if the reciprocal grooming saves you from dangerous infection by ticks. This is not of course a calculus that is made in any way by the individuals; it is simply that those whose brain programs are such as to make them spend too much time grooming others (or too little) will leave fewer offspring than those who are 'optimally altruistic'.

Conditions that are likely to favour altruism are found in human populations. Some of them, listed by Trivers, are (1) Long life, which will obviously increase the chance of later reciprocity; (2) Low dispersal, or the habit of living in groups (this also increases the probability of kin selection); (3) Mutual dependence, for instance in primate groups; (4) Usefulness of assistance in fighting, which provides special opportunities for altruism.[14]

Early pre-human populations may well have lived in conditions that favoured the survival of genes for altruism. The precise circumstances cannot be defined either theoretically or by anthropology. Certain aspects of the problem have been considered by sociobiologists such as Trivers, Wilson[15] and Dawkins.[16] In a population where altruism depends on the expectation of later reciprocal benefits it may 'pay' individuals to decline to give reciprocal benefits. For example, considering grooming by monkeys, Dawkins showed by computer simulation that under suitable circumstances the genes of such 'cheats' who never repay will displace those of the 'suckers' who groom everyone, and that this will perhaps lead to the extinction of the population by disease acquired from ticks. However, a third category of individuals, who recognize the cheats and withhold reciprocity from them ('grudgers') will in the end dominate the population.

Such models can be used to throw some light on the background of human attitudes and morals. The tendencies to selfishness are not in doubt and lead to temptation to cheat. This in turn leads to developments of devices to prevent cheating and to detect it. The facial and linguistic signs that indicate trust or suspicion are characteristic accompaniments of altruism. Emotional responses of gratitude for favours and insistence on reciprocal 'fairness' are common human characteristics. They help to guarantee that gifts do not unduly favour genes for selfishness.

It is obvious that our system of morals is directed towards the support of altruism and it is at least interesting to consider how far it provides conditions suitable to the spread of the appropriate genes. The capacity to experience guilt is a powerful agent of morality: it is a form of negative reinforcement that is not far from pain. Again, the readiness to be aggressive against those who offend against moral rules shows how fundamental behavioural capacities are involved in cultural developments.

iii. *Group selection*

One of the powerful factors that favours altruism is the division of the population into small groups. There has been much discussion of how far natural selection can operate upon actions that promote the welfare of a group at the expense of the individuals in it. Kin selection is a form of group selection with an obvious genetic basis. There is no theoretical limit to the size of population within which an individual may be said to be promoting the welfare of his own genes. In practice, groups of ten to a hundred are about the range of effective personal bonds. Groups larger than this are called demes and the possibility of group selection among them depends on complex social, geographical, and genetic conditions. Analytical models and computer simulations have shown that altruistic genes can spread by selection of those groups that contain them under certain rigidly prescribed conditions. The possibility depends, among other things, on the size of the whole population and the way in which it is broken up into many semi-isolated sub-populations. Similar considerations are obviously relevant to discussion of the significance of the division of human populations into both large and smaller groups. There is clearly a strong tendency for humans to associate in small family groups, which would favour kin selection. The possible genetic significance of tribes and nations is less easy to assess. If language is so important to human culture, how are we to explain the Tower of Babel phenomenon: the multiplicity of dialects and languages? Perhaps anthropologists and historians are the people best qualified to find answers, but they cannot ignore possible biological influences both through genetics and neurobiology.

These are some characteristic features of human behaviour whose genesis can be dimly seen in our limited knowledge of brain physiology. The really difficult problems begin when we look for the basis of the detailed system of ethics.

iv. *The language of ethics*

J. L. Mackie gives his excellent book *Ethics* the subtitle 'Inventing Right and Wrong'.[17] This I take to imply that he believes being valuable is not a property of objects in themselves. Indeed the first words of his first chapter are 'There are no objective values.' His book proceeds to show the great complexity of the issues of naturalism in ethics and at the end leaves me to conclude that in some sense some moral values do have what can be called partly objective bases in human brains.

The method that Mackie uses to disentangle the problems of defining objectivity is to distinguish between first- and second-order moral statements. Those of the first order indicate what are considered to be proper aims, such as to avoid cruelty, increase happiness or serve God. Second-order statements are attempts to decide the meanings of moral words or to analyse what is involved in making first-order judgements. Ayer puts a parallel distinction on the first page of *The Central Questions of Philosophy*, saying that ethics are concerned with what lies behind the prescriptions of human conduct: 'Not so much in formulating rules of conduct as in considering what basis there may be for them'.[18] This is another version of Moore's distinction between the question of what sorts of things are good, which can be answered in descriptive natural terms, and the question of what goodness itself is, which he held to be non-natural.

Using Mackie's distinction, some might say that causing pain for fun can objectively be described as cruel, but the second order question is, what is the relation between this fact and the *moral* fact that it is wrong? The wrongness does not follow as a logical or semantic necessity. How do we 'know' that it follows? Is there some natural faculty for moral perception or intuition or is it simply what has been learned from social condemnation? These were the sort of questions that led Moore to conclude that ethical judgements were non-natural.

It may be that progress can be made in answering such questions by evidence about the stages by which moral judgements emerge in children. There are probably few psychologists or neurologists who would be ready to postulate the existence from birth of fully formed faculties for recognition of 'good' or 'bad' actions between humans. Nevertheless the increased knowledge of the neural basis of emotional responses suggests some clues to underlying mechanisms. Learning the ethical values of one's group is presumably a higher cortical activity; but the cortex does not function alone: its operations are linked to those of the basal forebrain areas concerned with reward and emotion (Ch. 32.iv). A child's process of learning his 'intuitive' approval of loving behaviour and disapproval of cruelty may be reinforced by signals from basal forebrain regions concerned with love, or fear, or aggression, as the case may be. It is likely that both cortical and subcortical areas of humans are particularly suited for such activities; it is not implausible to suggest that humans are provided with brains that are ready to learn to respond in these socially desirable ways. It is relevant that the prefrontal lobes are the latest development of the human brain (hence our high foreheads). Among the clues to the function of these lobes is the fact that, in animals, cells there have been shown to be active during self-stimulation for rewards. The pathways involved in this activity include many fibres that ascend to the frontal lobes and others that descend from them. These pathways may be concerned with the positive rewards of pleasure and negative rewards of guilt that frame our social conduct. It is no accident that people may become socially unreliable after frontal leucotomy. Such patients may surprise the family by using four-letter words or saying things in public that are often thought but not usually said. These seem to be parts of the brain that are involved in learning what we 'ought' and 'ought not' to do, especially by providing appropriate rewards for restraint.

Much philosophical controversy over ethical naturalism has centred on the meaning and use of key words such as 'ought'. Hume's dictum was that no 'ought' can be derived from an 'is', and later workers have tried to express this more precisely. In Hare's well-known phrasing, a *descriptive* statement is bound to facts and cannot answer the question 'What shall I do?' Only a command can do this and that is a *prescriptive* statement. A

statement that has both meanings Hare calls *evaluative*.[19] Evaluation therefore includes some extra element beyond the characteristics described, which is once again what Moore wished to
emphasize when he said that 'good is good and that is the end of it.'

In relation to 'personal' value it is clear that the something
extra is indeed not there in the object (e.g. strawberries) but in the
person's reaction to them. A similar evaluation is implied in
ethical judgements, but its basis is not firmly fixed by inherited
set-points. There is no hypothalamic set of centres to tell me that I
ought to pay taxes. Nevertheless individuals depend upon society
and they 'want' to be approved by it. There is little physiological
information about how such needs operate, but they are real. The
'need to conform' is clearly there in a child and he quickly learns
the behaviour that satisfies it, according to the customs of his
society.

v. *What are morals for?*

This brings us to the problem of whether there are any natural
foundations for what Mackie calls first-order moral judgements.
There may perhaps be said to be two main themes in the discussion of the objectives of moral enquiry. Utilitarians of various
sorts assume with Thomas Hobbes that human affairs tend to go
badly and that morals are part of an attempt to help them along.
Others would suppose that ethics has a higher aim, to find the
fundamental goal(s) of life and help us to attain them, whether
they be human or divine.

In either case there can be no doubt that moral thinking starts
from some relation to social codes; its precepts are related to the
human condition and tend to the improvement and flourishing of
human life. Sidgwick defines ethics as the Science of Conduct;
morality, as Kant said, is about people; Warnock's phrase is that
it involves practical appraisal of the effects of human conduct.
He asks 'What is evaluation for? Certainly it is never pointless.'[20]
Quinton puts it rather differently: 'ethical theorists . . . search
for a formal criterion for the moral character of a judgement of
value.'[21]

vi. *Utilitarianism*

The classic answer to this problem is Utilitarianism, the doctrine
that the choice between courses of action should be that which

contributes the greatest quantity of happiness, or the least pain and distress. The advantages and difficulties of this prescription and of any calculus of happiness are obvious, and much discussed. For one thing it is particularly difficult for the individual to judge how wide to cast his search. The general welfare of mankind is too broad an aim to guide everyday conduct. Indeed the attempt to make such assessments is a purely intellectual exercise; it makes little use of the emotional influences which help to guide us in moral judgements in relation to those close to us. The very attempt to make such general judgements may bring conflict with more profitable ethical thinking nearer home.[22]

As we have discussed already, the capacity to take actions that help others as well as oneself almost certainly depends on specific human emotional properties. To quote Mackie again, 'A humane disposition is a vital part of the core of morality, it would surely have been an element in the *aidōs* that the gods, in Protagoras' myth, gave to men.'[23] But why postulate a god-given gift? Surely this special disposition has arisen by natural selection and 'manifests itself in hostility to and disgust at cruelty and unsympathy with pain and suffering wherever they occur'. Mackie is here giving a twentieth-century European view of morality; empathy and sympathy have been less prominent at other times and places. However, the quality of mercy has long been present, however strained, and it is interesting to speculate when and why these characteristics appeared in the evolution of man. More practically, we should try to advance understanding of how these are embodied in cerebral activities.

vii. *Learning morals*

We have already examined the system in the brain by which 'practical values' are determined for the individual, but ethics is concerned with the valuation by people of each other. In any social animal the behaviour of individuals to each other is a matter of fundamental concern for survival. Surely the relevant conduct must be determined by suitable brain programs, either inherited or learned. Let us consider how such programs are formed.

Human morality is presumably based on some inherited *capacity* for this sort of learning. Making moral appraisals is universal — there is honour even among thieves. The presumption is that

morals help to ameliorate the course of human affairs, assuming
with Hobbes that they tend to go badly. Resources are limited
and there is competition to satisfy needs. Warnock tried to identify
the limitations on human capacity to meet this human predicament.[24] He emphasizes two of them as the inadequacy of rationality on the one hand and of sympathy on the other. We have already
in earlier chapters given some consideration to the question of the
cerebral capacity for sympathy. The child smiles not only at its
mother but at any smiling individual. Surely this and our other
capacities for happy interaction provide the basis for the
sympathy that can limit our selfishness. The mutual pleasure
achieved is the reward for the individual for any sacrifice he may
be making. As we have seen, the brain has mechanisms that
classify events as pleasant or unpleasant: if one object or situation is bad, then others like it will be. The child learns a sequence
of values by linking them to primordial ones. So hugging is the
first lesson in good behaviour.

All people are capable of morality and have these capacities
to do good. Better knowledge about their sources and how to
develop them during education and in adults is surely likely to
help in amelioration of our predicament. Finding the best ways
for people to learn about moral responsibility becomes more
important as religious belief declines. As a basis for this it is
helpful to realize that 'doing good' is a natural human characteristic and that it brings its own reward.

People nowadays are encouraged to learn of the natural
sources of their wants and tendencies. They feel the lack of
'something that backs up and validates some of the subjective
concerns which people have for things' as Mackie says of Hare's
World without Objective Values.[25] They ask for something to
help them to reach decisions and solve problems of conflicting
aims. No one can provide any complete objective basis: all
action is a continual creative choice between alternative
possibilities. 'Morality is not to be discovered but to be made', as
Mackie wisely says.

Understanding of the factors that are at work in oneself and
others is surely of assistance. This is one way in which biological
knowledge can help ethics — by showing the historical origin
and functional rationality of our needs and aims. Some biologists
such as Huxley and Waddington who have discussed ethics have

tried to show that humans should follow some cosmic evolutionary aim. This seems to me to be a biological mistake. The aims of life are firmly set in individuals. 'Egoism is not amoral but forms a considerable part of any moral system.'[26] There is nothing wrong in following our own wants and needs, which are the directives for living that have been implanted in us over the ages. But we are *also* endowed both by nature and by custom with the need to respect the needs of others if we are to be free of the painful guilt-feelings that accompany activation of the negative reward systems.

The actions of individuals have produced the gradual increase both in complexity and quality of life that we discussed in Chapter 9 and which culminates in man. As we do not know how life began we cannot say whether this evolutionary progress, revealed *ex post facto*, represents some cosmic purpose. Aiming to increase the amount and variety of life is indeed a noble human ideal. But the more limited targets of individual life are a more realistic basis for ethics, and they are firmly set in the brain. It is perhaps too much to say that study of our cerebral capacities yet provides an objective basis for a set of fundamental social values, but there do seem to be natural tendencies for humans to co-operate as well as to conflict. There is a paradox in all social creatures between mutual sympathy and the selfishness that is natural to every living thing. Human life obviously depends fundamentally on co-operation. This suggests that the basic principle of morality should be 'that we should give a priority to policies whose end is to make well-off those who are badly-off', as it is expressed by Honderich.[27] He calls this the principle of equality, though he does not suppose that all men are the same, nor that the best results for the badly-off will necessarily be achieved by giving the same welfare to all. The principle is more important than the name and is not contrary to the biological history of man, in spite of all his past and present warlike propensities.

viii. *The childishness of man*

Discussion of ethics brings us to consider another striking characteristic of man — the long period of childhood, which is the time when we learn how to think morally as well as how to behave. Most mammals become sexually mature as soon as they have stopped growing, often even earlier. In man growth is slowed, and sexual development delayed for ten or more years; the great apes show a lesser delay. Then just before puberty there is the adolescent growth spurt: the individual becomes large and dominant.

The very long childhood is a specific human characteristic. It determines the whole character of human societies, ensuring that a large proportion of the population consists of small individuals unable to survive independently and constrained by their physical weakness to attend to the training that is given by their elders. We shall not be disturbed that these facts may generate wrong notions about the rights and freedom of individuals. The dominance of adults over children and the dependence of the latter are facts that cannot be avoided. This does not mean ignoring the need to treat children as individuals.

This particular pattern of life probably developed gradually from an ape-like condition three million years ago or more. It must be the result of specific neuro-glandular systems in the hypothalamus and pituitary, which are known to control the rate of growth and sexuality. A possible theory is that the delays are produced by an overriding inhibition of growth and sexual development by the amine substance melatonin, secreted by the pineal gland.[28] Evidence for this is that children with tumours of the pineal may become sexually mature at four years old or younger. The amount of melatonin in the blood has been found to decrease during puberty of both boys and girls,[29] while the sex hormones showed a corresponding increase.

I emphasize these facts to show that childhood is a specific feature of human life. Indeed, an ingenious theory suggests that the change from ape to man consisted essentially in neoteny, which is the reaching of sexual maturity of a larval form. Man is, as it were, a foetal ape, just as the Mexican axolotl is a sexually mature tadpole.[30] This process of neoteny has been shown to be quite a common evolutionary process.[31] By neoteny the ancestral stage is eliminated. We achieve manhood by never reaching apehood.

Such a change would explain our large head and brain and many emotional and behavioural facts. We are in a sense all children, even as adults, and correspondingly liable to obey; in fact to be moral. Readiness for attachment to others, initially to parents, is another human characteristic, related to the imprinting process that is found in many young birds and mammals. Bowlby has emphasized the fundamental importance of this attachment and the dangers involved in the converse separation, even though this is inevitable. The capacity for imprinting and attachment to others certainly involves particular parts of the brain in birds. It may be that these capacities are specially developed in humans. We remain prone to attachment throughout life (hence falling in love). The need for social approval and the guilt that comes from breaking social codes may be further developments of the same propensity, perhaps linked to the enlarged frontal lobes. Included in their complex functions is the capacity for restrained behaviour and attention to social values.

36. Social man

i. *Biology and sociology*

It is dangerous for a biologist to discuss problems of sociology, and this for several reasons. Firstly there is an enormous literature on the subject, with which he is not familiar. Next, he must avoid interfering where he is not competent: the practices of social life are very important to people emotionally and even legally. This should not in itself preclude discussion, but the point is that these complex situations are hard to analyse and biologists have little to say about them. The continuance of a social practice does not depend upon survival value in the usual Darwinian sense. Slavery did not end in America because of the loss of certain genes from the population.

The characteristics of humans today must be based upon those that originated by natural selection, but anthropologists still have few hard data as to conditions that were responsible in those remote times. In spite of all these caveats, I believe that knowledge of the brain can contribute something to understanding of social man, as we may see by looking at some things that biologists do understand, such as the special features of human anatomy and some general aspects of social behaviour.

ii. *What purpose do large brains serve?*

The outstanding physical characteristic of man is the large size of the brain, and there is good evidence that this has arisen rather recently (by geological standards). The brain of the Australopithecines, living from three to one million years ago, was hardly larger than that of an ape (about 450 ml cubic capacity). In *Homo erectus*, the cave men of Java and Peking, living from perhaps one and a half to half a million years ago, the brain reached about 1,100 ml, whereas in modern *H. sapiens* it is about 1,440 ml. It is reasonable to suppose that these large changes in size of the brain were related to the emergence of social man and to many of his characteristics such as consciousness, language and culture.

The development of the capacity for communication by language was one product of the growth of the brain, and elaborate social collaboration was made possible by language. The power to speak depends upon particular features of the shape of the pharynx and mouth. These allow the production of the vowels, fricatives, plosives and other sounds by the tongue and lips, which provide the relatively small range of forty phonemes that are used in human speech. These physical properties are necessary for the sounds of speech, but the real essence of our language depends upon the special way in which sound production is controlled by the brain. Human language involves the power to produce this variety of sounds in certain arbitrary sequences, enabling them to carry information, which we have defined as an abstract quality that assists in the maintenance of living organization. (Ch. 7). Fossil evidence shows that the shape of the skull changed over this period and the activity of the brain must have changed too. Unfortunately the endocasts of fossil skulls (usually damaged) show little about the detailed differences among these fossil forms. Differences between the two sides of the brain indicating possible specialization of the left side for language are said to have been present in *Homo erectus* about one million years ago. Changes that we cannot see from the casts must have led to fresh functional capacities. New selective brain powers were developed to allow groupings of the sounds to make words and the syntactic ordering of these by rules of grammar. These cerebral developments were the essential basis of language and so of society and culture.

iii. *Symbolism*

Something is known about the location of the power to produce and comprehend speech in certain parts of the brain (Ch. 15). Unfortunately we have very little understanding of the computation that goes on in these areas to endow the production of certain groups of sounds with their meanings and power to act as symbols. Symbols are signs that carry a message with an emotional significance for the sender and receiver. This is the source of the meanings of the words, of their semantics. It is this relation of words to the needs of individuals that gives them their power to act as the cement of society. Their transmission is part of the life pattern of the communicator. The computation that goes to produce meaningful speech cannot be purely cortical or syntactical: it is suffused with the life-preserving influence of the basal forebrain centres which give its emotional and so symbolic and semantic character. Symbolizing is the essence of human communication. Our words are not just sounds, each conveying a piece of practical information: the sentences we exchange do far more than this. They are the currency with which we conduct all the exchanges of everyday life, buying and selling the emotional as well as the physical goods that we need. This subtle interfusion of fact and value in language defeats the attempt of empiricists to give arbitrary definitions of meanings.

Words are tools with which we actively seek to do things, as Austin has insisted. They can be classified according to the effects that the speaker hopes they will produce. This complex and ambiguous character of language arises directly from the nature of cerebral operations. In speaking we are continually selecting sentences that shall express our needs of the moment. As I write this I seek to explain to you the reader the depth of my belief in the unity of action of all parts of the brain in the service of the life of an individual.

iv. *Group symbolism*

One of the striking characteristics of humans is their propensity to gather together for communal ceremonies. Often these are accompanied by symbolic acts of singing, dancing or more macabre ceremonials such as slaughter and drinking of blood, either actual or ritual. In many cultures the largest and most enduring physical artefacts are connected with ritual assembly, from Stonehenge to St Peter's or Olympic stadia. As I emphasized long ago in my Reith Lectures, all such assemblies and assembly points serve to symbolize the importance of communication.[32] They are an opportunity to renew contact with society, whether at daily, weekly or annual or longer intervals. Buildings such as churches or mosques or domed legislatures become the very symbols of the society concerned.

It would be rash to suggest that the human brain is specifically organized to bring people together in groups. But it is reasonable to suggest that as our personal interchanges involve symbolic use of words so we find satisfaction in the symbolic gathering together and exchanging of well-known symbols in singing, music or dance, or even simply in talk.

The ramifications of public symbolizing are endless, extending throughout religion, politics, law, warfare and the whole of social life. It would be unrealistic to pretend that we understand the interactions of the brains of people in their social activities. The tendency to use idealized concepts of human nature, epitomized as gods or present leaders, often forms the centre of communication. Lenin is a frequent central symbol, as is the image and name of Mary. We have already suggested that this focal interest in human nature may be a reflection of a specific inherited brain power to attend to the characteristics of our fellows (Ch. 4.i). This may at least form part of the readiness to accept the authority of deities, kings and leaders of all sorts.

v. *The evolution of culture*

The properties of the brain may provide the basis for religion and culture but they do not dictate its detailed forms. The plasticity of the brain is one of its most characteristic features yet the brain of the newborn child certainly does not represent a *tabula rasa*. It has definite tendencies to attend to human characteristics and to acquire language. It also seems to be very ready to adopt a culture, since all societies have one. But the particular form of that culture is a product of the influences of the environment and the history of the group in the recent past. The very variety of cultures may be the secret of their success in the Darwinian sense, though it is for historians to say whether such a concept is acceptable.

37. Beauty and the brain

The experience of beauty is so essentially subjective that it may seem absurd to connect it with the brain. Some people may feel that the very suggestion is a sort of sacrilege. Yet aesthetic appreciation like all mental processes must be accompanied by particular activities in the brain. If we can find what these are we may at least be helped to a better understanding of aesthetics. Better still, such knowledge might provide richer experience of the beautiful.

One clue that we may follow is that most sensory processes involve an active search. This is especially obvious for vision. The eyes are never still but continually seek for successive stimuli that combine to make a satisfactory and meaningful 'picture' (Ch. 24). Unfortunately there is very little information about the brain processes that go on as the 'meaning' emerges. They presumably involve among other things those areas in the base of the forebrain that are active when one is satisfied (Chs. 32–4). There is evidence that these centres are not limited to setting the targets for physical actions such as eating and drinking (Ch. 32.iv): they provide a system for monitoring *other* cerebral activities and indicating that life is 'going well'. Information about this is scanty and it is not understood how the operation of these centres assists in the selections that constitute seeing and appreciation of the beautiful. There is no obvious impression of 'reward' in the ordinary acts of vision, but from time to time, and indeed not too seldom even in daily life, something strikes one as looking 'good', or 'beautiful' or perhaps even 'wonderful' or 'glorious'.

According to our canon of the relations of the mental and the physical, when this happens there must be some associated activity in the brain. It is obvious to suggest that it comes from the basic reward centres.

This does not get us very far with the aesthetic question of 'why' some things are judged to be beautiful, whether seen, heard or touched; but the idea of a link between appreciation and the fulfilment of the aims of life is attractive. The design of our sensory apparatus dictates that we must use the equipment to search for meaning. The reward centres operate to give satisfaction when it has been found. It is encouraging to think that when we appreciate the beauty of some object or sound we are using the system that records that our life is 'in tune'.

The question of what is meaningful is obviously related to the problem of the nature of representations in the brain, which has worried us so much in earlier chapters. In a search by the eyes or hands presumably a 'meaning' is reached when there is some way to find a 'fit' between the incoming signals and the representations already there. One exclaims 'Good, I see it now' (notice the adjective). Perhaps one may add: 'How beautiful it is.'

The questions are essentially similar in hearing: the nature of meaning is very clear for speech, more difficult for music. The sounds that are judged to be musical in different cultures are perhaps in some way symbolic representations of the sounds of speech. The connection with the generation of emotion is very obvious for music. A part of the process of 'fitting' is the finding of associations with previous experiences of similar sounds.

An interesting sidelight on aesthetics may be found in smell. Odours are not usually referred to as beautiful or ugly, but some scents are intensely attractive and others repulsive. Both the 'good' and the 'bad' ones include many that have obvious biological connections, with food, sex or hygiene: there is no need to be more particular. Some scents that could reasonably be called beautiful are obviously connected with the reward centres. The beauty of a face or a voice somehow comes from those centres too, and also the beauty of a picture, though less directly.

Attention to the processes of perception helps also to understand creative artistic activity, for instance in the visual arts. We have emphasized that every occasion of seeing is an active process of selection, creating a representation in the brain that is satisfactory. Admittedly we do not fully understand what makes ordinary vision satisfactory, but it is somehow connected with the emotions, if only faintly. The artist is using the ordinary process of vision to guide his hands to make a representation *outside* the brain, and he is encouraging his emotion to enter the process. He is literally showing us *what he has seen and wants us to see*. The viewer may appreciate the result for various reasons. It may agree with his perception of the world and so, as it were, validate his own life processes. The squire seeing on his walls naturalistic pictures of his ancestors and his horses is reassured in his world. But the 'better' artist can intensify the viewer's perceptions.

Coming out of an art gallery one literally sees more in the world around. It is interesting to know that this is just what you would expect, given that the process of vision is an active selection. Indeed the artist can teach us not only to see more but to see in new ways, a process that has been going on for centuries in European art.

The artists who have perhaps the greatest impact on our daily lives are the architects. Whether they like it or not, they provide part of the visual experience of every individual. Their constructions almost inevitably become familiar symbols of one's life. Those who design the buildings we pass or in which we live carry a very heavy responsibility. Both the insides and the outsides are bound to influence everyone who uses them, even if unconsciously.

Much of the training of architects is inevitably devoted to practical considerations. Questions of cost are unfortunately apt to be foremost in the thoughts of patrons who instruct the architect. But the design of the buildings that result will give its stamp to the brain and so to the seeing, and indeed thinking, of all who come to use it. I hope that architects are trained to recognize the great influence that they have on the lives and brains of those who pass by their buildings, or enter them. Patrons who encourage the creation of beautiful buildings and surroundings should receive every social recognition and reward: those whose attitude is mean or merely monetary should be execrated as criminals who impoverish life.

38. Freedom and determinism

i. *Paradox*

Everyone has a firm conviction that in some sense he is free to decide his course of action; yet, as physical systems, our actions must be constrained by physical laws. Are we then deterministic creatures whose sense of freedom is an illusion? Several of the points stressed in this book may help to resolve this ancient paradox, which is still very much discussed.

ii. *Mental freedom implies physical selection*

First we can use our knowledge of the correlation of the mental and physical to great effect. Evidence has been produced that all mental processes are accompanied by events in the brain. We can argue therefore that since we feel free to choose between alternative courses of action there must be some comparable choice mechanisms in the nervous system; if we look hard enough we should find them. Indeed, the brain programs we have been describing provide precisely the material for individual choice. The concept implies that every brain contains neural systems that allow the performance of a wide range of possible actions, including variations of each of them. Selection is continually made among these many possibilities by the whole brain on a basis of the immediate needs as indicated by the hypothalamus and other centres, modulated by more enduring programs of social and personal values. These are the operations that are identified subjectively as the making of a free choice.

The act of making a choice is the product of the whole person, including his brain. We may follow the processes that might be involved in a trivial case: 'I feel restless' (the reticular system is in action); 'I want a drink' (the hypothalamus is signalling thirst and some centres conditioned by alcohol are at work); 'Let's see what he has in the cupboard' (scanning activities by the eyes); 'Ah, here are some bottles and glasses' (comparison of visual input with stored representation); 'I'd rather have gin than whisky' (selection according to stored system of values). And so on, to satisfaction and perhaps euphoria or worse.

Each mental event is accompanied by physical ones in lawlike correlation. The mental events could no doubt be analysed in more detail. The physical events individually can be broken down into electrochemical changes at synapses, which follow the laws of physics and chemistry. But each one of these mental occurrences involves a pattern of many millions of those physico-chemical events. The sequences in which they occur depend upon a vast series of past occurrences stretching back at least to the origin of life, perhaps 3,000 million years ago. The events in the brain can as yet only be vaguely defined. We begin to have a little knowledge of how groups of neurons may serve as representations, say of bottles of whisky or gin. The mechanisms involved in making the decision are even less known but can be suggested:

they are presumably based on the activity of the reticular system continually initiating action in various parts, directing attention to current needs and external circumstances. So the outcome of all these operations is not dependent only on the individual physico-chemical events but on the particular *combinations* in which they occur as a result of past history, constituting the possible programs among which choice can be made. The laws of physics and chemistry alone do not avail to forecast the outcome of this immense history, either to the individual himself or to others.

iii. *Living involves creative choice between alternatives*

The essence of freedom is unforced choice by an individual according to his own character and needs. Each living organism is provided with a repertoire of possible programs of action. Everyone agrees that decisions between these as to what course to take are not made at random but on a basis of past and present information. The decision depends on factors acting *within* the organism by some form of balancing operating, about which neuroscience can yet say little in detail. This is the accompaniment of the mental event that we call 'making up one's mind': it involves calling into play a series of representations of past situations and experiences.

The information that we use to decide whether to eat meat or fish, or which colour to paint the walls, is recorded in the coded memory systems of our brains. In the act of choosing, the various relevant representations are brought into play and balanced with the information coming from parts of the brain that indicate the needs of the moment. The outcome of this balancing operation depends entirely upon the characteristics of that individual, as built up over the centuries in the DNA of his ancestors and in the brain over his own years of growth. A basic property of a human person is that he must make choices. It is a responsibility imposed by our human nature and individual characteristics, and the choice is free within the limitations of that nature and character. It depends not *only* on the laws that control the chemical events that are followed but on the particular pattern of combinations in which they occur; and *that* is the unique result of events of the immediate and remote past.

In what sense then do the physico-chemical laws determine the free choice by the whole person? The answer to this question is not easy to find, and depends upon what is meant by 'determine'. All physical changes are interrelated and have 'causes' in the sense that they involve some change in the distribution of energy. The fundamental laws of physics and chemistry have been derived from study of simplified systems to provide idealized principles. Taken alone they are not sufficient to define the course of behaviour of actual complex systems. For example the movements of the land masses of the world by continental drift obey the fundamental laws of physics, but each event, say an eruption of Mount Vesuvius, is determined also by the history of the earth. Similarly the behaviour of an organism is influenced by its past history. It is therefore not easy to define the sense in which historical factors can be said to 'determine' the behaviour of any system.

We have seen that an essential feature of the process of living is the capacity to take action that is directed towards survival by selecting from a repertoire of possibilities. Even bacteria can adapt to a new medium (Ch. 8.vi). In this sense they make a 'choice' between a small set of possibilities. The selection depends upon properties *within* that individual, which may be different from those of all others (for example in a new mutant). The characteristics of the 'higher' organisms include an increasing variety of possible alternative actions, culminating in man (Ch. 9.vii).

It is characteristic of living things therefore that they have alternative possibilities of action, limited by their own characteristics and of course by the constraints of the external world. Their choices are thus made within themselves according to their needs. That is the sense in which they are free. They are 'determined' by the limitations imposed by their own nature and by the ultimate laws of physics and chemistry.

If this is the sense in which organisms are determinate how far are their actions determinable? The pattern of redistribution of energy in living organisms cannot be forecasted completely from the laws of non-living systems, because it is influenced by the encoded instructions that direct the performance of actions in such a way as to support life. Forecasting therefore depends upon knowledge of the state of these encoded memories, which determine the 'direction' or 'aim' of the organism at any given moment. These are the features that differentiate living systems from all others that are known. In simpler organisms we can analyse them and make reasonably accurate forecasts, though subject to the difficulty that we cannot investigate any organism fully without changing it. In higher animals the complexity of choice and of motivational factors makes forecasting increasingly difficult. An action of an individual of any species can be predicted approximately from its past behaviour and that of others like it, but will depend upon the remote and recent history of that individual. It is not determinate in the sense of being outside the power of the individual. It is creative in the sense that it is performed in accordance with the specific objective of promotion of life.

This description of the situation covers fully the individual's conviction that he can and must make free choices. The process of doing so involves selecting among the possible programs of his brain. This seems to provide a rational description of the sense in which we are free. It may not satisfy those who believe that the problem has a simpler answer and that humans possess some special faculty for free will.

iv. *Agents and spectators*

The conflict between free will and determinism is sometimes said to arise from the fact that different 'languages are used by the active initiator of an action and observers describing it as an event'.[33] The difference in point of view inevitably prejudices the possibility of accurate forecasting. The agent has recourse to information that is not available to an observer, namely that in his own brain. Moreover, even should it become possible for both to participate equally (which heaven forbid) neither would be able to make absolute predictions. The agent himself cannot know for certain what he is going to do until he does it and if he is influenced by a spectator's predictions those predictions may be falsified.[34]

v. *Human needs restrict the freedom of choice*

More interesting than theoretical discussion about choice is the study of the restrictions that limit our freedom. These may be divided into restrictions imposed by our nature and by our culture. We cannot be other than we are: the very existence of our lives depends upon the instructions inherited from the parental DNA, which make strong demands that we shall strive to continue to live and to reproduce. Subjectively we seek for warmth, food

and drink and sexual satisfaction. These demands are insistent.
We cannot stop breathing for more than about a minute. Most of
us want to eat and drink and have sexual satisfaction. Characteristically we meet these needs by creative choice of means suited
to the situation.

Again, our human constitution imposes restrictions on our
action in relation to others, and especially to those near to us. We
are prone to become so conditioned mentally and physically that
it is 'natural' for us to wish to do well for those we love. Moreover
it is also 'natural' to allow those actions of anger and rage to
appear when we or they are attacked. Such 'limitations on human
freedom' are the essence of drama, romance, and tragedy.

The human system for control of action is so constituted that
the individual is capable of denying or distorting the claims of
any or all of these needs. We express this by the phrase 'He can
control himself' (which is curiously paradoxical if you think
about it). He can dispense with sex, starve himself to death, or
even murder his mother. The power to act in such apparently
'unnatural' ways must, like everything else, involve activities in
the brain. The fact that the more fundamental biological needs
can be overcome does not mean that they are without influence.
No one can doubt that the choices of action of most human beings
for most of the time are limited by the urge before long to drink and
sooner or later to eat, to mention only the most obvious tendencies.

vi. *Limitations of freedom imposed by language and culture*

Those 'natural' restrictions imposed by our 'animal' nature are
obvious enough. But are these really the major needs that control
human actions? It is arguable that the greater part of human
living is motivated by the desire to achieve honour or respect
from other people rather than the satisfaction of physical needs.[35]
It is certainly difficult to realize how greatly one is limited by the
culture in which one is reared and the language and customs that
go with it. These are the agencies that impose the restrictions on
freedom that are the chief sources of controversy and it is not
possible for the biologist to say much about them. We understand very little about how the operations of individual brains
'influence' language and less still about their relations to culture.

The very words with which such matters are discussed have
meanings that vary with the culture; as Bennett says 'One's own

first language is all-encompassing.'[36] This becomes unhappily evident in the differing uses of 'truth' in religious controversy, or of 'democracy' in politics. If divergences can arise within the use of words of one language how much greater is the difficulty in achieving understanding by people whose culture and language have different ancient roots, as is the case with European, African or Oriental cultures. The biologist can only encourage the search for understanding by emphasizing that in spite of differences we are all one species.

vii. *Limitations of perception and rationality*

Obvious limitations are placed upon us by the nature of our sense organs, but these can be partly overcome. We cannot see ultra-violet light or hear ultrasound but by intelligent action can make instruments that detect both of these. There may however be fundamental limitations on the way the brain can be used to think and to reason. At several points it has been emphasized that there is evidence that the brain may be organized on a basis of the use of certain concepts, for instance about order or space. Admittedly at present we have no clear idea what it means to say this, but work such as that of O'Keefe and Nadel suggests that the neurons may be organized to form a spatial map (Ch. 28.vi). It is surely no accident that the arrangement of connections in the areas of the brain that relate to the outside world are laid out in regular spatial sheets. The nerve impulses provide an arbitrary code of signals, but they are displayed in ways that are partly isomorphic with the environment. It is difficult to know how far these inherited characteristics are ultimately limiting. Some people can understand non-Euclidean geometry or relativity, which run counter to common sense. There are no obvious limits to the human capacity to make and manipulate symbols, though language comes more readily than mathematics to most people. Euclid is easier to follow than calculus and quantum mechanics is harder still. The capacity of infant prodigies so readily to understand music or mathematics or indeed languages must surely depend upon some features of their brains. My forebear Thomas Young understood six languages at the age of four. Such forms of determinism are acceptable and indeed welcome, but we do not understand their origin.

39. What am I?

In conclusion you may ask 'If there are all these programs, what am I?' It may seem that even with all the descriptions of correlated mental and cerebral activities the ordinary feeling, suffering, loving person fails to appear. Certainly it is not yet possible to follow the activities of the brain that accompany all the depths and heights of human joys and sorrows. What I have tried to give is a brief account of how recent biological discoveries affect the interpretation of the words that we use to discuss some aspects of the human condition.

Our human systems of transmission of information by selecting words from an arbitrary code is a recent version of the communication system that makes possible the continuation of all life. So living precedes thinking and the fundamental basis of all human knowledge may be said to be awareness of life. 'Cogito, ergo sum' is better replaced by 'I know that I am alive', which emphasizes that knowledge is a property of the operation of the physical body, and this mitigates the problems of dualism (Ch. 6.i).

The fact of human consciousness seems to separate us from the rest of the living world, and yet there is abundant evidence that all mental events are correlated with brain processes. The peculiar human brain processes may be the ones that accompany intentional mental events, especially those referring to future ends. It may be that our brains have evolved special powers to contain representations of situations that are not yet present. This power of anticipation is obviously a very useful facility for survival and may have been the basis for the evolution of our consciousness. The most conspicuous use of this capacity to form representations is the power that it gives to recognize a consciousness like one's own in other people. This awareness of others provides the basis for our whole elaborate social, ethical and moral system and makes us naturally prone to what Strawson calls the participant attitude, in contrast to the objective or scientific attitude.[37] He believes that we must accept the pervasive existence of these two distinct 'stories' about human life, but perhaps further understanding of their neural basis may help to show the relations between them.

We are at present just beginning to understand how the brain operates to build representations of the world and of other people. Something is now known about the selective formation of connection between nerve cells during learning and the influence of those parts of the brain that specify the needs of the person and influence his moods and satisfactions.

Such information from biology and neuroscience helps towards a better understanding of oneself. It provides information about the sources of one's experienced life which could not be known only by introspection. It helps to provide a rational answer to the question: what am I? It tells me how I have come to my present state and something of the nature of the brain and its possibilities and limitations. This helps a lot by showing the implications of the fact that all we living things are very special self-maintaining homeostatic systems. We continually try to achieve the aim of promotion of life — especially our own. Human beings in particular have elaborate mechanisms in the brain and glands tending to make them act in the ways that they do. They are primarily selfish and may be aggressive, but as social creatures have special propensities to learn to love and to help each other.

As I say, I find all such knowledge helpful and I think it is time that people stopped talking about reductionism as if increased knowledge somehow subtracted from human dignity. On the contrary, reductionism consists in seeing ourselves in terms beyond the simple impression of the senses and so enlarging our knowledge of our nature. This adds greatly to understanding of our possibilities and limitations and hence ability to conduct ourselves wisely, and especially with the fullest respect for other human beings, and indeed for all life. However, by the same token no amount of reductionism can be applied to the study of subjective experience, since this is essentially one's own point of view.

The reality for me is my continuous living self, one entity experiencing a series of mental events, including those that indicate that I have a body and a brain. The evidence shows that I and my brain are one; without a brain I should be nothing. If the person is inseparable from his brain it is senseless to ask which of them controls the other. We should not confuse ourselves with such questions but devote our energies to increasing understanding of how best to describe ourselves and our brains and so to improve the quality of life.

Of course a simplified view of this sort leaves many problems to be discussed. None of our knowledge is certain or complete, all is provisional and subject to revision. We have learnt to distrust those who come with absolute certainties, whether in religion, science, politics or philosophy. Our culture has developed for a long time with some of these alleged certainties and many people find it hard to live without them.

Philosophers must tell us whether this scientific approach has been described coherently — probably not. I feel very anxious about it and conscious of its limitations, both scientific and philosophical. In particular, I must stress how little is yet known about the programs of the brain. The code has not yet been properly broken; but we begin to see the units of it. What is needed now is study of the ways in which many neurons interact in time and space, which is technically very hard to do. We can see that the code is somehow a matter of sequences of neural activities, providing expectancies of what to do next.

With all the limits, I believe that some such approach can help with the problems of various phases of life. Academic philosophy and science do not claim to issue detailed prescriptions for daily life, but they surely have a part to play in establishing a background, and should try to help in amelioration of the human condition.

I suppose people will want to give labels to the position I am outlining, calling it determinist, or materialist, monist or dualist, parallelist or epiphenomenalist or some other name and implying either praise or denigration. I wonder whether such labels are useful? Certainly it is very difficult to find the right words. As Collingwood said, 'Philosophical enquiry is the attempt to know better what we know already.' The more I try to deal with these problems the more I realize how necessary it is to have trained logicians and other philosophers who devote their lives to them. But please philosophers, do use what little we can tell you about your brains.

Notes

PART I: CODING AND REPRESENTATION

1. D. M. Armstrong, 'The nature of the mind', in *Readings in Philosophy and Psychology*, ed. N. Block, Harvard University Press, 1983.

2. J. and P. Medawar, *Aristotle to Zoos*, Weidenfeld and Nicolson, 1983.

3. G. Sommerhof, *Logic of the Living Brain*, Wiley, 1974.

4. C. Taylor, *The Explanation of Behaviour*, Routledge and Kegan Paul, 1964, p. 57.

5. W. H. Thorpe, *Purpose in a World of Change*, Oxford University Press, 1978.

6. A. M. Whiteley and E. K. Warrington, 'A clinical, psychological and anatomical study of three patients', *Jour. Neurology, Neurosurgery and Psychiatry* 40 (1977), 395–403.

7. J. C. Eccles, *The Human Mystery*, Gifford Lectures, Routledge and Kegan Paul, 1978.

8. A. J. Ayer, *Philosophy in the Twentieth Century*, Weidenfeld and Nicolson, 1982, p. 78.

9. J. R. Searle, *Minds, Brains and Science*, Reith Lectures, BBC Publications, 1984.

10. Ibid. 11.

11. Ibid. 18.

12. T. Honderich, 'Psychophysical lawlike connections and their problem', *Enquiry* 24 (1981), 277–303.

13. Searle, op. cit. note 9 above.

14. J. Z. Young, *Programs of the Brain*, Oxford University Press, 1978.

15. R. Granit, *The Purposive Brain*, MIT Press, 1977.

16. R. Reidl, *Order in Living Organisms*, trans. R. P. S. Jeffries, Willey, 1978.

17. S. W. Fox, 'Proteinoid experiments and evolutionary theory' in *Beyond Neo-Darwinism*, ed. M.–W. Ho and P. T. Saunders, Academic Press, 1984.

18. J. D. Bernal, *The Origin of Life*, Weidenfeld and Nicolson, 1967; A. G. Cairns Smith, *Genetic Takeover*, Cambridge University Press, 1982.

19. T. A. Sebeok, 'Zoosemiotic components of human communication', in *How Animals Communicate*, ed. T. A. Sebeok, Indiana University Press, 1977.

20. For further details of DNA and other aspects of biology, see B. Alberts, D. Bray, J. Lewis, M. Raff, K. Roberts and J. D. Watson, *Molecular Biology of the Cell*, Garland Publishing, 1983.

21. L. Wolpert, 'Pattern formation in biological development', *Scientific American* 239 (1978), 154–64.

22. S. J. Gould, *Ontogeny and Phylogeny*, Harvard University Press, 1977.

23. J. Z. Young, *The Life of Vertebrates*, Clarendon Press, 3rd edn, 1981.

24. D. C. Dennett, *Brainstorms: Philosophical Essays on Mind and Psychology*, Harvester Press, 1979.

25. J. R. Searle, *Intentionality*, Cambridge University Press, 1983.

26. R. Wollheim, *The Thread of Life*, Harvard University Press, 1984.

27. Searle, op. cit. note 9 above, p. 16.

28. Dennett, op. cit. note 24 above, p. 235.

29. Ibid.

30. S. Hampshire, *Thought and Action*, Chatto and Windus, 1982.

31. D. C. Dennett, 'Intentional systems in cognitive ethology: the "Panglossian paradigm" defended', *The Behavioural and Brain Sciences* 6 (1983), 343–90.

32. R. Seyfarth, D. L. Cheney and P. Marler, 'Monkey responses to three alarm calls', *Science* 210 (1980), 801–3.

33. H. P. Grice, 'Utterer's meaning and intentions', *Philosophical Review*, 78 (1969), 147–77.

34. Dennett, op. cit. note 31 above, p. 346.

35. Ibid.

36. Dennett, op. cit. note 24 above, p. 234.

37. Ibid.

38. P. F. Strawson, *Studies in the Philosophy of Thought and Action*, Oxford University Press, 1968, p. 23.

39. Dennett, op. cit. note 24 above, p. 247.

40. Ibid. 245.

41. J. D. Fodor, *The Language of Thought*, Harvard University Press, 1975, p. 17.

42. Dennett, op. cit. n. 24 above, p. 91.

43. Ibid. 101.

44. See the useful summary in B. Katz, *Nerve, Muscle and Synapse*, McGraw-Hill, 1966.

45. D. O. Hebb, *The Organization of Behaviour: A Neuropsychological Theory*, Wiley, 1949.

46. B. Libet, A. G. Curtis, E. W. Wright and D. K. Pearl, 'Time of conscious intention to act in relation to onset of cerebral activity (readiness-potential). The unconscious initiation of a freely voluntary act', *Brain* 106 (1983), 640.

47. R. Jung, 'Postural support of goal-directed movements. The preparation and guidance of voluntary action in man', *Acta. biol. Acad. Sci. hung.* 33 (1982) (2–3), 201–13.

48. G. A. Ojemann, 'Brain organisation for language from the perspective of electrical stimulation mapping', *The Behavioural and Brain Sciences* 6 (1983), 189–230.

49. G. A. Ojemann and C. Mateer, 'Human language cortex', *Science* 205 (1979), 1401–3.

50. I. Fried, G. A. Ojemann and E. E. Fetz, 'Language-related potentials specific to human language cortex', *Science* 212 (1981), 353–6.

PART II: PERCEIVING

1. A. J. Ayer, *The Central Questions of Philosophy*, Gifford Lectures, Penguin Books, 1973.

2. J. L. Austin, *Sense and Sensibilia*, Clarendon Press, 1962.

3. F. C. Bartlett, *Remembering: A Study in Experimental and Social Psychology*, Cambridge University Press, 1932.

4. Ayer, op. cit. Part II note 1.

5. J. Y. Lettvin, H. R. Maturana, W. S. McCulloch and W. H. Pitts, 'What the frog's eye tells the frog's brain', *Proceedings Instit. of Radio Engineers*, 47 (1959), 1940–51.

6. J. D. Fodor, *The Modularity of the Mind*, MIT Press, 1983.

7. Ibid. 53. Subsequent quotations from pp. 71, 103, 101.

8. For further information about the sense of touch, see G. Gordon, *Active Touch*, Pergamon Press, 1978.

9. C. S. Sherrington, *The Integrative Action of the Nervous System*, Cambridge University Press, 1906, repr. 1947.

10. See Gordon, op. cit. Part II note 8.

11. For a good account of the structure and functions of the cortex, see C. G. Philips, S. Zeki and H. B. Barlow, 'Localisation of function in the cerebral cortex', *Brain* 107 (1984), 327–61.

12. K. Brodmann, *Vergleichende Lokalisationslehre der Grosshirnrinde*, Barth, 1909.

13. See Gordon, op. cit. Part II note 8.

14. See R. Miller, *Meaning and Purpose in the Intact Brain*, Clarendon Press, 1981.

15. See Gordon op. cit. Part II note 8.

16. A. R. Luria, *The Working Brain: An Introduction to Neuropsychology*, Basic Books, 1973.

17. P. D. Wall, 'The gate control theory of pain mechanisms: a re-examination and re-statement', *Brain* 101 (1978), 1–18.

18. P. W. Nathan, 'Pain and nociception in the clinical context', *Philosophical Trans. Royal Soc. London* B 308 (1985), 219–26.

19. P. D. Wall, 'Future trends in pain research', *Philosophical Trans. Royal Soc. London* B 308 (1985), 393–401.

20. P. Lieberman, *The Biology and Evolution of Language*, Harvard University Press, 1984.

21. Ibid.

22. Ibid.

23. E. Knudsen, 'Space and frequency are represented separately in the auditory mid-brain', *Jour. Neurophysiology* 41 (1978), 870–84.

24. E. Baumgard, 'Threshold quantal problems', *Handbook of Sensory Physiology*, ed. Autrum *et al.*, vii.4, Springer, 1972, 303–30.

25. M. von Senden, *Space and Sight*, Methuen, 1960.

26. S. Zeki, 'Uniformity and diversity of structure and function in the rhesus monkey', *Jour. Physiology* 277 (1978), 273–94; 'Functional specialisation in the visual cortex of the rhesus monkey', *Nature* 274 (1978), 423–8.

26a. Sutherland, N. S., 'Visual discrimination of orientation and shape by the octopus', *Nature* 179 (1957) 11–13.

27. D. H. Hubel and T. N. Wiesel, 'Receptive fields of single neurons in the cat's striate cortex', *Jour. Physiology*, 148 (1959), 574–91.

28. K. K. de Valois, 'Interactions among spatial frequency channels in the human visual system', *Frontiers of Visual Science*, ed. S. J. Cool and C. L. Smith, Springer, (1978) 544–56.

29. C. G. Gross, C. E. Rocha-Miranda and D. B. Bender, 'Visual properties of neurons in infratemporal cortex of the macaque', *Jour. Neurophysiology* 35 (1972), 96–111.

30. D. A. Perrett, P. A. J. Smith, D. D. Potter, A. J. Austin, A. S. Head, A. D. Milner and M. A. Jeeves, 'Visual cells in the temporal cortex sensitive to face view and gaze direction', *Proceedings Royal Soc. London* B 223 (1985), 293–317.

31. R. Srebro, 'Localization of visually evoked cortical activity in humans', *Jour. Physiology* 360 (1985), 233–46.

32. M. Mishkin, 'A memory system in the monkey', *Philosophical Trans. Royal Soc. London* B 289 (1982), 85–95.

33. M. Alpern, 'Eye movements', *Handbook of Sensory Physiology*, ed. Autrum *et al.*, vii.4, Springer, 1972, 303–30.

34. A. L. Yarbus, *Eye Movements and Vision*, trans. B. Haigh, Plenum Press, 1967.

35. A. M. Treisman and G. Gelade, 'A feature-integration theory of attention', *Cognitive Psychology* 12 (1980), 97–136.

36. L. Weiskrantz, 'Varieties of residual experience', *Quart. Jour. Experimental Psychology* 32 (1980), 365–86.

37. J. Hochberg, 'Attention, organisation and consciousness', in *Attention: Contemporary Theory and Analysis*, ed. D. I. Mostovsky, Appleton-Century-Crofts 1970, 99–124.

38. S. Zeki, 'The construction of colours by the cerebral cortex', *Proceedings Royal Inst. Gt Britain* 56 (1984), 231–58.
39. M. M. Haith, 'Visual competence in early infancy', *Handbook of Sensory Physiology*, ed. Autrum *et al.*, viii, Springer, 1978, 311–56.
40. J. Kogan, B. Henker, J. Hen-Too, J. Levine and M. Lewis, 'Infants' differential reactions to familiar and distorted faces', *Child Development* 37 (1966), 519–32.
41. R. K. Yin, 'Looking at upside-down faces', *Jour. Experimental Psychology* 81 (1969), 141–5.
42. *Helmholtz's Treatise on Physiological Optics* (3rd edn, 1909–11), trans. J. P. C. Southall, Dover, 1962.
43. A. Sloman, 'Image interpretation: the way ahead?', in *Physical and Biological Processing of Images*, ed. O. J. Braddick and A. C. Sleigh, Springer, 1983.
44. N. S. Sutherland, 'Outlines of a theory of visual pattern recognition in animals and man', *Proceedings Royal Soc. London* B 171 (1968), 297–317.
45. D. Marr, *Vision*, Freeman, 1982, p. 99.
46. Ibid. 68. Subsequent quotations from pp. 51, 91.
47. Sloman, op. cit. Part II note 43, p. 381.
48. Ibid. 385.
49. Ibid. 386. Subsequent quotation, p. 390.
50. J. A. Feldman and D. H. Ballard, 'Connectionist models and their properties', *Cognitive Science* 6 (1982), 205–54.
51. T. Poggio and C. Koch, 'Ill-posed problems in early vision from computational theory to analogue networks', *Proceedings Royal Soc. London* B 226 (1985), 303–23.
52. R. Shepard and J. Metzlee, 'Mental rotation of three-dimensional objects', *Science* 171 (1971), 701–3. S. Kirkpatrick, C. D. Gelatt and M. P. Vecchi, 'Optimisation by simulated annealing', *Science* 220 (1983), 671–80.

PART III: LEARNING

1. Wollheim, op. cit. Part I note 26.
2. J. Z. Young, *A Model of the Brain*, Clarendon Press, 1964; 'Croonian Lecture: The organisation of a memory system', *Proceedings Royal Soc. London* B 163 (1965), 285–320; 'Learning as a process of selection', *Jour. Royal Soc. Medicine* 72 (1979), 801–4.
3. J. P. Changeux, *Neuronal Man: The Biology of Mind*, Pantheon, 1978; V. Mountcastle and G. E. Edelman, *The Mindful Brain*, MIT Press, 1978.
4. G. E. Edelman, 'Through a computer darkly: group selection and higher brain function', *Bulletin American Acad. Arts and Sciences* 36.i (1982), 21–49.

5. E. Kandel, *Cellular Basis of Behavior: An Introduction to Behavioral Neurology*, Freeman, 1976.
6. E. Filikova, 'Effect of light and visual deprivation on the retina', *Jour. Experimental Neurology* 35 (1972), 450–7.
7. F. Valverde, 'Rate and extent of recovery from dark rearing in the visual cortex of the mouse', *Brain Research* 33 (1971), 1–11.
8. L. L. Iverson, 'Amino acids and peptides: fast and slow chemical signals in the nervous system?', *Proceedings Royal Soc. London* B 221 (1984), 245–60.
9. J. Z. Young, 'The distributed tactile memory system of *Octopus*', *Proceedings Royal Soc. London* B 218 (1983) 135–76.
10. M. J. and J. Wells, 'The function of the brain of *Octopus* in tactile discrimination', *Jour. Experimental Biology* 34 (1957), 131–42; M. J. Wells, 'Functional evidence for neurone fields representing the individual arms within the central nervous system of *Octopus*', *Jour. Experimental Biology* 36 (1959), 501–11.
11. J. Z. Young, 'The evolution of the nervous system and of the relationship of organism and environment', in *Evolution: Essays presented to E. S. Goodrich*, ed. G. R. de Beer, Clarendon Press, 1938.
12. Edelman, op. cit. Part III note 3.
13. A. Brodal, 'Self-observations and neuro-anatomical considerations after a stroke', *Brain* 96 (1973), 675–94.
14. Iverson, op. cit. Part III note 8.
15. K. H. Pribram, M. Nuwer and R. Baron, 'The holographic hypothesis of memory structure in brain function and perception', in *Contemporary Developments in Mathematical Psychology*, ed. R. C. Atkinson, D. H. Krantz, R. C. Luce and P. Suppes, Freeman, 1974, 416–67; K. H. Pribram, *Languages of the Brain*, Prentice Hall, 1971.
16. B. Milner, S. Corkin and H.-L. Teuber, 'Further analysis of the hippocampal amnesic syndrome: 14-year follow-up study of H. M.', *Neuropsychologia* 6 (1968), 215–34.
17. J. W. Papez, 'A proposed mechanism of emotion', *Archives of Neurology and Psychiatry*, 38 (1937), 725–43.
18. J. O'Keefe and L. Nadel, *The Hippocampus as a Cognitive Map*, Clarendon Press, 1978.
19. Ibid. 220.
20. Ibid.
21. Ibid. 380.
22. See Miller, op. cit. Part II note 14.
23. W. Penfield, *The Mystery of the Mind: A Critical Study of Consciousness and the Human Brain*, Princeton University Press, 1975.
24. Helmholtz, op. cit. Part II note 42.

25. Haith, op. cit. Part II note 39, p. 313.
26. C. Blakemore and R. C. van Sluyten, 'Innate environmental factors in the development of the kitten's visual cortex', *Jour. Physiology* 248 (1975), 663–716.

PART IV: VALUING

1. G. E. Moore, *Principia Ethica*, Cambridge University Press, 1903.
2. See C. Lewy, 'G. E. Moore on the naturalistic fallacy', in *Studies in the Philosophy of Thought and Action*, ed. P. F. Strawson, Oxford University Press, 1968.
3. J. L. Mackie, *Ethics: Inventing Right and Wrong*, Penguin Books, 1977.
4. R. L. Franklin, *Recent Work on Ethical Naturalism*. American Philosophical Quart. Monograph no. 7. 55–95.
5. T. Honderich, 'The question of well-being and the principle of equality', *Mind* 90 (1981), no. 360, 481–504.
6. D. Davidson, 'Actions, reasons and causes', *Jour. Philosophy* 60 (1963), 685–700.
7. J. Olds, *Drives and Reinforcement: Behavioral Studies of Hypothalamic Functions*, Raven Press, 1977.
8. See Miller, op. cit. Part II note 14.
9. Wollheim, op. cit. Part I note 26.
10. C. H. Ashton, *Brain Systems, Disorders, and Psychotropic Drugs*, Oxford University Press, 1986.
11. B. K. Anand and J. R. Brobeck, 'Hypothalamic control of food intake in rats and cats', *Yale Jour. Biology and Medicine* 24 (1951), 123–40.
12. Mackie, op. cit. Part IV note 3, p. 51.
13. J. Maynard Smith, *The Theory of Evolution*, Penguin Books, 1975.
14. R. L. Trivers, 'The evolution of reciprocal altruism', *Quart. Review Biology* 46 (1971), 35–57.
15. E. O. Wilson, *Sociobiology: The New Synthesis*, Belknap Press, 1975.
16. R. Dawkins, *The Selfish Gene*, Oxford University Press, 1976.
17. Mackie, op. cit. Part IV note 3.
18. Ayer, op. cit. Part II note 1., p. 1.
19. R. M. Hare, *Applications of Moral Philosophy*, University of California Press, 1972.
20. G. J. Warnock, *The Object of Morality*, Methuen, 1971, p. 12.
21. A. Quinton, *Thoughts and Thinkers*, Duckworth, 1982, p. 375.
22. B. Williams, *Utilitarianism*, Cambridge University Press, 1973.
23. Mackie, op. cit. Part IV note 3, p. 194.
24. Warnock op. cit. Part IV note 20.

25. See Hare, op. cit. Part IV note 19.
26. R. Harré, *Social Being*, Blackwell, 1979.
27. Honderich, op. cit. Part IV note 5.
28. J. Z. Young, 'The pineal gland', *Philosophy* 48 (1973), 70–4.
29. F. Waldhauser *et al.*, 'Fall in nocturnal melatonin during prepuberty and pubescence', *Lancet* 1 (1984), 362–5.
30. Gould, op. cit. Part I note 22.
31. G. R. de Beer, *Embryos and Ancestors*, Clarendon Press, 1958.
32. J. Z. Young, *Doubt and Certainty in Science*, Reith Lectures, BBC Publications, 1951.
33. For discussion see J. R. Lucas, *The Freedom of the Will*, Clarendon Press, (1970), p. 17.
34. D. M. MacKay, 'On the logical indeterminacy of a free choice', *Mind* 69 (1960), 31–40.
35. Harré, op. cit. Part IV note 26.
36. J. Bennett, *Linguistic Behaviour*, Cambridge University Press, 1976.
37. P. F. Strawson, *Skepticism and Naturalism: Some Varieties*, Methuen, 1985.

Index

Where a page number is followed by figures in parenthesis, reference is to the Notes (see pp. 217–24), for identification of an author whose work is cited anonymously on the page in question.

acetyl choline, 61, 181
activity, as feature of life, 3
adaptation, 40, 45, 150
   in bacteria, 37
adaptiveness, 5
adenine, 34
adrenalin, 30
Adrian, Edgar, 61
aesthetic activities, 187
aesthetic appreciation, 176
aesthetics, 205
agent, exempt, 59
agents, 6–8
aggression, 187, 188
agnosia, 131
   visual, 145
aims, 32, 178
   as feature of life, 3
   of a program, 20
alcohol, 183
allosteric enzymes, 39
Alpern, M., 129 (II, 33)
altruism, 191
Alzheimer's disease, 16
amine transmitter substances, 186, 188
amino acids, 31, 36
ammonites, 46
Amoeba, 59
amputation, 102
amygdala, 127, 181, 187
analog brain models, 146
   codes, 70
Anand, B. K., 186 (IV, 11)
anger, 188
angiotensin, 187
angular acceleration detectors, 107
animal spirits, 64
annealing, simulated, 145
aphasia, 76
Aplysia, 150, 170

architects, 207
Armstrong, D. M., 1
artificial intelligence (AI), 137
artist, 206
Ashton, C. H., 183 (IV, 10)
asparagine, 36
assemblies of neurons, 72
attachment, 200
attention, 191
Austin, A. J., 126 (II, 30)
Austin, J. L., 79, 85, 203
Australopithecus, 203
autonomic nervous system, 107
aversive stimulation, 182
avoidance reflex, 66, 104
axolotl, 200
axons, 61
Ayer, A. J., 12 (I, 8), 79, 194

bacteria, 30, 210
Ballard, D. H., 145 (II, 50)
Barlow, H. B., 90 (II, 11)
Bartlett, F. C., 81
basal forebrain areas, 187, 195
basal ganglia, 93, 181
Baumgard, E., 116 (II, 24)
beauty, 205
bees, 84
belief, 53
believing, 190
Bender, D. B., 126 (II, 29)
Bennett, J., 212
Bentham, Jeremy, 189
Berkeley, G., 79
bilingual, 77
biochemists, 33
bird's brain, 114
bit of information, 27, 41
blind people and touch, 97
blind sight, 131

blindness, recovery from, 117
blink, 83
blood cells, 41, 150
bodily odours, 101
body and mind, 2, 9
body image, 96
bones, 150
Bowlby, J., 201
brain: contents of, 8, 22
  logic of, 63
  programs of, 17, 18
  records in, 49
brain death, 15
brain waves, 17
Braille, 92, 97
Brentano, F.C., 51, 52, 58
Brobeck, J. R., 186 (IV, 11)
Broca's area, 76, 91
Brodal, A., 159 (III, 13)
Brodman, K., 90
buildings, 207
  as symbols, 204

calcium and memory, 151
canaries, 152
cancer, 105
causation, 177
  of mentality, 14
causes, 14, 210
central sulcus, 90
cephalopod, 46
cerebellum, 70, 106, 157
cerebral cortex, *see* cortex
ceremonies, 203
Changeux, J. P., 149
chemical code signs, 30
  sense, 101
Cheney, D. L., 54
childhood, 199
childishness, 199
choice, 4, 208
  in bacteria, 210
Christianity, 11
chromosomes, 34, 43
cingulate cortex, 91
circuits and memory, 155
climatic change, 46
clitoris, 87
co-articulation, 114
cochlea, 84, 110
cochlear nucleus, 111

codes, 29–31
  analog, 70
  chemical, 30
  in learning, 111–13
  origin of, 30
code-signal, 29
coding, visual, 118–21
codons, 36
cognitive friendliness, 144
  map, 162–6, 171
  psychologists, 58, 85, 137
cogito, 24, 214
Collingwood, R. G., 3, 216
colour, 120
  in cortex, 124
colour vision, 132–4
  constancy, 133
columns in cortex, 124
commanding, 190
communication, 27, 54
  of information, 28
computer, 64, 137, 168
  and brain, 17
computer analogy, 146
concepts, abstract, 2
conditioned aversion, 99
  reflexes, 67
cones, 118
conscious occurrents, 14
consciousness, 12, 48, 107, 214
  of animals, 7
  and brain, 8
  and evolution, 214
consonants, 110
consummation, 178
continental drift, 210
contingent negative variation (CNV),
  73
continuity: between man and nature, 4
  of existence, 25
control, 33
co-operation, 199
Corkin, S., 162 (III, 16)
corollary discharge, 106
  for vision, 129
corpus callosum, 10
corpus striatum, 93
correspondence of mental and physical, 14
cortex: activation of, 93
  auditory, 113

binocular cells, 158
columns in, 94, 124
divisions of, 89
hot points in, 71
human, 68
motor, 68, 70
olfactory, 101
organization of, 166
precentral, 68
sensory, 71
signals from, 68
somatic sensory, 106
temporal area, 127
visual, 121–5
visual development, 158
cortico-spinal neurons, 70
creative choice, 211
creativity, 38
cruelty, 194
culture, 204
and freedom, 212
cupula, 108
cyanide, 100
cybernetics, 33
cytosine, 34

dance, 203, 204
Davidson, D., 177
Dawkins, R., 192
death, 16
de Beer, G. R., 200 (IV, 31)
decibels (dB), 110
decision, 4, 47
decoding, 61
degeneracy, 171
in cortex, 95
in hearing, 111
in memory, 158
of taste, 100
in visual cortex, 125
demes, 193
democracy, 213
dendrites, 69
Dennett, D. C., 49, 52, 54, 58, 59, 146
depression, 189
Descartes, R., 12, 23, 79
desire, 182
determinism, 4, 207–10
de Valois, K. K., 125
dialects, 193
directive correlation, 5

DNA, 6, 19, 30, 33–40, 60, 148
origin of, 35
dopamine, 94, 180
doubt, 16
dream, 17, 22
drinking, 185–7
drugs, 183–8
dualism, 11, 48

ear, 84, 110
earth, origin of, 31
eating, 185
Eccles, J. C., 11
Edelman, G. E., 149, 156
egg, 40
electric fields in the brain, 160
electroencephalogram (EEG), 17, 164, 171
elements, 5
embryology, 33, 40
emotion, 162, 178
enkephalin, 104, 160, 188
entropy, 28
enzyme, 31, 35
epilepsy, 75, 161
epistemology, 172
erythropoietin, 41
ethics, 190, 194
Euclidean space, 166
evolution, 40
exempt agent, 59
existence, continuity of, 25
expectation in perception, 81
experience, continuity of, 24
exploration and learning, 164
expression of genes, 37
eyes: colour of, 42
movements of, 121, 129
muscles of, 89

faces, 10
neurons for, 125, 146
facial expressions, 135
facial movements, 77
family groups, 193
feature detectors, 84, 112, 122, 153, 171
development of, 158, 169
feedback system, 40
Feldman, J. A., 145 (II, 50)
Fetz, E. E., 77 (I, 50)

field effects in the brain, 69, 160
Filikova, E., 152 (III, 6)
fingers, 87
fishes, 99
flexor reflex, 88
flower scents, 101
Fodor, J. D., 58, 85
forebrain bundle, 180
Fourier transform in vision, 125
fovea, 119
Franklin, R. L., 175 (IV, 4)
freedom, 207–10
frequency code, 63
Freud, S., 182
Fried, I., 77
frog's brain, 17
  eye, 84
frontal cortex, 91
frontal lobes, 102
function, 45

Gabor, D., 160
galactosidase, 37
Gasser, H., 61
gate-control, 104
Gelati, C. D., 146 (II, 51)
generalization, 154
genes, 35, 42
genetic code, 29–32, 42
geneticists, 33
genital odours, 101
Gerard, R., 17
gestalt, 136
giddiness, 108
glands, 30
glycine, 36
goal-seeking, 5
goat, drinking, 187
goodness, 174–6
Gordon, G., 86 (II, 8), 92 (II, 13), 96
  (II, 15)
Gould, S., 200 (IV, 30)
grammar, 32
grandmother cells, 126
Granit, R., 20
gratings, visual, 125
gravity receptor, 107
grey matter, 89
Grice, H. P., 54, 56
grooming, 192
Gross, C. G., 126

group selection, 193
group symbolism, 203
growth, 43
guanine, 34
guilt, 193–5

habitats, invasion of, 46
habituation, 125, 151
hairs, 87
Haith, M. M., 134 (I, 25), 168, 169
Hampshire, S., 53 (II, 30)
Hare, R. M., 195, 198, 199
Harré, R., 212 (IV, 35)
Head, A. S., 126 (II, 30)
hearing, 109
Hebb, D. O., 72 (I, 45)
hedonic effects, 183
Helmholtz, H. von, 136, 168 (III, 24)
hemisphere, right and left, 11
Henker, B., 134 (I, 40)
Hen-Too, J., 134 (II, 40)
heredity in brain, 143
hippocampus, 16, 91, 127, 177
  electrical stimulation of, 151
  and memory, 161
history, 30, 209
  as feature of life, 3
H. M., 161
Hobbes, Thomas, 196, 198
Hochberg, J., 132
Hodgkin, A., 61
holism, 90, 125, 147, 159
holographic memory, 160
holography, 125, 147
homeostasis, 29, 33, 39, 178, 184, 215
  and altruism, 191
  and emotion, 187–8
Homo erectus, 202
  sapiens, 202
Honderich, T., 14, 176 (I, 5), 199
honour, 212
hope, 53, 181
hormones, 179
Horsley, V., 89
Hubel, D. H., 123, 129
human descriptions, 13
  language and DNA, 32
  memory, 167
Hume, D., 12, 195
Hume's problem, 59
hunger signal, 186

Huxley, A., 61, 198
hydrogen sulphide, 101
hypothalamus, 67, 151, 157, 173, 178–80, 200
hypothesis, visual, 131, 145

illusions, visual, 142
image analysis, 139
immune system, 32, 156
imprinting, 201
indeterminism, 38
induction of an enzyme, 37
infant brain, 143
information, 5, 23–33
    amount of, 27
    as feature of life, 3
    increase of, 41
    measurement of, 89
    theory of, 29, 41
    visual, 119
inhibition, 66
input analysers, *see* feature detectors
insulin, 30, 36
intellectual activities, 181
intentional action, 73, 214
intentionality, 6, 51–8
    definition of, 53
interneurons, 65
intra-laminar nuclei, 103
introspection, limits of, 2
isomorphism, 50, 147, 313

James, William, 12
Java man, 202
Jeeves, M. A., 126 (II, 30)
joy, 181
Jung, R., 75 (I, 47)

Kandel, E., 150
Kant, I., 2, 79, 196
Kantian space, 166
Katz, B., 61
kin selection, 192
Kirkpatrick, S., 146 (II, 51)
kittens, feature detectors in, 158
    memory in, 169
knee-jerk, 105
knowing, 23
knowledge, 3, 9, 23–8, 176
    theory of, 172
Knudsen, E., 114 (II, 23)

Kogan, J., 134 (II, 40)

language, 32, 109, 112, 202
    and brain, 75
laser beams, 160
Lashley, K., 90, 161
lateral geniculate body, 121
laws of physics and chemistry, 210
Lawlike Correlation, 14, 208
learning, 42 (*see also* memory)
Lettvin, J. Y., 84 (II, 5)
leucotomy, 195
Levine, J., 134 (II, 40)
Lewis, M., 134
Lewy, C., 174 (IV, 2)
Libet, B., 73, 74
Lieberman, P., 110 (II, 20), 112 (II, 21), 114 (II, 22)
life, rhythm of, 22
light, 116–18
limbic circuit, 162
liver, 39
living, 24
living things, origin of, 31
locus coeruleus, 186
logic of the brain, 63
loving care, 187
Luria, A. R., 102

McCulloch, W., 146
Mackay, D. M., 211 (IV, 34)
Mackie, J. L., 175, 190, 194, 197, 198
macula, 119
map: cognitive, 162–6
    in owl's brain, 114
    visual, 121
Marler, P., 54
Marr, D., 135–46
Mateer, C., 77
materialism, 48
Maynard Smith, J., 192 (IV, 13)
Mayr, E., 47
meaning, 29, 113, 203
mechanism, 57
Medawar, J. and P., 4
medial geniculate body, 111
meiosis, 44
melatonin, 200
memory, 148 (*see also* learning)
    as a program for acting, 168
    in children, 168

circuits, 155
content addressed, 168
critical periods for, 170
differentiation of, 41
human, 167
in kittens, 169
localization of, 161
long term, 152
molecules, 152
place, 162
record, 30
and selection, 156
short term, 155
summary of, 170
tactile, 97
units of, 18
visual, 140
Mendel, G., 42
menstruation, 189
mental activity, timing of, 74, 77
mental images, rotation of, 146
mentalistic words, 1
mentality, 11
as property of brain, 13
Mesozoic period, 46
messages, 61
metabolism, 33, 38
metaphysics, 172
Metzlee, J., 146 (II, 51)
micrometre, 120
mid-brain, 132
Miller, R., 94 (II, 14), 166, 181 (IV, 8)
Milner, A. D., 126 (II, 30)
Milner, B., 162
mimic of taste, 99
mind, 9, 11, 49, 51, 172
and body, 2
not a thing, 13
Mishkin, M., 127
model, 147
in brain, 50, 70
modules, 71, 85, 95
for hearing, 112
and memory, 154
in vision, 141
molecular biologists, 33
Mondrian, Piet, 133
monkeys, face cells, 126
Montreal Neurological Clinic, 161
moods, 179, 182
Moore, G. E., 174, 194, 196

moral responsibility, 189
moral values, 190, 194
morality in children, 195–8
morals, 193
morphine, 104
Morse code, 29, 62
mother, 191
motivation, 93
motor cortex, 70, 91, 159
end-plates, 61
neurons, 62, 65, 70
skills, learning of, 159
movement programs, 74
movement receptors, 107
Mountcastle, V., 123, 149
muscles, 62, 150
music, 204, 206
mutation, 44, 210

Nadel, L., 162–6, 171, 213
Nathan, P. W., 102 (II, 18)
natural selection, 31, 45, 156, 191
naturalistic pictures, 206
fallacy, 173–5
Necker cube illusion, 142
need, 176
needs in bacteria, 37
neoteny, 200
nerve cells, numbers of, 156
nerve fibres, 61
impulse code, 61
neurons, assemblies of, 72
neuropeptides, 146
neuropil, 150
New Connectionists, 145
Newton, I., 132
Nisihara, M. K., 138
nociceptive system, 102
nose, 84
nucleotides, 31, 34, 44
nucleus, 43

obeying, 190
objects, 80, 85, 140
occipital cortex, 91
octopus, 45, 122, 152, 170
odours, 206
Ojemann, G. A., 76, 77 (I, 49, 50)
O'Keefe, J., 162–6, 171, 213
Optacon, 98
order, 27, 82, 213

organization, 27
ossicles, 110
ought, 195
owls, hearing in, 114

pain, 102–3
  internal, 104–5
pancreas, 36
Papez, J. W., 31 (I, 17), 162
paranormal phenomena, 16
parietal cortex, 91
Parkinson's disease, 94
participant attitude, 57, 214
patrons, responsibility of, 207
Pavlov, Ivan, 67
Peking man, 202
Penfield, W., 167
penis, 87
peptide, 104, 160, 188
perception, 26
  veracity of, 83
perfumes, 101
Perrett, D. A., 126 (II, 30)
personality, 172
persons, 12
pheromones, 101
Phillips, C. G., 90 (II, 11)
philosophers, 1, 216
phonemes, 77
phones, 112
phonetic structure, 112–14
photons, 116
physico-chemical laws, 209
Piaget, J., 166
pineal gland, 200
Pitts, W., 146
pituitary gland, 179, 200
place code, 63
  memory, 162
  tokens, 140
plants, signals sent by, 30
plasticity in brain, 149–50
pleasure, 181, 195
Poggio, T., 138, 146
polymerases, 35
polymers, 31
pontifical neurons, 126, 146
positional information, 40
Potter, D. D., 126 (II, 30)
prefrontal cortex, 195
premotor cortex, 71

pressure, 87
Pribram, K. H., 160 (III, 15)
programs, 5, 7
  brain, 17
  definition of, 20
  hearing, 114
  human visual, 135
  living, 19
  motor, 21
  movement, 74
  speaking, 21
  visual, 135
progress in evolution, 46
proprioceptors, 105
prosopagnosia, 10
Protagoras, 197
proteinoids, 31
proteins, 31
  structure of, 34
  and memory, 152
psychiatry, 174
psychic, 16
psychosomatic drugs, 183
puberty, 200
punishment, 182
pupil, 121
purines, 146
Purkinje cells, 156
purpose, 4–5, 48
pyramidal cells, 94
  and memory, 152
pyramidal tract neurons (PTN), 159

quantum evolution, 45
Quinton, A., 196

rage, 187
raphe nuclei, 181
rat in maze, 165
rational enquiry, limits of, 2
readiness potential, 73
reading, 131
reality, 16, 80
recovery in brain, 159
reductionism, 215
redundancy, 171
  in cortex, 95
  in hearing, 111
  in memory, 158
  of taste, 100
  in visual cortex, 125

reflexes, 65
Reidl, R., 27
releasing factors, 179
religion, 51
replication, 43
representation, 81, 171
    artistic, 206
    definition of, 138–9
    neurons for, 128
    visual, 117
representation: of environment, 45
    of world, 20
repression of genes, 27
reptiles, 46
respect, 212
reticular activation system, 21, 67, 94, 164
reticular formation and feeding, 186
retina, 84, 116, 119
reward centres, 182
    and aesthetics, 205
rhodopsin, 118
rhythm, 180
    of life, 22
ribosomes, 36
ritual assembly, 203
RNA (ribonucleic acid), 35
    and memory, 152
robots, 137
Rocha-Miranda, C. E., 126 (II, 29)
rods, 118
rotation of mental images, 146
Ryle, G., 1

saccades, 129
saccharine, taste of, 99
salt, hunger for, 99
satisfaction, 176, 180
    system, 185
scanning by touch, 88
schizophrenia, 180, 189
scientific attitude, 214
    discourse, 1
search for life, 47
Searle, J. R., 13, 14, 51
selection, 31, 36, 39
    in hearing, 113
    as feature of life, 4
    and memory, 149
    natural, 31, 45, 156, 191
selective system, 150
self, consciousness of, 55, 56

selfishness, 193
self-stimulation, 180
semantic functions in brain, 78
semantic information, 29
semantics, 203
semi-circular canals, 107
semiotics, 32
senescence, 105
sensitization, 151
septum, 164, 173
serotonin in brain, 151, 181, 182
sexual reproduction, 44
Seyfarth, R., 54
Shannon, C., 27
shape, 117
sham rage, 187
Shepard, R., 146, (II, 51)
Sherrington, C. S., 88
shivering, 184
Sidgewick, 196
sign, 32
signals: sent by bacteria, 30
    sent by plants, 30
singing, 203, 204
skin, senses in, 86
slavery, 201
sleep, 17, 49
Sloman, A., 138, 141
smell, 100, 206, 213
Smith, P. A. J., 126 (II, 30)
sociology, 201
Sommerhof, G., 5, 6
soul, 16, 51
sound, 108–10
smiling, 134
space, theories of, 166
spatial organization in cortex, 95
species, 46
speech, 76, 85, 91, 112
    origin of, 202
spinal cord, 65
spirits, 16
squids, 45, 122, 157
squint, 170
Srebro, R., 127 (II, 31)
stellate cells, 94
stem cells, 40
stimulus, 66, 80, 88
Strawson, P. F., 57, 214
striatum, 173, 180, 181
subfornical organ, 187
subliminal vision, 132

substance P, 160
substantia nigra, 180
sugar, taste of, 99
supra-chiasmatic nucleus, 180
Sutherland, N. S., 137
sweating, 184
symbol, 32, 203
sympathy, 198
synapse, 69
  inhibitory, 66
  memory changes, 152
  numbers, 156, 157
  modulated, 146
syntactic organization in brain, 78
system, 28

tabula rasa, 149
tactile map, 91
  memory, 97
taste, 83, 98
taste buds, 99, 175
Taylor, C., 6
teleology, 4
temperament, 171
temperature control, 184
  of rat, 185
temporal cortex, 91, 126
temporal gyrus and speech, 113
terminology of mind and brain, 12
testosterone, 152
Teuber, H.-L., 79, 162 (III, 16)
thalamus, 70, 93, 103
theologian, 11
thermodynamics, 28
thermostat, 185
theta waves, 164, 171
things, 24
thinking, 1, 21, 24, 56
  conceptual power of, 2
Thorpe, W. H., 8
thymine, 34
timing mental events, 74, 77
tobacco, 183
tooth pain, 102
topological code, 63
touch, 83
  cortical areas of, 91–2
transducers, 84, 88
translation, 29, 36, 61
transmitters, 61, 65, 186
Trivers, R. L., 192
truth, 176, 213

in hearing, 116
turnover, 38

utilitarianism, 196

values, 67, 175–8
  negative, 182
Valverde, F., 152 (III, 7)
van Gogh, Vincent, 123
Vecchi, M. P., 146 (II, 51)
vertebrates, 45
vertical lobe, 155
vervet monkeys, 53
Vesuvius, 210
vibration, 87
vision: in children, 134
  human, 127
  subliminal, 132
  theories of, 137
visual areas, 122
  injuries of, 10
visual arts, 206
voluntary action, 73
von Senden, M., 117 (II, 25)
vowels, 110

Waddington, C. H., 198
Waldhauser, F., 200 (IV, 29)
Wall, P. D., 32 (I, 19), 102 (II, 17), 104
wanting, 177
Warnock, G. J., 196, 198
Weaver, W., 27
Wells, J., 153
Wells, M. J., 153
Wernicke's area, 77, 91
whiskers, 87
white matter, 89
Wiesel, T. N., 123, 129
Williams, B., 197 (IV, 22)
Wilson, E. O., 192
Wollheim, R., 51, 149, 183
worshipping, 190
writing in the brain, 50

Yarbus, A. L., 130
Yin, R. K., 134 (II, 41)
Young, J. Z., 46 (I, 23), 149 (III, 2),
  152 (III, 9), 155 (III, 11), 200 (IV,
  28), 204 (IV, 32)
Young, Thomas, 119, 213

zebras, 49
Zeki, S., 90 (II, 11), 122, 134

OXFORD

MORE OXFORD PAPERBACKS

Details of a selection of other books follow. A complete list of Oxford Paperbacks, including The World's Classics, Twentieth-Century Classics, OPUS, Past Masters, Oxford Authors, Oxford Shakespeare, and Oxford Paperback Reference, is available in the UK from the General Publicity Department, Oxford University Press (JN), Walton Street, Oxford OX2 6DP.

In the USA, complete lists are available from the Paperbacks Marketing Manager, Oxford University Press, 200 Madison Avenue, New York, NY 10016.

Oxford Paperbacks are available from all good bookshops. In case of difficulty, customers in the UK can order direct from Oxford University Press Bookshop, 116 High Street, Oxford, Freepost, OX1 4BR, enclosing full payment. Please add 10 per cent of published price for postage and packing.

THE STANDING OF PSYCHOANALYSIS

B. A. Farrell

Psychoanalysis is a notoriously controversial and confusing subject. What are we to make of it? In this book, B. A. Farrell addresses the two central problems psychoanalysis raises. How believable is it as a doctrine? And how effective is it as a therapy?

Mr Farrell's book offers a view of what Freud's 'discoveries' amount to, and what psychoanalysis has achieved. It places the subject on our contemporary map of knowledge and belief by showing where it stands in relation to science, history, psychiatry, objective psychology, and common sense. And by clarifying the controversy that surrounds the subject, it dispels some of the confusions which perplex experts and laymen alike.

AN INTRODUCTION TO THE STUDY OF MAN

J. Z. Young

There are many ways of approaching the study of Man. Professor Young believes that biological knowledge provides a useful framework to help us to understand ourselves. Modern biology embraces many disciplines, and in this book a synthesis is made, tracing the sources of human activity from their biochemical basis to the highest levels of consciousness.

'Professor Young sticks to straight and informative science . . . is rivetingly interesting, and conveys a constant sense of the controlled, critical curiosity which is what science is about' *Guardian*

'an impressive performance' *Observer*

'a work of rare distinction' *Nature*

WHAT IS ECOLOGY?

D. F. Owen

Ecology has become a household word, but what is it all about? It is concerned with the growth of populations, plant and animal, and the resources available to them, and with the structure of communities and their relationship to an environment which is always in a state of flux, not least the hands of man.

Denis Owen begins with plants and animals—how they live and why they die. He goes on to consider man as a part of nature and explains how ecology affects us, and our supplies of food, oil, and other raw materials. Particular attention is paid to recent events which have changed our natural ecological balance: Dutch elm disease in Britain, for example, and oil tanker disasters.

'I recommend this informative book to anyone wishing to broaden his knowledge of ecology.' *New Scientist*

An OPUS Book

THE PROBLEMS OF PHYSICS

A. J. Leggett

This book attempts to give the non-specialist reader a general view of what physicists do, and of the problems which are still to be solved in contemporary physics. In contrast to many popular books on the subject, it concentrates not on the achievements of physicists, but on the exciting frontier areas of modern physics, and the fascinating work which is still to be done in this field.

An OPUS Book

THE PROBLEMS OF EVOLUTION

Mark Ridley

Is evolution true? If so, what is the force that drives it? Can natural selection account for so complex an organ as the eye—or is Darwin's theory merely what an eminent nineteenth-century astronomer called 'the law of higgledy-piggledy'? Is molecular evolution a random process? What is the real relationship between the theory of evolution and biological classification? Why do living things appear to become recognizable units called species, and how can one species split into two? Does evolution proceed gradually, or in jerks? What causes the grand patterns of change in the fossil record?

The Problem of Evolution sets out to identify such key questions and explains clearly and authoritatively the main answers that have been offered, whilst giving the rival merits of different theories their due.

An OPUS Book

THE SELFISH GENE

Richard Dawkins

'this fascinating book takes us on a journey whose purpose it is to join together in one vision the older truths of Darwinism and the new truth of another great idea, that of the self-seeking, self-replicating, and self-sufficient hereditary particle. On this magic carpet the author invites us to share his view of a world far below where ordinary animals and plants and people live and move and multiply' *Times Literary Supplement*

'this book should be read, can be read, by almost everyone. It describes with great skill a new face of the theory of evolution' *Science*

WATCH YOUR CHILD'S WEIGHT

Jennifer Ashcroft

Many children are unhealthy. Generally, their diet is too high in fat and sugar; too low in fibre. A good diet and adequate exercise are important in childhood and healthy behaviour patterns are best learned early in life. Inappropriate health habits can lead to weight problems, and emotional as well as physical distress.

The programme outlined in this book is geared specifically to children's needs. It describes their particular nutritional requirements, appropriate exercise, and how to make health-related behaviour changes easy and fun to achieve. It does this by considering the problem within the context of family, influences at school and social events.

CONCISE MEDICAL DICTIONARY

The *Concise Medical Dictionary* gives clear explanations of nearly 10,000 terms and concepts in all the major medical and surgical specialities, with very full coverage of community medicine.

' "no home should be without one" certainly applies to this splendid medical dictionary' *Journal of the Institute of Health Education*

'remarkable for the consistent clarity of its definitions . . . excellent layout and jargon-free style should commend it to a variety of readers' *Nursing Times*

WHAT IS PSYCHOTHERAPY?

Sidney Bloch

In this introduction to psychotherapy Sidney Bloch covers both theory and practice. He discusses the kind of people and problems that can be helped by treatment, the qualities needed in a therapist, and the ethical difficulties he or she has to face. He examines the three fundamental theoretical approaches from which all the many schools derive—the psychodynamic, the humanist-existential, and the behavioural, and outlines the findings of systematic research.

'This admirably clear and demythologizing introduction to the major approaches and, more important, just what we can expect from them, is more than welcome' *New Statesman*

SCIENCE AND TECHNOLOGY IN WORLD DEVELOPMENT

Robin Clarke

Published in association with Unesco

Foreword by Amadou-Mahtar M'Bow, Director-General of Unesco

In the developed world many of today's most urgent problems lie on the frontiers of science and technology. Robin Clarke's account—based on a Unesco report—examines the crucial relationships between science, technology, and society in both the developed and developing countries, and raises controversial questions about the nature of scientific advance and who really benefits from it.

THE PHILOSOPHIES OF SCIENCE:

An Introductory Survey

Second Edition

Rom Harré

The new edition of this survey of scientific thought contains a new chapter in which Dr Harré examines science as a social activity, analysing such problems as funding, and experiments on live animals.

'Harré's *The Philosophies of Science* offers a respectably cool, hard look at scientific throught and its relationship with the great historical schools of philosophy . . . both scholarly and lucid . . . and as good an introduction to the subject as could be wished for.' *Times Literary Supplement*

An OPUS book

A HISTORICAL INTRODUCTION TO THE PHILOSOPHY OF SCIENCE

Second Edition

John Losee

Since the time of Plato and Aristotle, scientists and philosophers have raised questions about the proper evaluation of scientific interpretations. A *Historical Introduction to the Philosophy of Science* is an exposition of positions that have been held on issues such as the distinction between scientific inquiry and other types of interpretation; the relationship between theories and observation reports; the evaluation of competing theories; and the nature of progress in science. The book makes the philosophy of science accessible to readers who do not have extensive knowledge of formal logic or the history of the sciences.

THE MAKING OF THE ATOMIC AGE

Alwyn McKay

For most of us the atomic age began in the 1940s with the dropping of the first atomic bomb, and in the post-war years when the first nuclear power stations came into being. What scientific discoveries lay behind these developments? Dr McKay, himself a pioneer nuclear scientist, reconstructs the story in absorbing detail, and also looks at the future of nuclear power in the context of world energy resources.

'written at a popular level . . . The writing is admirable. Not only are the technical points well explained, but the topics are skilfully selected so that the reader is given a clear overall picture of the discoveries and of the scientists who made them. I recommend this book unreservedly.' *British Book News*

THE STRUCTURE OF THE UNIVERSE

Jayant Narliker

Do black holes really exist? Why does the sun emit fewer neutrinos than expected? What is a quasar really like? Where do galactic radio sources get their energy from? Do the laws of physics, as we know them on earth, really apply on an astronomical scale?

Professor Narliker looks at the universe and its mysteries from two contrasting points of view. He describes how the modern astrologer investigates the structure of the universe and interprets what he sees; and he shows how the physical environment here on earth is so totally dependent on the structure of the universe that the study of that structure can provide valuable information for the earth bound scientist.

ENERGY: A GUIDEBOOK

Janet Ramage

'Dr Ramage sets out to provide a comprehensive, balanced guide to all the most important features of the energy world, present and future, in terms intelligible to a reader with no technical background . . . (she) is most obviously enthusiastic and splendidly lucid, when writing about the generation and use of electricity.' Ian Smart, *Nature*

'a clear, wide ranging and easy-to-read account of the energy scene . . . The book is not dogmatic or even provocative: Janet Ramage emphasises that a guidebook should not dictate the traveller's final destination, so this ends not with glib answers but with open questions about the world's energy future . . . the book provides plenty of meat for the teacher and sound supplementary reading for students and it will be a very useful acquisition for sixth-form, college and university libraries. *Physics Education*

An OPUS book

THE PROBLEMS OF BIOLOGY

John Maynard Smith

A unique book which explains the fundamental ideas of biology to a non-specialist readership, sixth-formers, and undergraduates in biology.

'He has provided us with a succinct and witty guide to what biology is all about . . . He lucidly conveys the strong sense of excitement among biologists that important things have been and are about to be discovered. That amounts to a very good reason for reading this book.' *New Scientist*

An OPUS Book

THE PROBLEMS OF MATHEMATICS

Ian Stewart

We are living in the Golden Age of mathematics. There are now more mathematicians alive than in all previous ages combined, and more research is being done than ever before. Yet many people still think that it is a static subject. In this astonishingly racy account of what's what in mathematics, Ian Stewart describes both the central problems of the subject and some of the exciting new discoveries being made. In doing so he has achieved the seemingly impossible—he has made maths fascinating and fun.

CRIME AND CRIMINOLOGY

A Critical Introduction

Nigel Walker

How much do we really know about crime and criminals? About the effectiveness—or otherwise—of the measures used by courts to deter, reform, or incapacitate offenders? In this critical introduction, refreshingly free of jargon or political bias, Nigel Walker tackles these and other central questions of the criminological debate. No respecter of accepted orthodoxies, he highlights the fallacies and failings of most explanations of criminal behaviour, and emphasizes the importance of rules as a determinant of human conduct, the crucial difference between rule-following and rule-breaking behaviour, and the special status of those rules that constitute the criminal and penal codes. After a comprehensive yet concise survey of the problems and their possible solutions, Nigel Walker goes on to explain the current popularity of 'just desserts' as an aim, and finally to ask whether we are leaving the war against crime, if there is indeed such a war, too much to the professionals . . . or if we do so at our peril.

An OPUS book

THE ROVING MIND

Isaac Asimov

This book offers a panoramic view of fringe science, technology, and the society of the future.

With extraordinary insight, Isaac Asimov examines:
* Creation versus evolutionism
* the Moral Majority and censorship
* scientific heretics and science fiction
* extra-terrestrial life, telepathy, and UFOs

Asimov offers an exciting view of the future where cloning, space colonization, and interplanetary travel are just some of the probabilities . . .

'vintage Asimov' *Publishers Weekly*

BETRAYERS OF THE TRUTH

Fraud and Deceit in Science

William Broad and Nicholas Wade

Why are scientists tempted to cheat? What leads a man who has devoted his life to the pursuit of the truth to fabricate evidence? Do rhetoric and propaganda play as large a role in science as they do in politics, law, and religion? *Betrayers of the Truth* analyses how the lure of fame and big money can lead scientists to abandon the ideals of their profession. Drawing on examples from astronomy, physics, biology, and medicine, the authors discuss scientific fraud as a historical phenomenon, perpetrated by men as separated in time as Ptolemy and Mendel, Newton and Sir Cyril Burt. They also explore fraud as a modern problem, endemic in the huge research factories which are part and parcel of modern scientific investigation.

'a highly responsible and well-argued contribution to the sociology of science' Peter Medawar, *London Review of Books*

CONCISE SCIENCE DICTIONARY

Over 7,000 entries provide full coverage of terms and concepts in physics, chemistry, biology (including human biology), biochemistry, palaeontology, the earth sciences, and astronomy, plus commonly encountered terms from mathematics and computing sciences. It is written in a clear and explanatory style to provide both straightforward definitions and invaluable background information.

'an essential tool for all school and college libraries, and in fact for anyone wanting to understand a wide range of scientific words and matters' *New Scientist*

THE MAKING OF THE MICRO

A History of the Computer

Christopher Evans

This is the story of how the mighty micro came to be: a book as much about people as about science and mathematics. The author describes not only the great inventions, but also the remarkable and often eccentric characters behind them, and the feuds and machinations that went on in their public and private lives.

'the author at his best—describing his subject and its history in a way that brings it immediately to life for even the most jaded reader' *New Scientist*

'Incisive account of the computer's evolution, from abacus to mighty micro, and the men involved.' *Sunday Times*

URBAN PLANNING
in Rich and Poor Countries
Hugh Stretton

Whose interests are served by the new planning bureaucracies? If some of them seem to do more harm than good, would they be best abolished, replaced, or reformed? Hugh Stretton suggests that many planning projects have not been effective in practice because they have not delved deep enough into the societies for which they were intended. Planners seek to understand the complexities of societies, their economic and political structures, he argues, and be aware of their own values and of governmental pressure.

Stretton has two main purposes: to help the readers to compare their own urban conflicts and policies with others round the world; and to enable them to stand back and consider the record of post-war planning and development as a whole.

THE MORAL STATUS OF ANIMALS
Stephen R. L. Clark

Most of us exploit animals for our own purposes. The Moral status of animals has long been a subject of heated debate. According to the great philosophers, morality has nothing to say about our relations with non-humans. Modern liberals, though have allowed that animals should at least be spared unnecessary pain.

In his lively and controversial book Stephen Clark argues that this liberal principle is powerful enough in itself to require most of us to be vegetarian. He discusses the arguments and rationalizations offered in defence of our behaviour in farms, laboratories, and at home, and reveals their roots in neurotic fantasy.

'an erudite, intriguing, provocative, disturbing book which deserves close attention' *Month*

NEURONAL MAN:

The Biology of Mind

Jean-Pierre Changeux

Neuronal Man was originally published in France as *L'Home neuronal* and was a best-seller for months; it also won the Broqùette-Gonin Literary Award from the Académie Française in 1983. The book is an extraordinarily wide-ranging synthesis of the most up-to-date knowledge we have of the human brain—an account of discoveries as revolutionary as those in atomic physics at the turn of the century or genetics in the fifties. But, more than a guided tour of the human brain, the book presents the author's radical and controversial hypothesis: that there is no 'mind' in man, nothing psychic, but rather only neurons, synapses, electricity, and chemistry.

'an excellent book . . . remarkably clear and easy to read . . . I know of no better book to serve as a guide to neuroscience for the layman.' *Times Higher Education Supplement*

'Writing with elegance and panache, he assaults dualist notions of a separate mind or spirit, the province of the philosopher and the theologian, like a latter-day knight errant riding through a land of misguided heathens.' *New Scientist*